Whatever became of...?

ELEVENTH SERIES

Whatever became of...?

ALL NEW ELEVENTH SERIES

100 profiles of the most-asked-about movie, TV, and media personalities.

Hundreds of never-before-published facts, dates, etc., on celebrities.

227 THEN-AND-NOW PHOTOGRAPHS

RICHARD LAMPARSKI

CROWN PUBLISHERS, INC.
NEW YORK

Published by Crown Publishers, Inc., 225 Park Avenue South, New York, New York
10003
CROWN is a trademark of Crown Publishers, Inc.
Manufactured in the United States of America

Library of Congress Cataloging-in-Publication Data

Lamparski, Richard.
    Whatever became of—? All new eleventh series : 100 profiles of the most-asked-
about movie, TV, and media personalities : hundreds of never-before-published facts,
dates, etc. on celebrities : 227 then-and-now photographs / Richard Lamparski.
        p.   cm.
    1. Television personalities—United States—Biography. 2. Motion picture actors and
actresses—United States—Biography.   I. Title.
PN1992.4.A2L33 1989
791.43′028′0922—dc 19
[B]   89-765

ISBN 0-517-57150-1
       0-517-57151-X (pbk)
10 9 8 7 6 5 4 3 2 1

First Edition

For Jean Nicolesco-Dorobantzou
Artist, Gentleman, Dear Comrade
1925–1988

Contents

NOTE: The superscript 8, 9, and 10 with the names in the text indicate that this personality is profiled in Whatever became of . . . ? EIGHTH SERIES, NINTH SERIES, *or* TENTH SERIES *by Richard Lamparski.*

Acknowledgments

The author gratefully acknowledges those who have helped to make this book possible:

Deborah Davis-Lipson
Wayne Martin
David DelValle
Bob Satterfield
Phil Boroff
Chris Dietrich
Ronnie Britton
Wayne Clark
Lester Glassner
Collectors Book Store
Robert F. Slatzer
Jim Brennan
Jim Janisch
Jim Jeneji
Copy King of Hollywood
Patrick Lobo
Doug Hart's Back Lot
Critt Davis
Gregory William Mank
Gary H. Grossman
Norman Lobo
Wayne Parks
Amaryllis Bierne-Keyt
Gawain Bierne-Keyt
Allied Artists Corp.
Paramount Pictures
Steven Arnold
Michael Back
Virginia Reidy
Roy Bishop
Beverly Hills Public Library
Eddie Brandt's Saturday Matinee
Mathew Tombers
Donna Schaeffer
Paul Schaeffer
Peter Schaeffer
Richard Schaeffer
Anne Schlosser and the staff of the Library of
    the American Film Institute
Tony Slide
Sons of the Desert
Twentieth Century-Fox Corp.

United Artist
Jon Virzi
Marc Wanamaker of the Bison Archives
United Press International Photos
World Wide Photos
Morgan Amber Neiman
Francia Neiman
Chapman's Picture Palace
Frank Buxton
Diana Serra Cary
R. T. Brier
Cinemabilia
Columbia Pictures Corp.
Warner Brothers
Bob Cushman
Shelly Davis
Samson DeBrier
Walt Disney Prods.
Tim Doherty
George Eells
Leatrice Fountain
Hal Gefsky
Aurand Harris
Michael R. Hawks
Howard W. Hays
Terry Helgesen
Charles Higham
Herman Hover
Corinne Lobo
Michael Knowles
Don Koll
Anton LaVey
Los Angeles Times
Dick Lynch
Bobby Downey
Luther Hathcock
Mike Marx
Metro-Goldwyn-Mayer
Iris Adrian
National Screen Service
Sloan Nibley
R. C. Perry

Dorothy Revier
Sarah Richardson
Linda Mehr and the staff of the Motion
    Picture Academy of Arts and Sciences
Bill Tangeman
Art Ronnie
Donovan Brandt
Nick Bougas
Lloyd Douglas
Milton T. Moore, Jr.
Chuck Williamson
Gerald Bastable
Ian Grant
Adam O. Robertson
Paul Taylor
Bryan Ough
Tom Hawes
Jim Yousling
Dave Singer
Beverly Churchill
Chapman's Picture Palace
Kirk Crivello
Jack Mathis
"Republic Confidential"
Jerry Siegan
Heidi Brandt
Dan Pattarson
Roy Moseley
IMP/GEH Still Collection
Harold Jacobs
Hamilton Meserve
Colin Williamson
David Quinlan
Howard Prouty
Sue Ellen Picker
William W. Granger
Chris Dietrich

Joe Lynch
Doug Warren
Robert F. Slatzer
Kenny Parker
Doug Hoerth
Movie World
Lynn Wood
Cary Schwartz
Jan-Christopher Horak
George Eastman House
Marty Jackson
Malcolm "Stuff" Leo
Clint Brown
Jeff Rose
Dale Crawford
Bob Siler
George Putnam
Paul L. Surratt, Jr.
Robert Coogan
Anton Hays
Pat Wilkes-Battle
Dale Horning
Wild River Publishing Company
Fangoria
Norman Maurer Productions, Inc.
Research Video
Peter Knego
Frank Lenger
Charles Naylor III
Ken Sephton
Piet Hein Honig
Stanton La Vey
Cody Morgan
John Carlyle

ELEVENTH SERIES

John Abbott's trademarks were his rich voice and outer reserve. On the screen he played with Bette Davis, Irene Dunne, Ingrid Bergman, and Joan Crawford. On Broadway he originated the leading role in Waltz of the Toreadors *in 1957.*

John Abbott

The distinguished character actor was born in London, England, on July 5, 1905.

As a boy he frequently, but secretly, acted out various roles in front of a mirror. John was mimicking the stars he was seeing in silent movies.

He studied art, however, not acting. Most likely he would never have gone on the stage had not a fellow student become ill. The boy had a role in an amateur production and John had been watching rehearsals. He stepped in on short notice and caught the attention of Sybil Thorndike, who said to a colleague, "Now *there's* a young man who knows how to make an entrance!" That remark was repeated to Abbott, who credits it with giving him the confidence to pursue a career.

By 1934, four years after his debut as an amateur, he was appearing in plays in the West End. In 1936, at the invitation of Tyrone Guthrie, John Abbott joined the Old Vic, a period he considers the high point of his life as an actor.

John's film debut was in support of Claire Luce and Erich von Stroheim in *Mademoiselle Docteur* (1937). His stage work was interspersed with such pictures as *The Return of the Scarlet Pimpernel* (1938), *This Man Is News* (1939), and *The Saint in London* (1939).

He was not conscripted at the outbreak of World War II because he had joined the Foreign Office. After a year in the British Embassy in Stockholm, doing coding and decoding, he journeyed through the Soviet Union to Canada. From there he went to New York City for a holiday, intending to return to England. On what he expected to be his last day in the United States, John was given a prominent role in *The Shanghai Gesture* (1941) with Phyllis Brooks.* He came to Hollywood to make the picture and has lived there ever since.

Mystery-film buffs know him as the menace to such master sleuths as "Sherlock Holmes," "The Falcon," "Mr. Moto," and "The Saint." Horror-film historian David Del Valle considers Abbott's starring performance in *The Vampire's Ghost* (1945) to be "classic horror-movie acting."

The actor believes he did his best filmed work in *The Woman in White* (1948) as the grandly foppish "Frederick Fairlie." Warner Brothers offered him a contract after his scenes were first screened, but he chose to free-lance.

He made more than fifty other features, including *Joan of Paris* (1942), *Mission to Moscow* (1943), *They Got Me Covered* (1943), *Mask of Dimitrios* (1944), *Saratoga Trunk* (1945), *Anna and the King of Siam*

(1946), *Humoresque* (1946), *Madame Bovary* (1949), *The Merry Widow* (1952), *Gigi* (1958), and *The Greatest Story Ever Told* (1964).

There were also many roles in B films. At the time John questioned the wisdom of having his name on the credits of pictures such as *The Gorilla Man* (1942), *Rubber Racketeers* (1942), *Get Hep to Love* (1942), *The End of the Road* (1944), *The Return of the Whistler* (1948), *Sideshow* (1951), and *Navy Bound* (1951). His agent assured him, however, that "nobody who matters will ever see this junk." The actor is amused to find himself now seeking out copies of the very movies he was once embarrassed to appear in. They are the ones he would most like to obtain on videocassette.

He was in the Broadway productions of *He Who Gets Slapped* (1946), *Monserrat* (1949), and *The Waltz of the Toreadors* (1957). John and Muriel Forbes, the late wife of Ralph Richardson, had the leads in the latter, a highly acclaimed farce by Jean Anouilh. He re-created this performance in the 1959 *Play of the Week* production on TV.

Tennessee Williams wrote the central character in *Auto-Da-Fé* for John Abbott and dedicated the one-act play to the actor. John played the part in a Los Angeles little theatre in 1950.

When he conferred with playwright Mary Chase about the lead in *Harvey,* she was still planning to have "Harvey," the huge rabbit, on stage. She was unable to convince the actor that it was plausible. *Harvey* most likely would have made Abbott a star, something he insists he never expected to happen. His original goal, he says, was "to do good work without having to run about looking for jobs."

John's first appearance on television was a role in *The Harmfulness of Tobacco,* which was aired on BBC-TV in June 1937.

On TV in the United States, he has been

Marty Jackson

John Abbott refers to his friend Queenie Leonard as "the quintessential English comedienne." Known in the United States chiefly for her work as a character actress in films, Ms. Leonard was married to and divorced from Tom Conway, brother of George Sanders. This photo was taken at Alan Napier's memorial service in August 1988.

seen in the anthologies *The General Electric Theatre, Studio One,* and *Hallmark Hall of Fame.* The television series he has been seen on include *Flipper, Bewitched, Get Smart, The Man from U.N.C.L.E., Beverly Hillbillies,* and *Star Trek.*

John Abbott has considered himself retired since the early eighties. "I haven't the slightest urge to act ever again," he said during an interview in 1987. He has found teaching and coaching young actors to be every bit as fulfilling as acting was for five decades. He is especially proud of his student Tom Schanley, who played the title role in *The Return of the Six-Million-Dollar-Man* (1987).

He and a friend frequently play debuts on the twin baby grands in his living room. He also does some composing on the piano.

Abbott's Hollywood Hills home is decorated with antiques and the oils he has painted of himself in character. His pet is "Tweedledee," the survivor of a pair of lovebirds.

A lifelong student of metaphysics, Abbott summed up his approach to life during a recent interview: "I always look for the good. Not perfection, but goodness. If it is a person, I always see it. If it is not, I turn away. I am only comfortable and creative with loving people."

One of the many challenges faced by the heroine during the fifteen chapters of The Perils of Nyoka *(1942) was to escape the clutches of the gorilla, "Satan." Her hirsute abductor was played by Emil Van Horn, whose wife became quite jealous of Kay Aldridge during the filming.*

Kay Aldridge

The cover girl and serial queen was born on July 9, 1917, in Tallahassee, Florida. Her great-grandfather on her mother's side was a Ward, one of the "old" families of Virginia. Her original name is Katharine Gratten Aldridge.

After Mrs. Aldridge was widowed, when Katharine was very young, she and her children went to live with two maiden sisters in Virginia. The home lacked plumbing and there was very little money, but the aunts were highly respected members of the community. They were what was known as "shabby genteel," a condition borne with a definite pride then, particularly in the South. Manners, speech, and refinement were emphasized.

In 1935 Katharine Aldridge had graduated from high school and was working at an office job in Baltimore when she broke her hip while horseback riding. When the small-town newspaper ran a story of the incident along with her photo, a relative sent the article to John Robert Powers, one of the world's top modeling agents. Powers wrote back expressing interest in seeing the girl in person.

Katharine visited New York City shortly thereafter and went to see Powers. Photographic modeling had only recently come into its own, and she had never heard of the profession. The agency head liked her coloring and features, but it was her air of innocence that convinced him she could be sold as the typical "All-American Girl."

Katharine Aldridge got her first modeling job without a composite. She had never been photographed professionally at the time she was hired. Within months her face was appearing in advertisements and catalogues, and on the covers of magazines such as *Redbook, Modern Romance,* and *Country Gentleman.* She was *Life*'s cover girl three times.

In 1937 producer Walter Wanger hired what he publicized as the "ten most photographed girls in the world" to appear throughout the lushly produced *Vogues of 1938* (1937). Katharine was the only one of the group to stay on in Hollywood. She did so to appear in a small role in *Rosalie* (1937) but remained when other studios showed interest.

When she was asked to test for the role of

"Scarlett O'Hara" in *Gone with the Wind*, Henry Fonda coached her.

She was pacted by Twentieth Century-Fox and cast in the lead opposite James Ellison[8] in *Hotel for Women* (1939), but she was replaced at the last moment by Linda Darnell. Instead, Katharine played the second lead. Under that contract she made eleven features, and was then dropped.

She frequently appeared on the screen as a wealthy, snobbish young woman. *Here I Am a Stranger* (1939), *Free, Blonde and 21* (1940), *Dead Men Tell* (1941), *Louisiana Purchase* (1941), *The Falcon's Brother* (1942), *DuBarry Was a Lady* (1943), and *The Phantom of 42nd Street* (1945) are among her screen credits.

During her eight years as a Hollywood actress she made twenty-one features. She is remembered, however, for the title role in *The Perils of Nyoka* (1942), one of her three serials.

Kay Aldridge was one of the very few women to star in serials during the sound era. Yet, when she made them she didn't even know what a serial was. When in 1978 fans screened some of the chapters of *Nyoka* for her, it was the first time she had seen any part of any serial.

The Perils of Nyoka was very popular among matinee audiences when it was first shown. Ten years later it was re-released as *Nyoka and the Tigermen* (1952), and the serial again drew loyal attendance week after week. In 1966 it was re-edited and presented as a feature under the title *Nyoka and the Lost Secrets of Hippocrates* in theatres and on TV. Countless numbers of prepubescent boys of at least three generations formed the first crushes of their lives as they longed to rescue Kay Aldridge as "Nyoka."

In *Daredevils of the West* (1943) and *Haunted Harbor* (1944) she was merely the hero's leading lady. The late Kane Richmond

Kay Aldridge in 1988 on her annual visit to Los Angeles.

Marty Jackson

was the central figure of the latter; Allan "Rocky" Lane, whom she has described as "the most conceited human being I have ever met," headed the cast of the former.

She dated James Stewart, Sterling Hayden, and Randolph Scott. Jack Carson proposed to her and Darryl F. Zanuck tried to seduce her. Howard Hughes was about to make a pass when she walked out on him.

Kay was helping her family financially with earnings from screen roles and would have continued in pictures if her first husband had not insisted she retire. Arthur Cameron was many years her senior and a self-made oil millionaire. They were married on Valentine's Day, 1945. They had two sons and two daughters before they separated in 1954. When they were divorced, she took no alimony.

In 1956 she became the wife of painter Richard Derby Tucker. The couple lived in her present home on the Penobscot Bay in Maine until his death in 1979.

The mining engineer she married in 1982 had first proposed to her forty-two years earlier. Within eight months she was again a widow.

Richard Allan is best known for playing Marilyn Monroe's lover in Niagara *(1953). He found her "very sweet off the set, but maddening to work with. My goal was to be professional. She was already a star and yet the most unprofessional person I've ever worked with."*

Richard Allan

The actor who played Marilyn Monroe's lover on screen was born on June 22, 1923, in Jacksonville, Illinois. His father owned farms in the area. Mrs. Allan was a dietician.

Richard began to take dancing classes when he was seven years old. At about the same age, he started going to movies. He preferred the musicals, and Fred Astaire and Ginger Rogers were his favorite stars. He saw each of their films "at least five or six times," frequently with the little girl who was his partner at dancing school. The pair soon began to get a great deal of attention locally, doing their versions of the Astaire-Rogers routines.

By the time Richard Allan won a scholarship to the University of Illinois, he had become rather well known in Jacksonville as a dancer-singer-actor. Shortly after he joined the university's Theatre Arts Department, he was drafted. The army unit in Italy with which he served was assigned the officers' laundry detail.

Immediately upon his discharge from service, Richard went to New York City. He was hired from the first professional audition of his life to dance in *The Red Mill* (1945). By the time its Broadway run and national tour ended, he was playing a speaking part.

Richard went immediately from his first show into another, the 1948 Los Angeles production of *Naughty Marietta*. He danced in that musical, which starred Susanna Foster,[8] and then remained in Hollywood, determined to get into movies.

He swam in the Esther Williams vehicle *Neptune's Daughter* (1949) and danced in *Love That Brute* (1950) with Jean Peters[9] and in *Let's Dance* (1950) with Fred Astaire and Betty Hutton.

When Richard met Montgomery Clift, for whom he doubled in *A Place in the Sun* (1951), the star looked at him and said, *"You should be playing the part!"*

During the filming of *Wabash Avenue* (1950) Richard became friendly with its star, Betty Grable. He was a lead dancer in that movie musical, as he was in *My Blue Heaven* (1950) and *Call Me Mister* (1951), both Grable vehicles. By the time he was in the latter, he had been signed by Twentieth Century-Fox.

During the five years he spent under contract, Richard was tested for many leading roles, the most notable being that in *The Egyptian,* a part that went to Edmund Purdom. The small roles he did play brought notice from fans and the publications that catered to them. "Promising" and "up-and-coming" was how his studio referred to him in press releases heralding his supporting parts in *With a Song in My Heart* (1952), *Bloodhounds of Broadway* (1952), and *Niagara* (1953).

Allan blames "lousy, lousy management, really lousy" for the fact that his career never developed further. But Fox dropped him after he refused to be photographed from a distance doing a hat dance that a star found too difficult to perform. And, when Tony Curtis was thought to be unavailable for *The Defiant Ones,* Richard was approached. But when told the producers wanted someone who looked like Curtis, Richard's response was, "Tell them to call me when they want someone who looks like Richard Allan."

Caterina Valente, who was then one of the German cinema's most important stars, had seen Richard in *The Snows of Kilimanjaro* (1952) and brought him to Europe. He supported her in *Casino de Paris* (1957), *Der Rest ist Schweigen* (1959), and *Das Einfache Mädchen* (1957). His other German films were *Und Abends in die Scala* (1957), *Der Czardas-König* (1958), and *Kleine Leute Mal Ganz Grosse* (1958).

Upon his return to Hollywood, he teamed up with Diane Hartman in a nightclub act. When the famed Ciro's closed its doors for the last time as a nitery in 1961, the marquee on the Sunset Strip read: "Mills Brothers . . . Hartman & Allan." It was also the conclusion of Richard Allan's career.

Richard Allan keeps the citation he received from Photoplay *magazine on display in his apartment. It proclaimed him "one of America's most promising newcomers" of 1953.*

By 1964 Richard was earning his living as a masseur. Kim Novak was the first to recommend his services to others in the industry. But gradually, Allan has developed a clientele who have no connection with show business.

During his tenure at Twentieth Century-Fox, Richard was considered "one of the family" by Barbara Rush and Jeffrey Hunter, who were then married. He is no longer in touch with anyone from his career, explaining: "When you aren't successful, people just aren't comfortable with having you around."

Recently Allan moved to Prospect, Kentucky, to be near his family. In 1987 he summed up his feelings about his life: "You need a really burning ambition to make it in Hollywood. When it's clear that you're not going to, that drive just dies. Then you're left with the most terrible emptiness. That never leaves."

Gloria Henry and Herbert Anderson played "Henry and Alice Mitchell," the parents of a very mischievous little boy, on all 146 episodes of Dennis the Menace. *Jay North starred in the title role.*

Herbert Anderson and Gloria Henry

Herbert Anderson was born in Oakland, California, on March 30, 1917.

He readily admits that he is still recognized frequently for his role as the father of "Dennis" in the TV series *Dennis the Menace*. It was not his favorite part, nor does he believe the series has any real significance.

Making those shows, however, he recalls with great affection: "That was a very happy set. Gloria [Henry], Sylvia Field, and the late Joe Kearns were always pleasant, punctual, and good company when you had to sit around. Jay [North] was so young we had to relate to him as a child, but he hit all his marks and knew his lines. Very professional."

He has remained in touch with both Henry and Field by mail and phone. Jay North used to drop by his home frequently when he was living in the San Fernando Valley. Since Anderson moved to Palm Springs, North has been to see him at least once a year. The older man is something of a father figure to North, a relationship that began on the set.

During the forties Herbert Anderson was under contract to Warner Brothers. His favorite roles in feature films were in *Navy Blues* (1941) and *The Male Animal* (1942).

Some of his other screen credits were: *'Til We Meet Again* (1940), *No Time for Comedy* (1940), *The Bride Came C.O.D.* (1941), *This Is the Army* (1943), *Give My Regards to Broadway* (1948), *The Benny Goodman Story* (1956), *Sunrise at Campobello* (1950), and *Hold On!* (1966).

The highlight of his career was as a member of the original cast of *The Caine Mutiny Court-Martial* (1954). Its author, Herman Wouk, and producer Paul Gregory, like Anderson both residents of California's Coachella Valley, encounter each other frequently.

Gloria Henry was born on April 2 in New Orleans.

During World War II she worked as an announcer on the local radio station, WDSU.

Gloria signed with Columbia Pictures in 1945. She was set to play the female lead in *The Return of October* and to be spotlighted with "Introducing Gloria Henry" in its exploitation. Almost simultaneous with the postponement of the film's production was her rejection of the advances of studio head Harry Cohn. Although she remained under contract for four years, almost all of the

Jay North,[8] star of the Dennis the Menace *series, and Tommy Rettig,[8] star of the original* Lassie *TV show, reunited at the party Crown Publishers gave celebrating the publication of* Whatever Became of . . . ? Tenth Series. *North is divorced and lives in Sherman Oaks. Rettig, also divorced, is the author of two books on computer software and heads his own computer firm. He lives in Venice, California.*

Gloria Henry in March 1988.

Herbert Anderson sold real estate for more than twenty years after making the Dennis the Menace *series. He shares his Palm Springs condominium with his poodle, "Gigi."*

"Martha and John Wilson," the long-suffering neighbors of "Dennis the Menace," were played by Sylvia Field and Joseph Kearns for the show's first season on television, 1959–62. Kearns died of a heart attack in 1962. Sylvia Field, the eighty-seven-year-old widow of Ernest Truex, posed with her companion "Charlie" in her Fallbrook, California, home in 1987.

more than two dozen pictures she made were Bs.

Her best-known movies are *Port Said* (1948) (in which she had a dual role), *Adventures in Silverado* (1948), *Miss Grant Takes Richmond* (1949), *Kill the Umpire* (1950),

and *Rancho Notorious* (1952).

Gloria is the mother of two sons and a daughter by an architect. Their twenty-five-year marriage ended in divorce in 1977. She and her three cats share a West Hollywood home that was once owned by the late Alice Reinheart, a radio actress best known for playing "Chichi" on the soap opera *Life Can Be Beautiful* in the thirties and forties.

Gloria played the girlfriend of the hero on *The Files of Jeffrey Jane,* a 1952 TV series, before becoming known to millions as the mother of "Dennis the Menace." She retired when the show ceased production in 1963 but has recently begun to reactivate her career. Gloria had a role in the feature *Doin' Time on the Planet Earth* (1988).

Ms. Henry enjoyed making *Dennis the Menace,* an experience she describes as "like having a second family." It confirmed her belief, however, that professional children are deprived children. She would not permit hers to act.

Visconti had Björn Andresen photographed lovingly in Death in Venice *but did not allow him a word of dialogue. Perhaps because of his virtual disappearance after the film's release in 1971, he has become the object of an international cult.*

Björn Andresen

The focal point of Visconti's film *Death in Venice* (1971) was born in Stockholm, Sweden. His birthday is January 26, 1955.

The teenager was studying piano and guitar when his grandmother began taking him to acting auditions. After Björn played a small part in *A Love Story* (1970), his photograph appeared in a directory of European actors. One of Luchino Visconti's assistants brought it to the director's attention. The boy was sent for, interviewed, and signed to play the central figure in the film version of the Thomas Mann novel *Death in Venice.*

Pederasty, long a forbidden subject for movies, was the central theme of *Death in Venice* (1971). Björn, as "Tadzio," was presented as a sex object. His androgynous looks were featured in all advertising for the picture and on the album cover of its recorded score (music by Gustav Mahler).

Dirk Bogarde played the aging composer who becomes undone by his secret yearnings for an adolescent Polish boy. In his autobiography, Bogarde recalled Björn during the making of the picture as a Beatles fan who chewed black bubble gum and whose wants were an electric guitar and a motorbike.

Andresen's remembrances of Dirk Bogarde are: "Such a kind, sensitive man. I was fifteen years old and so insecure about what was expected of me on camera. Being in a foreign country made matters even more difficult. He was so helpful and considerate. I will always be grateful to him."

The highlight of the *Death in Venice* experience for Björn was meeting Elizabeth II at the London premiere of the film.

In a published interview, one of the very few Björn gave in connection with *Death in Venice,* he was quoted as saying: "I couldn't care less if I ever made another film." The few he has made remain unknown to all but cinemagoers in Sweden, Norway, and Denmark.

In 1971 and 1972 he appeared frequently in TV commercials made for Japan, where the Visconti film was a major hit.

Björn considers himself a professional film

actor. He has no interest in acting on stage. The only lead he has had was in *Bluff Stop* (1977), which did not receive distribution outside of Scandinavia. He played an angel in *The Simple-Minded Murderer* (1982) and had another minor part in *Grass Widowers* (1982). His last features were *The King of Smugglers* (1985) and *Peas and Whiskers* (1986).

On Swedish television he has been seen during the 1983–84 season in the series *Swedish Crime* and in *Splendid Landing,* a made-for-TV thriller.

One of the rumors that has circulated over the years is that Björn was questioned by authorities after the 1976 murder of Sal Mineo. Canadian journalist Brian Linehan was told by "a top executive in the motion picture industry" at a Hollywood function several years ago that Mineo and Björn Andresen were having an affair and had been together only hours before the fatal stabbing.

As this story was being repeated to Björn, the actor interrupted to ask who Sal Mineo was. His only comment was to say that he had never in his life been in the United States.

In 1984, *Films in Review* published David Del Valle's interview with Helmut Berger, in which the actor said of Björn Andresen: "He died of a drug overdose." Berger had given similar information to other journalists.

During an interview conducted over the telephone to Stockholm in March 1988, Björn Andresen commented on the reports of his death: "I was shocked at first, as were my friends and family. But I believe I know the reason. We first met when we were seated across from each other at the dinner given after the premiere of the film in Rome. He was very rude, which confused me completely. I couldn't understand how someone could dislike me when we were total strangers. I learned later that he wanted to play

Joakim Strömholm

Björn Andresen is a film actor living in Stockholm, Sweden.

'Tadzio.' One version has it that Luchino had actually promised him the role. I'm told that sometimes I am supposed to have been killed in an auto crash, and once it was a plane crash. I am alive and well!"

Married since 1983, Björn and his wife separated in 1986, after their firstborn, a son, died of sudden infant death syndrome. As of July 1988, they were living together again in Stockholm with their daughter, Robin.

11

John Archer had the lead in Lerner and Loewe's first Broadway musical, played the title role on the radio show The Shadow, *and headed the cast of some B movies. But when he is recognized today, it is usually for his appearance in the cult film* Destination Moon *(1950).*

John Archer

The leading man of the forties was born Ralph Bowman on May 8, 1915, in Osceola, Nebraska.

Archer was drawn to motion pictures at an early age, but his interest was in the technical end of the profession. He studied cin-ematography at the University of Southern California but was unable to find a position at any studio.

He was supporting himself as an assistant to an aerial photographer when Ben Bard, director-drama coach and husband of silent-serial star Ruth Roland, spotted him in a restaurant. Bard, lunching with Jack Carson, had just boasted that he could turn anyone into an actor. Challenged, he approached the young Nebraskan and offered him a scholarship to his acting school.

Fifty years after that incident Archer said: "I had never for a moment considered acting. I was twenty-two years old and making $60 a month in a job that was going nowhere. So, I gave it a try. Ninety days later I was doing a walk-on in a 'Charlie McCarthy' movie. Then I had bit parts in the serials *Flaming Frontiers* (1938) and *Dick Tracy Returns* (1938). Within six months I was making a living."

"John Archer" and "Alice Eden" were the names bestowed upon the winners of a talent contest on *Gateway to Hollywood,* a radio program produced by movie pioneer Jesse Lasky. The final selections were made after weeks of competition listened to by movie fans coast-to-coast. Hugh Beaumont, Linda Darnell, and Charles Drake were among those who were eliminated. Both winning contestants were signed to a stock contract by RKO Pictures.

Dropped by the Gower Street lot after a year, Archer free-lanced until he was signed by Twentieth Century-Fox. Although he was cast in three of that studio's A releases in 1943—*Hello Frisco Hello, Crash Dive* and *Guadalcanal Diary*—John was dissatisfied with how his career was developing.

Reasoning that he would get better screen roles if he had experience on Broadway, Archer and his wife moved to New York City. (In 1941 he had married the actress Marjorie Lord.)

His deep voice became familiar to radio listeners during the forties. Archer played "Lamont Cranston," alias "The Shadow," on the show of the same title from September 24, 1944, through April 15, 1945—thirty episodes in all. He also guested in character as the invisible crime fighter on the quiz show *Quick as a Flash*.

John returned to Hollywood to make such pictures as *The Lost Moment* (1947) with Robert Cummings,[9] *Colorado Territory* (1949), *The Great Jewel Robbery* (1950), and *High Lonesome* (1950) with John Barrymore, Jr.* By 1951, the year he and his wife separated, the Archers had moved back to Hollywood. Two years later they were divorced.

The actor's favorite features are *White Heat* (1949), *Destination Moon* (1950), and *Ten Thousand Bedrooms* (1957). Among his other screen credits are: *Career* (1939) with Anne Shirley, *Scattergood Baines* (1941), *The Eve of St. Mark* (1944) with Michael O'Shea,[8] *My Favorite Spy* (1951), *The Big Trees* (1952), *The Stars Are Shining* (1953), and the Elvis Presley starrer *Blue Hawaii* (1962).

He was a regular on *Gangbusters* and *Counterspy* and created the role of "field agent Sheppard" on *The FBI in Peace and War*.

After his Broadway debut in *The Odds Against Mrs. Oakley* (1944), John Archer was directed by Elliott Nugent in *A Place of His Own* (1945) and by Jed Harris in *One-Man Show*.

In 1947 he played opposite Joan Tetzel in *Strange Bedfellows*. Three years later he was Edna Best's leading man in *Captain Brassbound's Conversion*, his last Broadway appearance. In 1960 Constance Bennett and Archer headed the cast of *Happenstance* at the Tappan Zee Playhouse.

One near-miss in his career came when he

Bobby Downey

John Archer in the den of his home in Thousand Oaks, California.

turned down the lead opposite Betty Field in what was to become a Broadway hit, *Dream Girl,* to sing Lerner and Loewe songs with Irene Manning in *The Day Before Spring*. Another was when he tested for a role in the Joan Crawford starrer *The Damned Don't Cry,* which went to the late Kent Smith. He also made a screen test as "Ashley" in *Gone with the Wind* and did a pilot opposite Barbara Stanwyck for a series that never sold. His biggest disappointment was losing the costarring role with Claudette Colbert in *The Egg and I* to Fred MacMurray.

Since 1968 Archer has been a sales executive with a trucking firm owned by his brother.

He readily admits: "I still miss acting. I didn't give it up. It gave me up."

Since 1956 he has been married to Ann Leddy, who had a career in Chicago as an actress on radio. Neither their son nor their daughter ever expressed an interest in the entertainment industry.

13

Lenore Aubert's appearance in Abbott and Costello Meet Frankenstein *(1948) was the first time a mad scientist was played on the screen by an actress, according to film historian David Del Valle. Most of her roles in pictures were more glamorous.*

Lenore Aubert

The continental movie actress was born on April 18 in Yugoslavia. Her father, a general in the Austro-Hungarian army, was stationed in the town of Celje, her birthplace. Her original name was Eleanore Maria Leisner.

Aubert was raised in Vienna and educated at convent schools. She was stagestruck at a very early age, but her parents tried in vain to discourage her from a career as an actress.

In 1938 she married another young, aspiring actor. Because her husband was Jewish she fled Vienna for Paris with him after the Anschluss. Shortly afterward they came to New York, where she immediately found work as a fashion model.

Lenore came to Hollywood on a bus. She was in a production at the Bliss-Hayden Theatre when a scout for Samuel Goldwyn arranged for her to be screen-tested.

When Lenore was signed to a contract with Samuel Goldwyn Pictures, she was led to believe that she would be introduced to the public as a new star in the mold of Hedy Lamarr. It was not until she lunched with her producer that she learned all of his plans for her.

Goldwyn also expected that she would be his mistress. She declined, pointing out that she took her marriage vows and her Roman Catholicism seriously. She was then told that, since he had to pay her, she would appear in movies. "But," he added, "you will never, ever be a star for me or anyone else."

Her agent, Gummo Marx, interested Metro-Goldwyn-Mayer in buying her contract, but Goldwyn refused their offer. Shortly after, he sold her services to RKO, "not for more money," said Lenore more than forty years later, "but because he hated Mr. Mayer and thought it less likely RKO could do anything with me. He couldn't bear the thought of being shown up. He was the great Goldwyn."

She was introduced to screen audiences in *They Got Me Covered* (1943), playing a seductive Nazi agent to Bob Hope's takes and wisecracks. After *Action in Arabia* (1944) and *Having a Wonderful Crime* (1945), Lenore played the title role in *The Wife of Monte Cristo* (1946) with Martin Kosleck.[8]

She made *The Catman of Paris* (1946) and then supported Barbara Stanwyck and David Niven in *The Other Love* (1947). Among her other credits are *Abbott and Costello Meet the Killer* (1949) and *Barbary Pirate* (1949).

Lenore Aubert was considered for the leading roles in *For Whom the Bell Tolls* and *Saratoga Trunk,* both of which went to Ingrid Bergman. She was also tested for the role Marlene Dietrich played in *Golden Earrings* and the Merle Oberon part in *A Song to Remember.*

Of her thirteen Hollywood films, her favorite is *I Wonder Who's Kissing Her Now?* (1947). In it she portrayed Fritzi Scheff, the international musical star of the early part of this century. Aubert is both chagrined and amused that she is best known for *Abbott and Costello Meet Frankenstein* (1948).

Lenore virtually abandoned her career when she left Hollywood in the late forties at the insistence of her husband, who had little success as an actor. The couple moved to New York City, and he went into the garment business. Four years later, just as he was becoming a millionaire, they were divorced. She spent the remainder of the fifties in Eu-

Jim McPherson

Lenore Aubert in her apartment in the Yorkville area of Manhattan in 1987. She has lived by herself since divorcing her second husband in 1974.

rope, where she made *Falschmünzer am Werk* (1951) in Germany and *Fille sur la Route* (1952) in France.

Lenore returned to the United States in 1959 as the wife of an American businessman. They maintained a penthouse in Manhattan and another home in Florida throughout the fifteen years they were together.

Lenore Aubert was considered by both fans and professionals to be a "lost" screen personality until her first published interview since leaving Hollywood broke in the *Toronto Sun* in late 1987. Jim McPherson got the exclusive.

At the request of Ms. Aubert, Jim McPherson wrote in his article: "She is delighted to know that she is still remembered by movie fans—but it's not possible for her to meet them or to acknowledge letters.

"About four years ago, she suffered a stroke and, while there is no physical evidence whatsoever, it has seriously impaired her memory and her powers of concentration—even the simple business of signing a photograph is a major undertaking."

Although he was still in his twenties at the time, Harry had to wear a hairpiece when he appeared in the first Kay Kyser feature, That's Right, You're Wrong *(1939). Some of the other movies they made together were* You'll Find Out *(1940),* Playmates *(1941), and* My Favorite Spy *(1942).*

Harry Babbitt

The vocalist of the big band era was born in St. Louis, Missouri, on November 2.

Babbitt was on staff at KWK, the Mutual radio network's affiliate in St. Louis, when he got his "big chance."

Kay Kyser was already a well-known name in popular music when his *Kollege of Musical Knowledge,* a popular radio show, came to St. Louis in 1938. His male singer, Bill Stoker, who went on to train Johnny Mathis, gave notice. Harry was auditioned and hired to take his place.

He quickly became very much a part of Kyser's weekly network radio program. Babbitt sang duets with the band's songstress, Ginny Sims, and joined in the teasings of the aggregation's comic, "Ish Kabibble."

When Kyser was away from the bandstand Babbitt led the musicians. When Harry enlisted in the navy in 1944, Kay asked him to audition and hire his own replacement. He chose a young singer named Michael Douglas, who eventually became nationally famous as TV host Mike Douglas.

Babbitt and the Kyser outfit earned gold records for their World War II hit recordings of "I've Got Spurs That Jingle, Jangle, Jingle," "Three Little Fishes," "Who Wouldn't Love You?," "Mairzy Doats," and "Praise the Lord and Pass the Ammunition."

Harry was the emcee of *Bandstand Revue,* an early telecast of pioneer west coast TV station KTLA. The weekly variety show provided comics Rowan and Martin with their first TV exposure.

From 1948 until 1960 Harry Babbitt had his own morning radio show over KNX, the CBS outlet in Los Angeles. During much of the run it was called *The Second Cup of Coffee Club.*

The feeling of "family" that Kay Kyser and his people were capable of projecting to the public on the air and in the movies was a reality. Until Kyser's death in 1985, Babbitt,

Sims, and Merwyn A. Bogue (the real name of "Ish Kabibble") remained in touch with the former band leader turned Christian Science practitioner and lecturer. Babbitt, Bogue, and Sims have worked with each other off and on over the years in the real estate business. "Ish," as he is always referred to, and Harry have been sales executives for the various land development ventures of Don Easterbrook, the husband of Ginny Sims.

Throughout the years Babbitt has performed with the Freddy Martin and Les Brown groups and at benefits. In 1988, with the blessing of Georgia Carroll, Kay Kyser's widow, he regrouped some of the former members along with additions and took the band on tour as "Harry Babbitt and the Kay Kyser Orchestra."

"Ish Kabibble" planned to join them for cruises scheduled later in the year, if his wife's health were to improve.

Harry and his wife, who have been married for more than fifty years, were childhood sweethearts. They have three sons and six grandchildren.

In 1960 the Babbitts settled in Newport Beach. A tennis enthusiast, Harry was the manager of the swank Newport Beach Tennis Club for three years. He is active in civic affairs and as a realtor.

He is frequently recognized by prospective clients when he shows properties. His stock reply to the inevitable question of whether he still sings is, "If you'll sign—right here—I'll sing *whatever* you like."

Marty Jackson

Harry Babbitt, Maxine Andrews, and Jimmie Rodgers toured the United States together in early 1988 for four months.

Mary Brian[8] and Thomas Beck (right) supported Warner Oland, who had the title role in Charlie Chan in Paris *(1935). Beck had similar roles in three other "Charlie Chan" features and two of the "Mr. Moto" series.*

Thomas Beck

The young leading man of the thirties was born in New York City on December 29, 1909. He was raised in Baltimore, where his father supervised the Maryland Workshop for the Blind.

While at Johns Hopkins University, Beck appeared in plays both on campus and with the famous University Players. Other members of the Players at that time included James Stewart, Margaret Sullavan, Joshua Logan, and Henry Fonda.

He received a B.A. degree during the depths of the Great Depression. When he could not find work as an engineer, Beck took a role in the Broadway play *Mademoiselle* (1932), which starred Grace George and Alice Brady. His contract with Fox Films came about after a scout for the studio saw him in *Her Majesty the Widow* (1934) as the son of Pauline Frederick. His movie debut was in *Hell in the Heavens* (1934) with Conchita Montenegro.*

The late filmologist Don Miller once commented on the screen career of Thomas Beck: "Fox used him every which way—small parts in big pictures and big parts in small pictures. With those clean-cut looks, he was pleasing to the family trade and perfectly cast as the love interest or best friend. He could never play a villain, but was perfect for the gal to fall back on, when 'Charlie Chan' or 'Mr. Moto' would come up with the surprising solution to the case. He was never shown to advantage at his home lot or in the B films he made after leaving Fox."

Among his screen credits are: *Lottery Lover* (1934) with Peggy Fears,* *Music Is Magic* (1935), *My Marriage* (1935) with the late Kent Taylor, *Crackup* (1936) with Peter Lorre, *Every Saturday Night* (1936) with June Lang,* *Under Two Flags* (1936), *White*

Thomas Beck in the front yard of his home in Miami Shores, Florida.

Fang (1936), *Heidi* (1937) with Shirley Temple, *Seventh Heaven* (1937) with Simone Simon [10],* *Walking Down Broadway* (1938), *Road Demon* (1938), *The Family Next Door* (1939) with Joy Hodges, and *I Stand Accused* (1939) with Bob Cummings.[9]

Beck was a casualty of the change of regimes at his studio. When it became Twentieth Century-Fox, the new production head, Darryl F. Zanuck, passed over Tom when casting major films. Important leads were assigned to more recent contractees such as Tyrone Power, Henry Fonda, and Richard Greene.

Recently he talked about his years at Fox and the abrupt end of his career: "I was less than happy with my parts and pictures from the beginning. When Katharine Hepburn offered me a role in *The Philadelphia Story* on Broadway, I went to the studio manager and suggested we terminate my contract. He became very disagreeable and refused. But twice when my option came up for renewal, I was asked to forgo the raise I had coming because of the financial state of the studio. The third time I refused and was let go."

Tom left Hollywood on Labor Day, 1939. By 1940 he had enlisted in the U. S. army as a private. When he was discharged five years later, after serving in the Pacific Theatre with the 98th Infantry, he held the rank of major.

Beck returned to Broadway in *Temper the Wind* (1946) with the late Blanche Yurka. Shortly after the play closed, he was standing

Marty Jackson

Mary Brian,[8] once publicized as the "Sweetest Girl in Pictures," with the late George Chandler[10] at a Screen Actors Guild function.

in line at the unemployment office reading the *New York Times*. "It was a long line," says Tom, "and I had plenty of time to finish an article on the tremendous prosperity of postwar America. It made me wonder what I was doing with my life."

Soon afterward he went into the advertising business. He worked both as a space salesman and an art director with the same New York agency for almost twenty years. After retiring to Redding, Connecticut, in 1965, Beck took out a real estate license. He ran his own office from 1966 until 1977, when he moved to Florida. Until recent years Tom sold real estate in Miami Shores, where he lives. By 1986, when his companion of more than thirty-five years died, Beck had retired.

His home contains his collections of Sepik River New Guinea carvings and Puerto Rico Santos. Beck paints in oil and watercolor. In 1988 he began a portrait of Ivan Lendl as World Tennis Champion. His pet is a stray marmalade cat named "Jim Boulton."

Recently, after discussing his career with the author, he commented: "I sometimes go for several years without a thought about those days. But when it is brought back to me, the experiences seem very fresh. I've enjoyed the times since then, but those were particularly happy years."

Adults, a large part of Molly Bee's following, were attracted by her wholesomeness and the modesty of her clothes. When she cut her famous pigtails in 1959, she received letters of protest from all over North America. "It was like having twenty thousand parents and grandparents," said the twenty-year-old singer at the time.

Molly Bee

The country western performer was born Mollie Beachboard in Grand Coolee Dam, Washington. Her birthdate is August 18, 1939. Her mother is a registered member of a tribe of Choctaw Indians.

She learned to sing and yodel from her older brother at a very early age. In 1949, shortly after her family moved to Tucson, Rex Allen* heard her sing in a grammar-school play and invited her onto his local radio show.

William Holden, who was in the audience when the ten-year-old performed at the Davis-Monthan Air Force Base, immediately sent a letter of praise and recommendation to Howard Hughes. The men on the base were so sure of her talent that they took up a collection for her trip to Los Angeles, where she was to appear on the TV show *Hollywood Opportunity* on KTLA, Channel 5.

One of her prizes as winner of that televised talent contest was a spot on the *Doye O'Dell Show,* a country music program on the station. Tennessee Ernie Ford and his manager/producer Cliffie Stone saw it and signed her for their show *Hometown Jamboree,* where she was to appear frequently for the next eight years. She was also with Ford on his Monday-through-Friday daytime NBC-TV show for four seasons. For more than two years Molly, as her name came to be spelled, was on Pinky Lee's* television show. When she left, it was to become a regular on Steve Allen's syndicated series. Then she spent the 1963–66 seasons on Jimmy Dean's variety show on ABC-TV.

Molly Bee was a familiar name and face to television viewers before she had ever actually watched a TV show. It was not until she guested on Ed Sullivan's *Toast of the Town* that she sat and viewed the celebrities who preceded her on the monitor. It was the first time she realized that she was one of them.

Recently she explained: "I was just too busy, what with my school lessons and all the jobs I was getting. We didn't have TV at our home then. Most people still went to their relatives' or neighbors' to see important shows."

Her closest friend and classmate at Hollywood Professional Children's School was Jimmy Boyd. After his recording of "I Saw Mommie Kissing Santa Claus" hit the charts, he worked with Molly on the same song. Her label, Capitol, recorded her rendition, which resulted in a gold record in 1952.

Her first date was with Stan Freberg. Her first romance was with Tommy Sands, another Cliffie Stone "find." The teenagers sang duets on TV and were featured in fanzines and on their covers, but drifted apart due mainly to the strong disapproval of Sand's professional management.

Americans watched Molly Bee grow up on their television screens. The problem, as the singer perceived it, was that her audience did not really want her to grow up. A large number of her following were adults, who liked the respectful way she related to her elders and appreciated the modesty of her clothes. She wore high necklines and kept her pigtails for so long that she was referred to in print as the "world's oldest teenager."

Country western music had not yet come into widespread popularity throughout Middle America in the early sixties. Many in the northern states associated the term with comedy of the *Beverly Hillbillies* sort. When she showed up for rehearsals on the *Jackie Gleason Show,* Molly found that she was expected to sing in front of a backdrop on which an outhouse had been painted. She refused to perform until it was removed.

Her recording of "Single Girl Again" brought her a Grammy nomination in 1965. She appeared in *Summer Love* (1958), *Man's Favorite Sport* (1964), *Chartreuse Caboose* (1960) with Ben Cooper,[9] and *Going Steady* (1958). Molly would have been in an Elvis Presley picture, but she was committed to tour with Jack Benny. She was the comedian's opening act, as she had been for George Burns and Dean Martin. Molly Bee proved to be a big draw to the rural crowds who attended state fairs as well as to the more sophisticated audiences at Chicago's Drake Hotel and Houston's Statler-Hilton.

Francia Nieman

On New Year's Eve, 1986, Molly married Bob Muncy, whom she met through her brother. Her husband, a gift manufacturer, had lived in Hawaii for several years during the early seventies. At that time his closest friend was Tommy Sands.[10] Neither of the couple has been in touch with Sands for some time.

It was in the late sixties that she began to withdraw from the profession. Recently she explained: "I had my first baby when I was twenty-nine and liked the experience a whole lot. So, I had another. Then I lost part of my nose to cancer, which gave me the reason and the time to really think about my life. My dad had died a few months after we first came to Hollywood. So, I had been the sole support of my mother and two brothers ever since I was ten years old. I had another baby, a boy, and have hardly sung since. I don't even listen much to music."

During the seventies she lived in the Pacific Northwest. Molly, her mother, son, two daughters, and fifth husband are now settled in a large hillside home in Oceanside, California.

Asked if she ever missed performing, Molly Bee replied: "There is a twinge every now and then. But I believe that when I was doing what I did, I was doing it the best. Now there are many real talents and they are every bit as well known as I was. What I had spoiled me. I think I'll just leave it at what I remember, because it really was a ball!"

In the early twenties artist Penrhyn Stanlaws called Madge Bellamy "The Most Beautiful Girl in America," and columnist Louella O. Parsons wrote of her "soulful eyes and holier-than-thou look." Yet the star is best remembered for a shooting incident that occurred years after her career on stage and screen had ended.

Madge Bellamy

The star of silent pictures was born Margaret Philpott in Hillsboro, Texas, on June 30, 1900. Her father coached athletics and taught at a college.

The Philpotts' only child was determined at a very young age to become an actress. She got her early training at Elitch's Gardens, a prominent stock company in Denver.

Producer Daniel Frohman noticed Madge in a chorus line and put her under personal contract. When Helen Hayes left the cast of *Dear Brutus,* she was replaced by Frohman's "discovery," who had been renamed Madge Bellamy. Her reviews in the role were on a par with those received by Hayes, whose rep-

utation was established in that Broadway hit of 1918. Indeed, several critics preferred Madge's interpretation.

In most of Madge Bellamy's starring roles during the twenties she personified innocence. She had the title role in the film version of the classic *Lorna Doone* (1922). She costarred opposite George O'Brien in *The Iron Horse* under John Ford's direction. After that western became a major box-office attraction when released in 1924, the studio brought them together again in *Havoc* (1925). *Summer Bachelors* (1926) and *Ankles Preferred* (1927) were also vehicles for Madge.

Madge Bellamy says she was promised the lead in *Seventh Heaven.* When it went to Janet Gaynor she complained bitterly to William Fox, who told her, "I'm not in business to please you."

Fox thought enough of her potential, however, to present Madge in the first dialogue feature produced by his studio, *Mother Knows Best* (1928). It was the screen version of an Edna Ferber novel that was based on the life of Elsie Janis, an international star of vaudeville.

In it Madge sang, danced, and did impressions of Anna Held, Harry Lauter, and Al Jolson (in blackface). But it did poorly with the critics and the public.

Fox acquired the screen rights to *The Trial of Mary Dugan,* but his star adamantly refused to make a picture of the play that had been a hit on Broadway in 1927.

After the Fox-Bellamy contract was terminated, Madge was forced to sell her home at auction. Called "The Cedars," it had been built by director Maurice Tourneur and was a copy of the Duke of Alba's Spanish castle.

When Madge was re-signed by Fox Films in the early thirties, there seemed to be the possibility of a comeback. But after being cast in small parts in several low-budget productions, she refused even to accept calls from the studio.

Among her few talkies were the Buck Jones serial *Gordon of Ghost City* (1933); *Gigolettes of Paris* (1933); *The Daring Young Man* (1935) with James Dunn[8] and Mae Clarke;[8] *Under Your Spell* (1936); and *Northwest Trail* (1945) with Bob Steele,[9] her last.

The film for which she is best known, because of its cult status, is the B horror film *White Zombie* (1932), which starred Bela Lugosi.

Originally, Universal Pictures was to have produced *The Great Ziegfeld* with Madge as Anna Held. When M-G-M filmed it, the part was played by Luise Rainer and brought her an Academy Award.

Madge was married in 1928 to a stockbroker. She found his interests "prosaic" and his tastes "vulgar." When her husband suggested they pool their finances, the star immediately moved out of the house, even though she owned it. They were together for less than three days.

Almost sixty years after making the decisions that changed her professional and domestic life, Madge Bellamy said: "I was so full of myself and quite stupid really. M-G-M bought *Mary Dugan* from Fox and gave it to Norma Shearer, who made a huge success in it. But I have no regrets about leaving my husband. From what I have seen of marriage, it seems to require that both parties give up a great deal of their individualities. I could never give up my independence for anyone. So, marriage and I were incompatible."

It was her strong feelings for a man, however, that brought the silent star's name back to the front pages in 1943. After a five-year affair with Madge Bellamy, her lover, a wealthy lumberman, married another woman. Days later, as the millionaire was leaving the Union Club on San Francisco's Nob Hill, his jilted mistress shot him.

Madge Bellamy (left) *with Gloria Stuart at the party given by Crown Publishers on December 5, 1986, for all of the personalities ever profiled in a* Whatever Became of . . . ? *book. For Ms. Bellamy, a resident of Ontario, California, it was the first "personal appearance" in more than fifty years.*

Marty Jackson

Eventually, Madge was given a suspended sentence and placed on probation, but the press made much of her virginal public image while the crime and proceedings were news. "Madge the Immaculate" and "Pistol Packin' Madge" were how two of William Randolph Hearst's newspapers referred to her. His *American Weekly* featured the shooting in a two-page spread.

But it was the star who had the last word: "I only winged him, which is all I meant to do. Believe me, I'm a crack shot."

Since 1946 Madge Bellamy has lived in Ontario, California, and until recent years she owned and operated a large junk yard. Retired, she now lives alone in a house guarded by two large dogs. Her only contacts with Hollywood are regular telephone conversations with her contemporary Dorothy Revier.

Madge is an atheist and a vegetarian. She describes her politics as "Left, far Left. Too far Left for most people." She claims never to have loved anyone except her parents and close friends.

In 1987 she explained: "I've avoided all my life the romantic stuff which novels and movies are about. Never went in for that mush. Of course, I've missed what most people would call the ultimate human experience. But then, I've remained my own person, which at my age is a very satisfying state."

On Yancy Derringer, *a TV series of the late fifties, X Brands played "Pahoo-Ka-Ta-Wah." Although he specialized in portraying American Indians, he is of German-Dutch descent.*

X Brands

The Caucasian actor who made a career on the screen as an Indian was born in Kansas City, Missouri. His birthdate is July 24, 1927.

His original name is Jay X Brands. The middle letter is his name, not an initial.

Since 1743 there has been a tradition within the Brands family to have one male member known as "X." Throughout his life he has been called "X."

In 1936 the Brands family moved to Glendale, California. When he was old enough to ride, X was given his own horse. Before he joined the navy at the outbreak of World War II, X had ridden in a number of rodeos.

During the Korean War his reserve unit was activated. When he was discharged, Brands enrolled at Ben Bard's Players under the G.I. Bill of Rights. He studied acting there for two years.

All of his free time was spent at the Hitching Post Café, a hangout for western stunt men and bit players. When a Columbia casting director called the restaurant looking for a young actor over 6 feet tall who could ride a motorcycle, X applied. He made his debut as one of Marlon Brando's sidekicks in *The Wild One* (1954).

X worked as an extra and did stunt work and walk-ons. Sometimes he worked on two TV shows in one day. Screen Gems and Gene Autry's Flying "A" productions were his main employers. He was Bill Williams'[9] double on the *Kit Carson* series.

His stunt work in *Hondo* (1953) led to a long, happy association with John Wayne. X appeared in almost every movie the star made thereafter and had dialogue in some, such as *The Conqueror* (1956).

By the mid-fifties Brands had done enough speaking parts that he decided to concentrate on acting exclusively. Casting directors and producers found X most effective as an American Indian. After he was signed as Jock Mahoney's Indian aide on *Yancy Derringer,* a CBS-TV show of the 1958–59 season, his agent told him that he was so typecast he could no longer be considered for other parts. Even when he appeared on *Tales of the Bengal Lancers,* it was as an East Indian.

X Brands is the Chief Flight Instructor and Pilot Examiner at the Van Nuys Airport.

X was perfectly satisfied with that professional niche and worked until American Indian groups began to voice objections to being played on the screen by white actors made up to look like them (some of whom even had to wear contact lenses to hide their blue eyes).

As westerns on television were almost completely phased out and few features were being made, X found himself unemployed and virtually unemployable in TV or movies.

In 1969 another out-of-work actor, who was supporting himself as a dispatcher at a small airport, suggested that Brands get a job as a flight instructor; flying had long been his hobby.

By 1971 he had flown more than 12,000 hours. It was, in X's own words, "the perfect job. I could take off if an acting job came up, and since it was an airfield there wasn't a drop of alcohol for miles around." (Brands had developed a problem with drinking while "waiting for the phone to ring." He attributes one of his two divorces to alcohol. He has not had a drink since 1968.)

Among the features he made are *Escort West* (1959) and *Comanche Territory* (1950).

Now and then X Brands still lands acting jobs. He played Rock Hudson's lawyer, who flies their plane into a mountain, in *Avalanche* (1978) and recently portrayed a pilot on a segment of *Dynasty*.

Occasionally he has business at the Van Nuys Airport, where he is Chief Flight Instructor and Pilot Examiner, with personalities from his original profession. He "checked out" John Denver recently and gave a demonstration ride to David Crosby, who expressed astonishment that X did not know his name or his music.

He is still a close friend of Brummett Echohawk, a spokesman for the Pawnee Indians. The two met in 1959 when X was Grand Marshall of the Homecoming in Pawnee, Oklahoma. Echohawk once wrote an open letter to Hollywood producers commending Brands on the authenticity of his performance and complimenting his pronunciation of the tribe's language.

X concluded a 1987 interview by saying: "I supported myself for years portraying American Indians. But in recent years I have come to realize that I owe them another debt of gratitude. I did not have a religious upbringing, nor do I now attend a church. But you cannot come to know these great people, as I have been privileged to do, without coming to believe in God."

Keefe Brasselle starred in movies, including the title role in The Eddie Cantor Story *(1953), hosted TV variety and quiz shows, headlined in Las Vegas, produced sit-coms, and wrote novels. Shortly after he died in 1981, journalist Jim Trombetta wrote of him in the* Los Angeles Times *as "charming, cunning, tireless . . . [his] achievements were literally meteoric—flaring like a shooting star and fading just as fast."*

Keefe Brasselle

The highly controversial show business jack-of-all-trades was born John Brasselli in Elyria, Ohio. His family used the name Brasselle and called him Keefe. His birthday was February 7, 1923.

After his father was killed during a fight in a local dance hall, his mother moved to Hollywood. By the time Keefe came to Hollywood during the late forties, Marie Brasselle was well known in her profession as Betty Grable's favorite hairdresser.

Keefe was brought up by his paternal uncle. After he left home during his teens to tour with a band, that uncle was arrested for child molestation.

Biographer Doug Warren, his next-door

neighbor during grammar school, remembers his former playmate as a "snide brat who—if he had the edge—was a bully."

In high school Keefe excelled as a cheerleader. He also liked to play pool, which was how he made spending money.

When Warren saw him in Hollywood, Brasselle had married a fifteen-year-old girl. While waiting for his card from the musician's union he sold tires across from the Palladium.

When he switched to acting Keefe claimed to be single, although he and his wife were living together and by then had a daughter. After Betty Grable talked him up to Louella O. Parsons, he was tested for the lead in *Knock on Any Door*. Another piece of publicity in a fanzine drew the attention of Ida Lupino.[10]

Director-producer Lupino represented Brasselle as her "discovery," teaming him with Sally Forrest[10] as the leads in *Not Wanted* (1949), *Never Fear* (1950), and *The Young Lovers* (1949).

Lupino sold his contract to M-G-M, where he appeared in *Dial 1119* (1950), *The Unknown Man* (1951), and *Skirts Ahoy!* (1952). His later credits include *Three Young Texans* (1954), *Mad at the World* (1955), *Battle Stations* (1956), and *West of Suez* (1957). He was hopelessly miscast as the scion of an old-money Wasp family in *A Place in the Sun* (1951).

Brasselle believed strongly in his abilities, especially as a song-and-dance man. He expected that playing the title role in *The Eddie Cantor Story* (1953) would make him a major star. Instead, the film musical was a disappointment to all concerned, including Eddie Cantor. Yet, when he did his act at the Thunderbird Hotel in Las Vegas, Keefe drew reviews and business good enough to get him booked back more than once.

What brought him the most money and

notoriety was his close relationship with James Aubrey, who became president of CBS-TV in 1959. The liaison was always subject to much unsavory speculation.

On CBS-TV he hosted the variety shows that were summer replacements for Jackie Gleason in 1962 and for Garry Moore the following season. In 1964 Brasselle produced and hired Rudy Vallee as emcee.

During its 1964–65 season CBS-TV carried *The Cara Williams Show* and *The Baileys of Balboa,* sit-coms that Brasselle's production company produced. The same network during the same period ran *The Reporter,* an hour-long dramatic series, also sold to them by Keefe. What drew attention within the industry was that the inexperienced producer had managed to sell three shows without investing in one pilot.

By the end of 1965 all of the Brasselle productions had been canceled, and James Aubrey had been removed from his position.

In 1968 Brasselle wrote *The CanniBalS,* † which *Variety* referred to as a "bitter, thinly disguised novel" about life at the top in a TV network. His second novel, *The Barracudas,* was described by its publisher as "the blistering story of Hollywood and New York and their play-for-pay girls who will do anything if the price is right." The latter was a reference to the widely circulated rumors that the CBS head was dismissed just in time to avoid a major sex scandal.

Keefe reveled in publicity, good or bad. A 1956 divorce from his first wife and the alimony hearings that followed were fully reported, as was his marriage to Arlene DeMarco of the singing DeMarco Sisters the same year. His separation from Arlene and the subsequent litigation over child support frequently made the papers, especially when Arlene accused him of stealing $40,000 worth of her jewelry.

Male bisexuality was one of the themes of

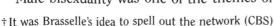

Until shortly before he died in 1980, Keefe Brasselle made appearances at events such as golf tournaments and tributes. This photo was taken in 1980, when he officiated for the fifth and final year at Burbank's Easter parade.

Arlene DeMarco's 1971 roman à clef *Triangle,* a novel with a show-business background. In interviews promoting her book she denied that any character in it was based on Brasselle. She spoke, however, with great bitterness about "girls I know, who married guys who really prefer men or boys."

Throughout most of his career Keefe was reputed to have underworld connections. The late David Susskind said, "He came on like a 1965 George Raft."

In 1971 Keefe Brasselle was back in the news when he shot and wounded a stunt man during an argument in a San Fernando Valley bar. After a woman, who identified herself as his wife, testified in his behalf, he was fined and placed on three years' probation.

Keefe received therapy for his heavy drinking and for a while attended Alcoholics Anonymous meetings. The cause of his death on July 7, 1980, was listed as cirrhosis of the liver.

Friends insist he had no financial problems and lived well until the end of his life. Yet the home he had bought for his mother was taken from her and sold.

A one-time press agent for Keefe Brasselle, who had kept in touch over the years, believed he was not lonely in later years because "he worshipped himself. He was never alone as long as he had Keefe Brasselle."

† It was Brasselle's idea to spell out the network (CBS) in the title.

27

Jim Brown played "Lt. Rip Masters" and Lee Aaker was "Col. Rusty" in all 164 half-hour segments of The Adventures of Rin Tin Tin *produced for TV in the mid-fifties. The show's central figure was the great-grandson of the original Rin-Tin-Tin,* a major attraction of silent movies. When the shows were re-packaged in 1976, Brown appeared with Rin-Tin-Tin VII in the openings and closings.*

Jim Brown

The screen actor was born in the tent city that sprang up during the oil boom in Desdemona, Texas. His birthdate is March 22, 1920. Jim attended the Schriner Military School in Kearville and spent two years at Baylor University.

Having won several tennis championships, he earned his first trip to Hollywood by playing for expense money in tournaments along the way. When a photo of him taken with a debutante at the Los Angeles Tennis Club appeared in the newspaper, he was immediately contacted by three agents.

It was the fabled Henry Willson whom he chose for representation. Jim was screen-tested by Twentieth Century-Fox and seriously considered for the lead in *The Outlaw,* but when no firm offers were forthcoming, he returned to Baylor University.

The following year, when Jim returned to Hollywood, Willson got him a contract with Paramount Pictures, where he was to replace the rebellious Sterling Hayden. Jim was immediately given a role in *Young and Willing* (1943).

Brown was glad at the time to be signed by a major studio but was soon unhappy over the way Paramount used him. He was tested for *So Proudly We Hail,* but Claudette Colbert, the film's star, nixed him as being too young to be her leading man. After Warner Brothers bought his services from Paramount for one feature a year, he was tested for *Destination Tokyo.* But the part went to John Garfield, because Paramount wanted Jim for another assignment. He was announced to star in the remake of *The Virginian,* but after its budget was increased, Jim was replaced by Joel McCrea. When *Thirty Seconds Over Tokyo* was offered to him, Paramount again refused the loan-out.

During the making of *Going My Way* (1944), the actor poured out his frustrations to Bing Crosby. Although he never knew for certain, Brown believes it was Crosby who arranged for his release, something he and Willson had been refused repeatedly during his five years on the Marathon lot. But his freedom came at a time when the movie industry was cutting back on production. He now views the move as a mistake.

His part as Gary Cooper's deputy in *High Noon* (1952) proved a major disappointment:

Both of his big scenes were edited out of the release print.

Among his thirty-four feature films are: *Air Force* (1943), *Springfield Rifle* (1952), *The Charge at Feather River* (1953), *Wild Blue Yonder* (1952), *The Forest Rangers* (1942), *Corvette K-225* (1943), *Sands of Iwo Jima* (1949), *Our Hearts Were Young and Gay* (1944), *The Woman They Almost Lynched* (1953), *Anna Lucasta* (1949), *Objective Burma* (1945), *The Groom Wore Spurs* (1951), *20,000 Eyes* (1961), and *Targets* (1968).

He received his greatest exposure on *The Adventures of Rin Tin Tin*. During the six years he played the adult lead on the series, Brown had only 1½ days off.

"The dog's hours were closely watched by his owners," remembers Jim. "And Lee, being a child, had a mother and a tutor looking after his time and energies. So I was the one to be worked ragged. I loved all of it and am still proud of the good stuff we had in those shows for kids, but it was exhausting."

Jim Brown believes he has been hampered by his name from the outset of his career. Henry Willson pleaded in vain with Paramount to rename him when he was signed. After his stint with *The Adventures of Rin Tin Tin* he wanted to use his character's name professionally, but the producer refused his request. Today, because of the prominence of soul singer James Brown and the football player Jim Brown, he is billed as James L. Brown.

Brown has three daughters by Verna Knopf, a model and Howard Hughes contractee whom he married in 1942. Immediately upon his divorce in 1947 he married a nonprofessional. The childless couple were divorced in 1971. Two years later he married his present wife in a ceremony performed by the father of John Davidson. They live in Woodland Hills, California.

James L. Brown recently with western heroine June Storey.

Marty Jackson

Johnny Crawford (left), *best known for TV's* The Rifleman, *with Lee Aaker. The juvenile star of* Rin Tin Tin *is a professional carpenter, a divorcé, and a resident of Sylmar, California.*

Clint Brown

When he is asked for an autograph, it is invariably because fans know him from *The Adventures of Rin Tin Tin* or as "Detective Sergeant Harry McSween" on *Dallas*. Jim has played what he refers to as "J.R.'s crooked cop" on almost fifty episodes of the series.

Sonny Bupp and Ruth Warrick played the son and wife of "Charles Foster Kane," the central figure in the highly esteemed Citizen Kane *(1941). The actress had a brief affair with its star-director, Orson Welles, shortly after they made the film.*

Sonny Bupp

The child actor best known for his role in *Citizen Kane* (1941) was born in New York City on January 10, 1928. His original name was Mayer MacClairn Bupp.

In 1930 the Bupp family moved to Los An-geles. Shortly thereafter Mrs. Bupp began taking Sonny's older sister on the rounds of casting offices. She had more success, how-ever, with his older brother, Tommy.

Sonny was still very young when he began appearing in productions at the Pasadena Playhouse. More than fifty years later he stated that he never cared for making movies but very much enjoyed acting on stage. His parents, who were in the process of breaking up, considered the plays he did as merely a way for him to get experience. Their goal for both boys was work in motion pictures.

Fans of the "Three Stooges" know Sonny for his part in the short *Goofs and Saddles* (1937). The following year he supported

Humphrey Bogart in *Swing Your Lady*. In the Hopalong Cassidy feature *Renegade Trail* (1939), he appeared as the boy sidekick to the cowboy star. His brother Tommy played roles in a number of westerns.

The picture that Sonny's family believed would establish him as a child star became instead the greatest disappointment of his career. *No Place to Go* (1939) was originally entitled *Not Wanted*. Dennis Morgan[8] received top billing, but Sonny had a prominent role. It was a human-interest picture, a genre thought to have plummeted in box-office appeal after war broke out in Europe. The studio so lost interest that the feature was given very few bookings and was never even released in California.

He also had small roles in *Three Faces West* (1940), *Father's Son* (1941), and *The Devil and Daniel Webster* (1941).

Being chosen to play in *Citizen Kane* was a unique experience for the twelve-year-old. He was picked from a group of boy actors by Orson Welles. The film's star-director was so struck by Sonny's resemblance to him that he cast the boy before he even heard him speak.

Shortly after he made *Citizen Kane*, Sonny moved to northern California with his mother and stepfather. Despite the film's controversy and eventual success, Bupp was virtually unaffected by it, professionally and personally.

In 1988 Mayer Bupp, as he is now known, celebrated his fortieth year with the Ford Motor Company. His title is Faculties Mechanization Manager, Parts & Service Division.

Bupp and his wife have been married since 1972. The childless couple live in Southfield, Michigan.

The former child actor's only contact with his past was an exchange of letters and photos in 1982 with Ronald Reagan. He wrote to the president, reminding him of their work-

Bupp has not been called "Sonny" since he left the acting profession. Family, friends, and co-workers call him "Mac."

Marty Jackson

Viewers of daytime TV know Ruth Warrick for her long-running role of wealthy matriarch "Phoebe Tyler" on All My Children. *She is single and lives in Manhattan, where she is an active member of the Democratic Party. Ms. Warrick has been married five times, twice to the same man, and has had two face-lifts.*

ing together in Reagan's first film, *Love on the Air* (1937). Like the president, he was originally liberal politically but now considers himself a conservative.

31

Janis Carter had the lead opposite Glenn Ford in Framed *(1947). The cast also included Karen Morley.*

Janis Carter

The leading lady of the forties was born Janis Dremann in Cleveland, Ohio. Her birthday is October 10, 1917.

After receiving a degree in music from Western Reserve University, Janis moved to Manhattan. Her goal was to sing at the Metropolitan Opera. When her audition did not go well, she decided on a career in the theatre.

While waiting to be cast in a Broadway show she modeled, at first as a "Conover Girl." When John Robert Powers opened his agency in partnership with future president Gerald Ford, Janis was one of the ten original models to sign with them.

She made her Broadway debut in the Vivienne Segal[8] starrer *I Married an Angel* (1938) but continued to model. She was seen as the Bostonian Girl and in advertisements for Raleigh cigarettes and Ipana toothpaste at the same time she was appearing on stage. Her second show was *DuBarry Was a Lady*

(1939). Songwriter-producer Buddy DeSylva squired her about town and gave her the nickname "Dish" Carter. But it was her part in *Panama Hattie* (1940) that got her a contract with Twentieth Century-Fox.

Studio head Darryl F. Zanuck, who had spotted her in *Panama Hattie,* permitted a loan-out to M-G-M, where she re-created her stage role in the movie version of *I Married an Angel* (1942). On her home lot she made only B pictures, usually as the "other woman."

Some of her Fox films were: *Cadet Girl* (1941), *Secret Agent of Japan* (1942), and *Girl Trouble* (1942).

Weary of supporting roles, Janis had her contract dissolved by mutual consent. She then signed with Columbia Pictures with the guarantee that she would play leads. Three days after signing she was cast opposite Chester Morris in *One Mysterious Night* (1944), a programmer. Then she was leading lady to Richard Dix in *Mark of the Whistler* (1944) and to William Gargan in *Night Editor* (1946). She appeared in *Slightly French* (1949), but Dorothy Lamour was the female star; likewise, Rosalind Russell got top billing in *A Woman of Distinction* (1950). She was

Glenn Ford entering Spago, where he attended the party given annually by agent Irving Lazar on the night the Oscars are given out.

Janis Carter and her husband, Julius Stulman, who is head of the World Institute.

leading lady to Randolph Scott, who dominated *Santa Fe* (1951). *Her Wonderful Lie* (1950) was a vehicle for the singing duo Jan Kiepura and Martha Eggerth.

Released from her commitment to Columbia, Janis Carter signed with RKO, which was then owned by Howard Hughes. At the time she was dating Noah Dietrich, overseer of the Hughes empire.

For RKO she made *The Woman on Pier 13* (1950), in support of Robert Ryan and Laraine Day. Next she did *My Forbidden Past* (1951), which starred Robert Mitchum and Ava Gardner. She had the female lead in *Flying Leathernecks* (1951), but it was a John Wayne-Robert Ryan picture. The film that might have put her over was *The Half-Breed* (1952). She played opposite Robert Young and had a chance to sing several songs, but the western did not do well with critics or the public.

Her RKO contract concluded, she was immediately signed as Revlon's first TV pitchwoman and appeared for thirteen weeks on behalf of their new "kiss-proof" lipstick on Jane Froman's TV show.

She toured for five months in *Put Them All Together* with Fay Bainter and William Prince. By the end of the run she was acting in the play in the evenings and substituting weekdays for Bess Myerson on the TV quiz show *Big Payoff.* From that program Janis got the cohost job with Bud Collyer on

Feather Your Nest, which lasted for two years. When *Panama Hattie* was done as a television special in 1955, Janis re-created her Broadway performance.

In 1951 her nine-year marriage to musician-composer Carl Prager ended in divorce. In 1956 she became the wife of lumber and shipping tycoon Julius Stulman.

The Stulmans travel frequently. They have made more than two dozen trips to Israel and have been to Europe more than fifty times.

Janis is on the executive board of Florida's Asolo State Theatre and the Asolo Opera Guild. She is also a director of the Ringling Brothers Museum.

The Stulmans spend much of their time in a condominium on Longboat Key, Florida. It has been described by Janis's longtime friend Ann Savage[9] as "lush outside and luxe within."

Another close friend of the Stulmans' is Jack Valenti, longtime president of the Motion Picture Association of America. Janis also remained in touch with Jeff Donnell.

The Stulmans' other home is a large apartment directly across from Duke University in Durham, North Carolina. The couple commute frequently, leaving their lavender-point Siamese cat in Longboat Key.

In the plays and sketches he appeared in between picture assignments, Chick Chandler took parts that would be considered "playing against type." He tried, but without success, to change his professional image from that of the affable, energetic nice guy.

Chick Chandler

The screen actor was born Fehmer Chandler in Kingston, New York. His birthdate was January 18, 1905.

His father, a surgeon, sent both of his sons to Manlius Military Academy, which served as a preparatory school for West Point. Chick, as he was already called, was very active in shows put on by the cadets. When he decided on show business rather than the military as a career, both of his parents were very supportive.

His first job was as assistant cameraman on some Pearl White films made at the New York City studios of William Fox. After being fired he went into burlesque as a comic. Then he toured in a vaudeville sketch, *I'm the Guy,* which featured Hugh Herbert.

Being the nephew of Howard Chandler Christy gave Chick a great advantage in New York City. Christy was one of the best-known illustrators and portrait artists of his day.

The young actor met most of Manhattan's elite at soirees in the Christy studio. At one party he became acquainted with Jean Frontai, a former Earl Carroll girl who had a part in *Once in a Lifetime* on Broadway. In 1933 they were married.

Chick had a role in *Pleasure Bound* (1929), a Broadway play that starred Jack Pearl, that showed him off well as a young, breezy leading man. He had the title role in *The Great McGoo* and was in rehearsal for the show when he was offered a contract with RKO. After a replacement was found, he left for Hollywood.

He had been signed at the urging of Fannie Brice, who admired his work on stage. David O. Selznick, who headed the studio during a brief period, saw his potential but soon left to join M-G-M. Chandler made *Melody Cruise* (1933) with Phil Harris,[9] *Blood Money* (1933), and *Murder on a Honeymoon* (1935), and was then dropped.

Chick made *Alias Mary Dow* (1935) for Universal and then joined the newly formed Twentieth Century-Fox, where he remained into the forties.

His wife appeared in shorts in support of Edgar Kennedy, Clark and McCullough, and Charlie Chase, and then left the profession.

In *Hollywood Cavalcade* (1939) Chandler was the assistant to the cameraman, who was played by Stuart Erwin. In *Remember the Day* (1941), which starred Claudette Colbert and John Payne, he was a reporter. He was to play those same roles many times throughout his career.

His other screen credits include: *Sing and Be Happy* (1937) with Dixie Dunbar,[8] *Portia On Trial* (1937) with Walter Abel,[10] *City Girl* (1938) with Phyllis Brooks,* *Alexander's Ragtime Band* (1938), *While New York Sleeps* (1938) with Joan Woodbury, *Swanee River* (1939) with Al Jolson and Don Ameche, *Tom Brown's School Days* (1940) with Jimmy Lydon[8] and Freddie Bartholomew,* *The Bride Came C.O.D.* (1941), *Springtime in the Rockies* (1942), *Action in the North Atlantic* (1943), *He Hired the Boss* (1943) with Evelyn Venable, *Hi Diddle Diddle* (1943) with Pola Negri, *Irish Eyes Are Smiling* (1944), *Johnny Doesn't Live Here Anymore* (1945) with James Ellison,[8] *Do You Love Me?* (1946), *Mother Wore Tights* (1947), *Family Honeymoon* (1949), *The Great Rupert* (1950) with Ruth Terry,* *Battle Cry* (1955), *Aaron Slick from Pumpkin Crick* (1952), *The Naked Gun* (1958) with Willard Parker,[10] *It's a Mad, Mad, Mad, Mad World* (1963), *Nightmare in the Sun* (1964), and *The Girl Who Knew Too Much* (1969).

A new generation came to know Chick in *Soldiers of Fortune,* the syndicated television series that premiered in early 1955.

Occasionally, Chick Chandler had the lead, such as in the B mystery *Seven Doors to Hell* (1944). Of the series features, he appeared in *Mr. Moto Takes a Chance* (1938), *Maisie Goes to Reno* (1944), *The People vs. Dr. Kildare* (1941), and *Leave It to Blondie* (1945).

Chandler was never placed on suspension and maintained he recalls no negative experiences with the many stars and directors he worked with. Nor was he greatly disappointed by missing out on any roles.

His favorite screen part was in support of

Marty Jackson

Chick Chandler in late 1987 on the front porch of his home in Laguna Beach, California.

Humphrey Bogart and Irene Manning[10] in *The Big Shot* (1942).

The Chandlers had no children but often looked after the daughter (by John Carroll) and son (by Dennis O'Keefe) of their long-time friend Steffi Duna.[9] Marc Lawrence[9] is another friend of many years.

On *Soldiers of Fortune* Chick Chandler played the older, humorous sidekick of John Russell, who handled most of the heroics and romance. The fifty-two half-hour episodes of high adventure were dubbed into Portuguese and Japanese and telecast throughout the world.

He continued to act on television into the late sixties. By then the Chandlers had sold their home in Beverly Hills and moved to Laguna Beach. Their house, which they bought from director Michael Curtiz, is only a few minutes' walk from the Pacific Ocean. The sketch his uncle made of him in 1929 hung on the living room wall.

During his last interview, which was conducted in his home in February 1988, Chandler said he spent his time "playing an occasional game of golf, but mostly sitting on my ass and enjoying every minute of it."

He died on September 30, 1988, one day before the death of his wife.

Robert Coogan (right) *was ten years younger than his brother. Jackie Coogan* (left) *was the first child in history to earn more than $1 million while still in grammar school.*

Robert Coogan

Jackie Coogan's little brother was born on December 13, 1924, in Glendale, California. His father was an eccentric dancer. His mother had been well known during the late nineteenth century in vaudeville as "Baby Lillian" Dolliver.

By the time of Robert's birth his older brother, whose movie career had been launched playing opposite Charlie Chaplin in *The Kid* (1921), was the most popular child star in the world. The Coogans lived in a mansion, and Mr. and Mrs. Coogan each had a Rolls Royce.

"But," Robert insisted, "they never went Hollywood like most people who made a fortune overnight. When Jackie was not on a movie set he was not around picture people. Mother had been a headliner on stage and was not all that impressed with movies or film folks. My parents were Catholics and were interested only in the business side of the business."

The Coogans were approached a number of times about having Robert, too, in films, but they refused until *Skippy* (1931). The picture and its star, Jackie Cooper, were both nominated that year for Academy Awards. In it Robert played "Skippy's" friend "Sooky." *Skippy* was such a box-office success that Paramount Pictures made a sequel, *Sooky* (1931), with the same cast: Jackie Cooper, Robert Coogan, and Jackie Searl. Coogan remembers Searl as being "a bit of a shit."

After Robert appeared in two more features, *The Miracle Man* (1932) and *Sky Bride* (1932), Mrs. Coogan took her son on an ocean cruise to the Orient.

In 1935 Mr. Coogan and juvenile star Junior Durkin were killed when the roadster they were riding in went over an embankment. Only the driver, Jackie Coogan, survived. Not long afterward Mrs. Coogan married the business manager of the family corporation.

In 1938 Jackie Coogan sued his mother and stepfather, claiming that large sums of money had been withheld from his inheritance. His accusation brought about legislation regulating the earnings of minors that is still referred to in California as "the Coogan law."

Keith Coogan and his grandfather, the late Jackie Coogan, were honored at the Youth in Film Awards in 1982. Jackie Coogan died on March 1, 1984.

Robert Coogan photographed in North Hollywood shortly before his death in 1978.

It was nine years before Robert Coogan made his next film, *Johnny Doughboy* (1942). Upon its completion he went into the U.S. Army. His next picture, *Kilroy Was Here* (1947), was the first and only time the brothers acted together.

Robert was never serious about a screen career. His explanation was: "Working in pictures was fun, but it never occurred to me I could become any more than what I was—a bit actor."

He played the comic character "Humphrey Pennyworth" in two "Joe Palooka" pictures and then moved to Europe for almost ten years. Abroad, he photographed auto races for the Shell Oil Company and acted in some pictures made on the continent but never released in the United States. After returning to Hollywood he continued to do small parts. His last was in the original version of *Little Shop of Horrors* (1961).

He and his wife, a nonprofessional, were married in 1967. The childless couple spent most of their time on the 40-foot sloop they owned. He wrote several articles for sailing magazines about cooking aboard a boat and worked on a novel.

Robert Coogan and his wife lived in a large apartment house owned by his mother in the San Fernando Valley. Whenever Jackie visited from his Palm Springs home, he stayed with Lillian Coogan. Despite the litigation, the Coogans remained close.

Yet, when Dickie Moore interviewed Jackie for his book *Twinkle, Twinkle, Little Star (But Don't Have Sex or Take the Car),* Jackie Coogan's parting words to him were, "Don't forget—stay away from mothers!"

Robert Coogan survived his mother by seven months.

Shortly before he died, on May 12, 1978, Robert Coogan was asked about his relationship over the years with his famous brother. He replied: "There were too many years between us for any rivalry or competition. I always felt lucky to have Jackie Coogan as my big brother. He was great in the part, by the way. We were and are very good friends."

Jonathan Coogan, Robert's son by an earlier marriage, is an actor. Keith Coogan, Jackie's grandson, has appeared in several movies.

Ellen Corby is best known to TV viewers as "Grandma Walton" on the long-running series, The Waltons.

Her portrayal of a Norweigian spinster in I Remember Mama *(1948) brought a nomination for the Best Supporting Actress Oscar and established her as a character actress in Hollywood.*

Ellen Corby

The award-winning character actress was born Ellen Hansen to Danish parents in Racine, Wisconsin. Her birthdate is June 3, 1911.

After the Hansens separated, when she was a child, Ellen moved with her mother to Philadelphia.

Many years later she said of her school years: "I was in every amateur contest there was and won most of them. I even won a beauty contest. I wasn't really beautiful, I just had a following."

She danced for a brief time in the chorus of an Atlantic City nightclub before coming to Hollywood in 1932. Both Ellen and her mother, who moved west with her, were determined that she would become a screen actress.

Two weeks after they arrived, Ellen got a walk-on in a movie.

Ellen played a few more bit parts, such as the maid in *Little Women* (1933), but in order to earn a steady income, she became a script girl. She acted in that capacity for some of the Laurel and Hardy shorts and *Our Gang* comedies.

Within a few years she married Hal Roach cameraman Francis Corby. By then, Ellen had become a script supervisor at RKO. Occasionally she managed to contribute to the writing of a picture. In *Twilight on the Trail* (1941), a Hopalong Cassidy western, she was credited as coauthor of the screenplay as well as a member of the cast.

The last script she worked on as supervisor was *Murder, My Sweet* (1944). When she told director-star Dick Powell that she would henceforth be available only for acting assignments, he gave her a party and a part in his next picture, *Cornered* (1945).

Ellen had been studying at The Actors' Lab, where she was cast in *Liliom*. She sent handwritten notes to fifty of the producers and directors she had worked for, inviting them to the production. Two of the three who came to see her, Edward Dmytryk and Val Lewton, cast her in their pictures.

A few years later another producer, Harriet Parsons, who had known her as a script supervisor, gave Ellen Corby the role that established her. Playing a Scandinavian spinster in *I Remember Mama* (1948) brought her the nomination for that year's Best Supporting Actress.

The part lifted her from the ranks of bit players, and there followed roles in the remake of *Little Women* (1949), *Raged* (1950), *On Moonlight Bay* (1951), *The Big Trees* (1952), *Shane* (1953), *A Lion in the Streets* (1953), *About Mrs. Leslie* (1954), *Sabrina* (1954), *Illegal* (1955), *Slightly Scarlet* (1956), *The Seventh Sin* (1957), *Macabre*

(1958), *Saintly Sinners* (1962), *The Caretakers* (1963), *The Strangler* (1964), *The Family Jewels* (1965), *The Glass-Bottom Boat* (1966), and *The Night of the Grizzly* (1966).

She was tested for the part of "Laura" in the first screen version of *The Glass Menagerie*, but nothing as important as *I Remember Mama* ever came to her again in features. Ellen worked frequently, however, playing such roles as a prissy schoolmarm, a frightened witness, or a nosy neighbor. By 1969 her face, if not her name, was familiar to regular moviegoers. When she was interviewed that year by Jim McPherson of the *Toronto Star,* he asked about her fame.

The actress replied: "I'm funny. I want the recognition, but I'm not willing to pay the price. So, I have to be content with what I have. I believe everybody is exactly where their thoughts have led them. Now if I want to change things, I have to start thinking differently and behaving differently—and I'm too lazy for that. I don't *want* to have to go to the studios every day and have lunch with the 'right' people."

Two years later she appeared in a made-for-television movie, *The Homecoming: A Christmas Story*. In it she played opposite Edgar Bergen, who had been her suitor in *I Remember Mama*. The show was so favorably received that CBS-TV ordered a series, using the same actors. When Bergen declined the role of "Grandpa Walton," Will Geer was cast opposite Ellen's "Grandma Walton." *The Waltons* ran on the network from 1972 to 1981 and is still in syndication.

Ellen Corby was nominated six times as television's Best Supporting Actress. She received the award for the 1972–73, 1974–75, and 1975–76 seasons.

In early 1976 Ellen Corby suffered a massive stroke. On *The Waltons* her absence was explained by having "Grandma" hospitalized.

Marty Jackson

Ellen Corby at a meeting of the Hollywood chapter of the Sons of the Desert, a group of Laurel and Hardy enthusiasts. The actress is an honorary member of the organization, the largest movie fan club in the world.

Her return late that year was greeted by the cast and crew as a joyous homecoming. It brought the series one of its highest ratings and drew moving tributes in the press, lauding Ms. Corby's professionalism and courage. There was no attempt to disguise the severe limitations that the stroke had caused.

Ms. Corby appeared on four more segments of *The Waltons* before it went off the air.

Her Emmys are on display in the living room of the house she shares in West Hollywood with a friend of more than thirty-five years. Earl Hamner, Jr., creator and narrator of *The Waltons*, has remained in close touch, as have Anne Francis and Ann Doran.[9]

Despite her condition, which has greatly hampered her speech and agility, Ellen Corby goes out to a movie at least once a week and frequently attends lectures on Science of Mind. Although even signing her autograph is done with some difficulty, the actress has handwritten a novel based on her two world tours. Her book, *The Pebble of Gibraltar,* was published in early 1988 by Vantage Press.

Most of her fan mail is generated by *The Waltons*. The part in *I Remember Mama,* however, is her favorite—not "Grandma Walton."

Hazel Court has been proclaimed the "British Fay Wray" by David Del Valle. The filmologist also points out that she is the only actress to play opposite Boris Karloff, Vincent Price, Peter Cushing, Christopher Lee, and Peter Lorre.

Hazel Court

The scream queen of English films was born in Birmingham, England, on February 10, 1926. Her father was a professional cricketer.

She was taken to the theatre from an early age. During World War II Hazel was a prominent member of a group of amateur thespians who raised more than £4,000 for Mrs. Churchill's Aid to Russia.

After graduating from the Lamada Academy of Musical and Dramatic Art, she got experience in repertory theatre.

Anthony Asquith, impressed by her photograph, called Hazel in for an interview. He sent her to Ealing Studios, where she was given a bit part in *Champagne Charlie* (1944). After a few other small roles, she was

cast in *Showtime* (1948), supporting Ann Todd and Richard Greene.

Pacted by J. Arthur Rank, Hazel was promoted throughout Great Britain as "Miss 1948."

The following year she married Dermot Walsh, who was to be her costar in several English movies. The couple were together in the West End production of *Random Harvest* (1942). It was such a success they then toured in the play throughout the British Isles and West Germany. Hazel had the title role in *Laura,* which she performed with Dennis Price in brief engagements at several theatres in England in the late forties.

Divorced in 1960, she and Walsh have remained friends. Their daughter, an artist, manages a Beverly Hills gallery.

Her favorite film role from the early years was in support of Sally Gray *[10] and Michael Wilding in *Carnival* (1946). It brought her an acting award from *Picturegoer* magazine.

Among her other films are *Dear Murderer* (1948), *Undercover Agent* (1953), *Model for Murder* (1960) opposite Keith Andes,* and *The Hour of Decision* (1957).

One deep disappointment came after Hazel spent six months in intense training for classical ballet. She was the original choice for the pivotal role in *The Red Shoes,* but the script was rewritten in the meantime. The final version required a professional ballerina. The role went to Moira Shearer* and brought her international recognition.

With her lush complexion and ample proportions Hazel attracted monsters, mad scientists, and gothic dandies in such fare as *The Curse of Frankenstein* (1957), *The Man Who Could Cheat Death* (1959), *Dr. Blood's Coffin* (1961), *The Raven* (1963) and *Masque of the Red Death* (1964). When the latter was reviewed in *Time* magazine there was a reference to Hazel Court, "in whose bosom you could sink the entire works of Edgar Allan

Poe and a bottle of his favorite booze at the same time."

Devil Girl from Mars (1955) is another of her motion pictures that has a cult following, this one among science-fiction enthusiasts.

Patrick O'Neal and Hazel Court had the title roles on *Dick and the Duchess,* a series that ran on CBS-TV from September 1957 to May 1958. She believes she was the first to wear a baby-doll nightie on U.S. television. The shows were filmed in England and, according to Ms. Court, were the first to show a woman actually getting into bed with her husband.

Hazel met her real-life husband, Don Taylor, during a trip to Hollywood. It was one of four times she was brought over to appear on an *Alfred Hitchcock Presents* teleplay. Taylor was her director. Later they costarred in *The Tweed Hat,* which he wrote and directed for the *General Electric Theatre.*

The Taylors were married in 1964. After the birth of a son in 1968, Hazel made an appearance on *Mission Impossible* and then retired. The only acting she has done since was a one-line scene in *The Final Conflict* (1981), which she did at the insistence of the director Graham Baker, a friend.

British filmologist David Quinlan believes her green eyes, red hair, and lush complexion, "a Technicolor technician's dream," were wasted playing "shy spinsters and heroines of second-feature crime dramas." Hazel readily agrees but is very pleased by her screen career on balance.

In May 1988 Hazel Court said: "I am remembered for horror films, which in my opinion were among the very last of the really well done examples of the genre. I loathe the things they're doing now, like *The Witches of Eastwick.* My husband has been in some important films, but I happen to think that his will date much quicker than mine and he reluctantly agrees."

Marty Jackson

Hours after posing for this photograph in May 1988, beside Marilyn Monroe, *one of her sculptures, Hazel Court left for Italy. She spends two months each summer studying under Silverio Paoli in the thousand-year-old village of Pietrasante.*

Hazel and Vincent Price headed the casts of *The Raven* (1963) and *Masque of the Red Death* (1964). They became friends then, but she believes he began really taking her seriously only after seeing her paintings. She refers to him as "my mentor in art."

She has painted in oil for many years and has had several one-woman shows. In 1980 a friend, the widow of Richard Basehart, persuaded her to sculpt. Although she still paints, Hazel devotes most of her efforts to sculpting in alabaster and marble. The grounds and interior of the Taylors' home contain many of her works.

The couple live in a three-story English manor house Taylor bought when he was married to Phyllis Avery. Built in the twenties by one of Paul Whiteman's sidemen, it is set on two acres of land approximately a mile from the Pacific Ocean in Santa Monica.

Ms. Court admits to missing movie-making from time to time, but adds, "Of course, I miss England too at times, which is not to say I'd rather live there. To learn, as I have, that one has another talent is tremendously exciting. A second career is so reassuring—just at the age you need it most."

During 1967–68, Batman's second and final season on ABC-TV, Yvonne Craig played "Batgirl," another character from the Bob Kane comic strip. Although she frequently aided the dynamic duo, neither "Batman" or "Robin" knew her real identity, which was "Barbara Gordon," librarian and daughter of the police commissioner. Her tights, like the Yamaha Batcycle she drove, were purple.

Yvonne Craig

Television's "Batgirl" was born in Taylorville, Illinois, on May 16.

Yvonne took to dancing from her first class. The Craigs lived in Columbus, Ohio, during her childhood. When her parents decided to move to Texas, she made them promise she could attend the prestigious Edith James School in Dallas.

She was thought to be very promising at the dance academy and was featured in its Christmas show. The guest of honor, the prima ballerina absoluta Alexandra Danilova, was so impressed she set up auditions for the teenager with George Balanchine and Fergei J. Denham. Both made offers, but Yvonne chose to go with Denham's Ballet Russe de Monte Carlo.

In 1957 she left the Ballet Russe de Monte Carlo in what she describes as a "snit." The company was playing the Metropolitan Opera, when at the last minute she was replaced as the second lead. Feeling that Mme. Danilova, who had ordered the change, had broken her promise, Yvonne walked out on her contract.

She intended, when she moved to Los Angeles, to continue her study of dance, but shortly after her arrival she was "discovered" while dining with a producer. Another producer and the son of director John Ford approached her with an offer to test for a part in a picture opposite Patrick Wayne.

That film, *The Young Land,* was shot in 1957 but was not released for two years. In the meantime she had been cast in *Eighteen and Anxious* (1957) with Luana Patten.[8]

The movies that followed were *Gidget* (1959) with Sandra Dee; *The Gene Krupa Story* (1959), in which she seduces Sal Mineo who played a seminarian; *By Love Possessed* (1961); *Seven Women from Hell* (1962); *Quick Before It Melts* (1965) with the late Doodles Weaver;* *One Spy Too Many* (1966)[10] with Dorothy Provine;*[10] *In Like Flint*

(1967); and *How to Frame a Figg* (1971).

In *High Time* (1960) she danced with Bing Crosby and became involved with Jimmy Boyd, who was then a roommate of Lindsay Crosby. Boyd had become famous as a boy when in the early fifties his recording of "I Saw Mommie Kissing Santa Claus" was a huge seller.

According to Yvonne: "We fell in lust and got married. We were too young and dumb to heed the advice that John Forsythe gave us, which was to live together for a while first. That wasn't being done much in 1960. Jimmy was a lot of fun, but during the two years we were husband and wife he never once worked. I was responsible for everything, including his personal debts."

Yvonne dated Elvis Presley when she appeared with him in *It Happened at the World's Fair* (1963) and *Kissin' Cousins* (1964), but their relationship was never serious. She considered marriage to Mort Sahl, who was her lover for more than three years, and later was deeply involved with Bill Bixby.

When the green-eyed Yvonne Craig is recognized today it is usually for portraying "Batgirl" on the television show *Batman*. She brought great exuberance to the role and played it with a sense of camp that is rare in so young an actress.

Of her experiences as "Batgirl" she said recently: "I was very well paid and it was a happy set. They even let me do most of my own stunts. I loved working with stars such as Milton Berle, Ethel Merman, and Rudy Vallee. And contrary to what had been predicted, it did not typecast me. Unlike Adam West and Burt Ward, I worked a lot after the show ceased production."

After *Batman* she guested on *Star Trek, Starsky & Hutch,* and *The Six Million Dollar Man.* But when Yvonne began turning down roles that she refers to as "the bubblehead in the bikini," no other parts were offered.

Gawain Beirne-Keyt

Yvonne Craig beside one of the works of Frank Gallo that adorn the walls of her apartment in the Champagne Towers, a building in Santa Monica owned by Lawrence Welk.

For a time she functioned as coproducer of industrial shows and an independent feature. Since then she has been in the real estate business. In the mid-eighties she made herself available for parts again but found that most of the contacts she once had at studios were no longer there.

In Ms. Craig's opinion, "It's much easier to start a career than to reactivate one. Agents I approached explained that to me and I know they're right. Perhaps if I were not such a reclusive person, I'd have more of a chance, but I am, and I have no desire to change. The truth is that acting came easily to me and I really enjoyed it, but the rest of what went on was a bore. Today I wouldn't have the patience to put up with all the bullshit."

Yvonne Craig married an attorney in early 1988. They share their ocean-view apartment with a long-haired tortoise cat.

43

Linda Cristal was the leading Latin American actress in Hollywood during the late fifties and early sixties. In movies she played opposite John Wayne and James Stewart. On TV she was Leif Erickson's [10] wife on the series The High Chaparral.

Linda Cristal

The Latin-American actress was born Marta Victoria Moya Burges in Buenos Aires, Argentina. Her birthdate is February 23, 1935. She was not yet in school when her parents fled to Uruguay, after her father, a publisher, became involved in a political dispute with the ruling party.

The family was living in Mexico City in 1948 when her French mother and Italian father died in what was considered a suicide pact. Linda believes otherwise. She suspects that Mrs. Burges, a diabetic, became comatose from lack of insulin. Mr. Burges was deeply humiliated by his failure to provide for his family in exile. Linda's theory is that after discovering his wife dead, or dying, he turned on the gas.

Orphaned, the teenager was about to be taken into a convent when she was noticed by the son of Mexico's president. He headed the largest film studio in the country and decided to make her a star. It was he who changed her name. (Linda pronounces her surname Cree-stal.)

Top-billed in more than ten features made in Mexico, Linda was a star throughout the Spanish-speaking world before coming to Hollywood.

When she learned that United Artists was about to produce a western with a leading role for a Latin woman, Linda took a crash course in English and then contacted the producers. The picture was *Comanche* (1956) with Dana Andrews* and Henry Brandon.*

More than thirty years later she commented: "It was a very Hollywood experience, which I've come to appreciate. *Comanche* made me a name in the United States. But I went back to Mexico in a fury because I could not collect the rest of my salary. Then someone at Universal liked me in it and they brought me back with a contract."

Linda admits that she never relied on professionals for career guidance and insists that all her important roles came about through her own efforts or mere chance.

John Wayne noticed her leaving an office, introduced himself, and asked her name. The star then informed her that he would like to use her as his leading lady in his next production. Two years later he contacted Linda and cast her in *The Alamo* (1960). On the set of that picture John Ford engaged her for his production of *Two Rode Together* (1961). Again she played opposite John Wayne, but rode off into the sunset with James Stewart at the film's climax.

Her motion pictures include *From Hell to Texas* (1958), *The Last of the Fast Guns* (1958) with Gilbert Roland, *The Fiend Who Walked the West* (1958), *The Perfect Furlough* (1959), *Cry Tough* (1959), *Legions of the Nile* (1960), *The Pharaoh's Woman* (1962) with John Drew Barrymore,* and *Panic in the City* (1968).

Linda had been inactive and considered herself retired when she was offered the role that gave her more exposure than any other. On *The High Chaparral,* a TV series that ran on NBC from 1967 to 1971, she played the young wife of rancher Leif Erickson.[10] The show has since been seen throughout much of the world.

U.S. audiences saw very little of Linda Cristal after *The High Chaparral* ceased production. She returned to Mexico for a six-month stint on a soap opera and then went to Argentina for another that went on for years.

Linda has had one annulment and several divorces. Her two sons are by Yale Wexler, one of the nation's leading real estate developers, whom she married in 1960. They separated six years later.

Even when traveling, which she does frequently, Linda spends mornings watching financial news on TV and talking with her stockbroker.

Linda's Beverly Hills home is guarded by Doberman pinschers. She has another residence in Palm Springs and keeps a flat in Buenos Aires, which she visits four times a year. She is a U.S. citizen, but feels "my soul is Argentinian."

Linda is less than satisfied with what she achieved professionally. In March 1988 she stated: "Someone inside of me was always

Marty Jackson

Linda Cristal recently leaving a screening at the Academy of Motion Picture Arts and Sciences.

shooting to miss. The feeling probably comes from a basic lack of self-confidence. I never date actors because they're all looking for the same thing in a woman that I seek in a man—someone to reassure me. It all comes from my mother, who was very cruel to me. I would tell her of my hopes and dreams and she would dismiss them with laughter or scorn. I've never really felt secure because of what she did."

A personal manager who represented Linda Cristal for a time said of her: "Never mind the women she played. She is no vine clinging to a macho man. She is very decisive and turned down almost everything I came up with. It's hard to argue with someone who made her Hollywood career happen and then parlayed most of the money she made into a real fortune. But it soon became clear she had neither the creative nor financial need to act."

In the spring of 1988 Ms. Cristal admitted to herself that she would like to perform again. She signed with an agency that took a full-page advertisement in the trade press announcing her availability.

THESE TOM THUMBS ARE COLOSSAL!
FIRST TIME ON ANY SCREEN!

with BILLY CURTIS
as THE SHERRIFF OF
TINY TOWN

JED BUELL'S MIDGETS

THE TERROR of TINY TOWN

Screen Play by FRED MYTON
Directed by SAM NEWFIELD

ASTOR PICTURES CORP.

Billy Curtis played the hero of **The Terror of Tiny Town** *(1938), a full-length western in which all the roles were taken by "little people," as they preferred to be called. It was produced by Jed Buell, who was also responsible for* **All-Colored Cast** *westerns starring* **Herb Jeffries.**[9]

Billy Curtis

The "Mayor of Munchkinland" and the star of *The Terror of Tiny Town* was born in Springfield, Massachusetts. His birthday was June 27, 1909.

Throughout his career he had been known as Billy Curtis, the name he had legalized. He did not reveal his original name for publication.

Billy was the second youngest of six children born to Italian immigrants. His younger sister was smaller than he. The others in the family were of average size.

Curtis was working as a shipping clerk in a shoe store when a member of a local stock company suggested him for a part in one of their productions. Her name was Shirley Booth.

The 4-foot-2-inch actor soon gravitated to New York City, where he was seen on stage with Jimmy Durante and Libby Holman. On Broadway he appeared in *Let 'Em Eat Cake* (1933), *Anything Goes* (1934), *See My Lawyer* (1939), and *Every Man for Himself* (1940) with Milton Berle.

Billy Curtis was crossing Hollywood Boulevard and Vine Street when he encountered an agent who told him M-G-M was looking for little people to appear in the musical version of *The Wizard of Oz* (1939).

"I'll never forget it," he said in 1988. "There was the director, Victor Fleming, the producer, Mervyn LeRoy, and the head of the goddamned studio. They all looked at me and then Louis B. Mayer said, 'That's him. He'll be the Mayor of Munchkinland.'"

Curtis was pleased to be known and recognized for the part he played in *The Wizard of Oz,* but it was neither his best part nor his longest. Nor was it his favorite screen role. For many years, however, it was the one for which he was best known.

Until recently, the picture in which he played the lead, *The Terror of Tiny Town* (1938), was rarely shown publicly. This western became a cult classic in the years since its original release and is now televised frequently; it is also available on videocassette.

During an interview in May 1988, Billy

Curtis used *The Terror of Tiny Town* as a case in point about little people in Hollywood: "When I was first offered the role of the sheriff they didn't want to pay my established salary. Then we were all directed like we were children. Small, in the minds of stupid people, is kiddie stuff. So first they try to exploit little people. Then they patronize you. And when the picture comes out, then the audience laughs at you. Why? Not because we were low-budget, because most westerns then were Bs. Because we rode ponies. What would a person my size ride—a stallion? I played the good guy who put the bad guy behind bars in the end—just like John Wayne. And I kissed the pretty girl—just like he did. So what the hell's so funny?"

He had appeared in more than sixty features, frequently without billing. In more than half a century of movie-making the only director he disliked was John Brahm. Curtis singled out Rod Serling, host-creator of *The Twilight Zone,* as the "all-time cheapskate" he had encountered.

Billy had been married for almost twenty years to a former actress he described as looking "just like Betty Grable." Mrs. Curtis is 5 feet 5 inches in height.

For years the Curtises lived next door to Grady Sutton in Hollywood. In spring 1988 they sold their home and moved to Dayton, Nevada. They took with them their pets: a mongrel, a poodle, and three spaniels.

Billy believed he was most frequently recognized by blacks for the part he did in the Clint Eastwood starrer *High Plains Drifter* (1973) and that Latinos usually know him for appearances in Hal Roach comedies, particularly the "Our Gang" ("Little Rascals") shorts. Film buffs remember him for Hitchcock's *Saboteur* (1942) and *The Incredible Shrinking Man* (1957). He also had one of the leads in *Little Cigars* (1973).

His favorite screen appearance was in *Meet*

Marty Jackson

The late Mervyn LeRoy (center), *who produced* **The Wizard of Oz,** *posed with Jerry Maren (left) and Billy Curtis shortly before he died in 1987. Curtis, who played the "Mayor of Munchkinland" in the film, retired to Dayton, Nevada, in 1988, and died shortly thereafter.*

John Doe (1941). Said Billy, "It's not that I had a big part. It's because I know the picture will live. *Oz* will always be fun, but Frank Capra made pictures that were *about* something. I'm very proud to have been even a small part of it."

Asked what he thought his life might have been like had he been a foot taller, the seventy-eight-year-old actor replied, "How the hell would I know? What would *yours* have been like if you were a foot shorter?"

Billy Curtis died on November 9, 1988.

47

"Too pretty to be a boy," was what both press and fans said about Philippe de Lacy when he was in motion pictures in the twenties and early thirties.

Philippe de Lacy

The Freddie Bartholomew of silents and early talkies was, according to what he has been told, born on July 25, 1917, in Nancy, France. He was found huddled in a shellhole by Edith de Lacy, a Red Cross nurse. His mother and five brothers and sisters had been killed by a German bomb. The fifty-two-year-old woman adopted the sixteen-month-old boy and brought him to the United States after the armistice.

A friend of his adoptive mother, who was also close to singer Geraldine Farrar, invited Ms. de Lacy and Philippe onto the set of *The Riddle-Woman* (1921). In some accounts it was the director who noticed the child and chose him to play in the picture. Others have it that the star herself "discovered" him.

Within two years Philippe de Lacy was ap-

pearing in films such as *Rosita* (1923), a Mary Pickford vehicle directed by Ernst Lubitsch. Free-lancing throughout the decade, the boy appeared in some of the era's most prestigious films.

In the hugely successful *Peter Pan* (1924), Philippe played "Michael," one of the "Darling children" with Esther Ralston[8] and Mary Brian.[8] He was also in the original version of *Beau Geste* (1926) and supported John Barrymore and Mary Astor in *Don Juan* (1926), the same year he starred in a highly acclaimed short, *The Elegy,* about a boy and his dog. Lubitsch directed him again in the very popular *The Student Prince* (1927), which starred Norma Shearer and Ramon Navarro. He played the son to Greta Garbo's "Anna Karenina" in *Love* (1927) with John Gilbert and was one of the children deserted in *The Way of All Flesh* (1927), the first Hollywood movie to star Emil Jannings.

Among his other credits are: *The Shooting of Dan McGrew* (1924), *Is Zat So?* (1927), *The Happy Warrior* (1925), *The Four Feathers* (1929), *The Broken Mask* (1928), *Royal Rider* (1929), *One Romantic Night* (1930), and *Mother McCree* (1928).

His looks, which made him a particular favorite of some moviegoers, became an embarrassment to Philippe as he entered puberty. While fans were writing in to plead for one of his tossed curls, the young actor was envying boys he knew with straight hair.

De Lacy dismisses the adage of actors being threatened by children: "I can't think of one adult I ever worked with who was not a thorough professional, and I remember many who were especially nice to me."

Sarah and Son (1930) had Philippe and Ruth Chatterton* in the title roles. The Broadway actress had risen to such popularity among movie audiences that she was being publicized as "The First Lady of the Talkies." It had the prestige of being a David

O. Selznick production and was a box-office hit. Philippe believes it was his best picture, yet it was the virtually the end of his career as a movie actor.

He appeared on Broadway in *Growing Pains* (1933) and *Strangers at Home* (1934), and then disappeared from both the marquees and the media for the next twenty years.

Philippe joined the staff of filmmaker Louis de Rochemont when he was nineteen years old. He began working on the popular *March of Time* series and then assisted in the production of features.

He and Freddie Bartholomew have frequently been compared. They had the same delicate features and refinement. Both were adopted and raised by spinsters. Bartholomew played the role of Garbo's son when she remade the Tolstoy classic under its original title, *Anna Karenina,* as a talkie in 1935. Both had long and successful careers as advertising executives. The two have never met, however.

De Lacy directed TV shows at channel 11 in Los Angeles for several years in the early fifties, leaving to rejoin de Rochemont. The public saw his name on the movie screen again as director of the feature *Cinerama Holiday* (1955), which de Rochemont produced.

Phil, as he has been known throughout his adulthood, then spent the next twenty-five years at the J. Walter Thompson advertising agency as a broadcast supervisor.

De Lacy kept in touch with Anita Louise until her death in 1970. They had worked together in *Marriage Playground* (1929). His only other contact from those years is Frank "Junior" Coghlan.*

Coghlan did not fully realize how completely de Lacy had put his career behind him until they were invited to a screening of *Square Shoulders* fifty years after it was

Marty Jackson

Philippe de Lacy and his wife, Marion, live in a small town in northern California. Their home is set behind a high wall at the end of a quiet street.

made. They had costarred in the part-talkie and gone on a promotional tour with it in 1929 when it was first released. "Phil had absolutely no interest in seeing it," said an incredulous Coghlan. "I remembered the filming and our travels around the country as a lot of fun. I thought it would be great to kind of relive it for an evening. What he gave was a very polite 'no,' but it was a very definitive one as well."

De Lacy once explained his attitude in an interview: "I enjoyed making films. I liked acting and other actors. The painful part came at the end when I was entering what casting directors called 'the gawky period' for juveniles, which was early teens in my case. All at once it seemed that no one wanted me. It was some years before I really understood what had happened. I was devastated by what I took as rejection. I'm extremely grateful I had the opportunities I had as a child, and they led to a very satisfying second career. I also appreciate that some of the work I did in pictures still entertains people."

When de Lacy met his wife in junior high school she already had a crush on him from seeing his movies. They have no children.

The de Lacys lived in the San Fernando Valley until his retirement in the early eighties. He prefers that his exact whereabouts not be made public. Philippe and his wife now reside in a small community in northern California.

In the group photograph, taken at the Chaplin studios in the early twenties, Sydney Chaplin is lying on the ground. Dinky Dean is holding the hand of Jack Dempsey, then the heavyweight boxing champion of the world. Kneeling beneath Dempsey is Benny Leonard, then holder of the lightweight boxing crown.

Standing (from left to right) are: Henry Bergman, a Chaplin crony and restaurateur, an unidentified employee, Rollie Totheroh and Chuck Reisner on either side of Dempsey, long-time Chaplin associates, and Alf Reeves, the manager of the Chaplin studios.

Dinky Dean

The "Boy's Boy" of the silent screen was born on November 3, 1918. His parents were visiting with the famous Foy family in New Rochelle when his mother went into labor.

One of the "Seven Little Foys," Charlie, drove his mother to the hospital in Manhattan.

His mother was Miriam Hope, who had met his father, Chuck Riesner, when they headed the cast of the road company of *Stop, Look & Listen*.

"Dinky's" earliest memory of his career was on stage in vaudeville. At age three he toured the country in a comedic boxing skit in which he sparred with Jack Dempsey, who at the time was the heavyweight boxing champion of the world.

When the act played Los Angeles, Mr. Riesner met Charlie Chaplin. He was to work with the star in various capacities over a number of years. His son was cast in the Chaplin starrer *The Pilgrim* (1923), and his name was changed to Dinky Dean. The origin of his well-publicized title "Boy's Boy" is unknown.

The moppet also appeared in some shorts and starred in the feature *A Prince of a King* (1923). Mrs. Riesner was concerned lest he develop "klieg eyes," a condition caused by the brightness of the lights on a movie set. But most likely his acting in pictures would have continued if his early career hadn't come to an abrupt end when their only child casually asked the Riesners, "How was I in the rushes?" More than half a century later he explained: "My father spent his days with stars. He was not about to come home to one." Dean was in high school before he was allowed to act again.

Dean believes the time he spent in London was the pivotal period of his life: "Here I was living at the Dorchester and being directed in a picture by my dad. I wore clothes made by Hawes and Curtis. We shared a magnum of champagne with the great tenor John McCormack in his dressing room. Ivor Novello's mother was my vocal coach and I was being schooled in lovemaking by an adult American movie star—whom I met through my mother! Never mind that I was still in my teens, I knew instinctively that things just don't get any better than that."

The English movie he made was *Everybody Dance* (1936). His lover, the older woman in his life, was Alice White. Another of his early affairs was with Barbara Read,* one of the *Three Smart Girls* in the film that launched Deanna Durbin's* screen career.

Upon his return to the film capital, Dean became what he calls "a drunk with an avocation for screenwriting."

Family friend Bryan Foy gave Dean a job as a scriptwriter at Warner Brothers. His first screen credit as a scenarist was on *The Code of the Secret Service* (1939), which starred Ronald Reagan. Recognition came from the screenplay of *The Fighting 69th* (1940). *Bill*

Francia Nieman

Dean Riesner wrote the screenplay for the Whoopee Goldberg starrer Fatal Beauty *(1987) on the Universal Studios lot where, more than sixty years before, he acted in silent pictures as Dinky Dean, "Boy's Boy."*

and Coo, which he wrote and directed, won a special Academy Award in 1947, but the Oscar and the acclaim went to its producer, Ken Murray.

Among the other motion pictures written by the former child star are: *The Helen Morgan Story* (1957), *Paris Holiday* (1958), *The Man from Galveston* (1964), *Coogan's Bluff* (1968), *Charlie Varrick* (1973), and *The Enforcer* (1976).

Dean Riesner wrote some of the "Joe Palooka" TV series and *So This Is Hollywood,* an NBC-TV show that starred Mitzi Green and Jimmy Lydon[8] for thirty-six weeks in 1955. His best-known television credit was as author of the miniseries *Rich Man, Poor Man* in 1976. Probably his most fondly remembered credit was *The Big Slide,* a *Playhouse 90* presentation in 1956 in which Red Skelton played a star of silent comedies whose career is on the wane.

Dean attributes his sobriety to "accepting the responsibility for someone else." He married for the first time in 1959 and has consumed alcohol only once since then.

His surname is pronounced "Rys-ner." Old friends still call him "Dink."

51

Carolina Blues (1944) was one of more than forty features Jeff Donnell made while under contract to Columbia Pictures. In that Kay Kyser starrer she was teamed with "Ish Kabibble" (above), who did comedy with Kyser's aggregation and sang novelty tunes such as "Mairzy Doats" and "Three Little Fishes," major hits of World War II.

Jeff Donnell

The feature player of the screen was born in a boy's reformatory in South Windham, Maine. Her father was a penologist and her mother a schoolteacher. Her birthdate is July 10, 1921. In 1923 her family moved to Maryland.

Her name was originally Jean Marie Donnell, but when she was fifteen she began calling herself Jeff.

After attending Leland Powers Dramatic School in Boston she enrolled at Yale University's School of Drama for one year.

Jeff was playing in summer stock, intend-

ing to return to Yale in September, when she was "discovered." Producer Max Gordon and casting director Max Arnow saw her on stage in New Hampshire and thought she was right for the screen version of *My Sister Eileen* (1942). Wearing pearls loaned by Josephine Hutchinson, she was directed by studio head Harry Cohn in her screen test, a scene from *Claudia*. She spent the next six years under contract to Columbia Pictures.

Jeff married in 1940. Her husband had taught drama until Cohn signed her to a contract, but when they moved to Hollywood he became a dialogue director. They were divorced in 1950.

The leads Ms. Donnell played were always in B pictures. Because of the exceptional versatility she showed, Jeff was soon established as a young character actress, a category that traditionally drew very little publicity. But both Louella O. Parsons and Hedda Hopper encouraged her in print and on the air, both in her career and in her love life.

Her romance with Aldo Ray and their sub-

"Ish Kabibble" has been licensed as a realtor under his real name, Merwyn A. Bogue, since Kay Kyser disbanded in 1952. For many years he was associated with a developer who is the husband of Kyser's vocalist, Ginny Simms. "Ish," as he insists on being called, lives with his wife of more than fifty years in Indio, California.

Shortly before she died in April 1988, Jeff Donnell was photographed as she left the public library in West Hollywood.

sequent marriage in September 1954 were well publicized. Both were under contract to Columbia. The unpretentious Jeff seemed perfect for Ray, a young man who had been a small-town constable before becoming a movie actor. The two were introduced by George Cukor when he directed them in Aldo's screen test. They were divorced in 1956.

In 1988 Jeff said: "Although we haven't been in touch in a long time, I think of Aldo a lot and always with a heavy heart. Hollywood and marriage were just too much for him."

The parts she wanted very much went to Terry Moore in *The Return of October* and to Betsy Blair[10] in *Another Part of the Forest*.

She appeared in the following features: *A Night to Remember* (1943), *Three is a Family* (1944), *Over 21* (1945), *Tars and Spars* (1946), *In a Lonely Place* (1950), *The Fuller Brush Girl* (1950), *Walk Softly, Stranger* (1950), *Because You're Mine* (1952), *The Blue Gardenia* (1953), *My Man Godfrey* (1957), *Force of Impulse* (1961), *The Comic* (1969), *Tora, Tora, Tora* (1970), and *Stand Up and Be Counted* (1972).

Jeff Donnell wanted the role of "Alice" on *The George Gobel Show* sufficiently to agree to a cut in salary. Playing the star's wife gave her the most exposure she had ever had and proved her comedic skills, but it did not lead to the career breakthrough she had hoped

for. In 1958, after four seasons, she left the popular series.

She made five appearances on television's prestigious *The United States Steel Hour* during the fifties.

In her other series, *Matt Helm,* which ran on ABC-TV during the 1975–76 season, Jeff played a key role.

Fans of *General Hospital* knew Jeff as "Stella Fields" in a long-running part on the TV soap.

Divorced for more than twenty-five years, Jeff Donnell lived with "Lily," a tortoiseshell cat, in West Hollywood, until her death.

Asked in April 1988 to comment on her career, Jeff Donnell said: "I wasn't the pretty type and I certainly wasn't glamorous. So, I always felt fortunate to be acting. My first concern was for my family, so I never developed a driving ambition. Phineas and Sally, who are by my first marriage, have turned out splendidly. I have two beautiful grandsons and I still work now and then. I consider myself a very lucky person."

Seventy-two hours later Jeff Donnell died in her sleep.

Among those who attended her memorial service were: George Gobel, Marie Windsor, Jimmy Lydon,[8] Ann Savage,[9] and her closest friends, Edith Fellows[8] and Barbara Hale, who was accompanied by her son, William Katt.

The Debbie Drake Show *and* Debbie Drake's Dancercize *were shown on TV worldwide through the early
seventies. She coauthored four books and made four
LPs on exercise. There were Debbie Drake dolls sold,
as well as a line of undergarments bearing her name.
She guested frequently with Johnny Carson, Merv
Griffin, and Mike Douglas.*

Debbie Drake

The creator and hostess of TV's original exercise show was born on March 28, in Corpus
Christi, Texas. She was the fourth of eight
children born to poor parents who adhered
strictly to the rules of their church, Assembly
of God. Throughout her school years she was
never allowed to see a movie, use cosmetics,
or wear shorts, even in gym class.

About the time she took her first job, at
age fourteen, she began calling herself
"Louise." In her late teens, fearing that she
might become stout like her mother, she began to exercise.

In 1959, when she debuted over a Dayton,
Ohio, TV channel, it was as "Debbie Drake."
At that point she was married to her partner
in a chain of twenty-eight health spas. By
1960 *The Debbie Drake Show* was a daily presentation of WISH-TV in Indianapolis, In-

diana. Almost immediately its five sister stations began telecasting her programs too. By the early sixties she was being seen in 130 markets, including many in foreign countries.

Her second series, *Debbie Drake's Dancercize,* offered women at home a chance to "hula, frug, or jerk your weight away." It enjoyed an even greater success in worldwide syndication than her first program and predated the aerobics craze by several years. Until Debbie conceived the idea for the show, she had never danced.

The last of her thirty-minute shows aired in Australia in 1978. Nine years later Debbie spoke of her career and of her life since then: "I was a rich woman married to a very wealthy man, yet I couldn't seem to afford time to enjoy my life. Until I went off the air almost everything I did was work or about work. From my first job I had always enjoyed what I did and had a strong desire to succeed. But I never got to the point, as so many have, that I believed that money and fame were all there is. Since I quit, I've traveled all over the world and really enjoyed myself."

During that same period she also got a divorce and then married a psychologist. They divorced in 1986 after eight years. Debbie refuses to disclose how many times she has been wed, but she refers to the man she married in 1987 as "my final husband." He is a realtor whom she met through her son.

Her only regret is that she and her only child could not have spent more time together during his formative years. (He was brought up by his grandparents.) "But even with my son," Debbie has said, "I was blessed because we've become very close in recent years. He understands how sorry I am that I wasn't there for him. But I am now and I was a few years ago when his first wife and two children were lost in a plane crash."

Of her parents Debbie Drake says: "Mom

Debbie holding Cindy Hernandez, the daughter of her housekeeper. Ms. Drake has a home in Englewood, Colorado, and a condominium on South Padre Island, Texas.

Shelly Davis

pretty near died when she first saw me on television in leotards, but she eventually came around. She and Daddy lived to see five of their kids become millionaires, so they knew they'd done something right. I go to various churches now and am interested in all religions, but I feel deeply commited to Christ. I'm glad I never strayed very far from what I learned at home."

Debbie is very complimentary of Jane Fonda's exercise technique and professionalism, while emphasizing that they are at opposite poles politically. She still works out regularly and has become more conscious of nutrition.

Ms. Drake believes she has never missed being in public life because "the entire quality of my life improved immediately. I developed other interests and became more sensitive to people. I found the more concern I had for others, the better I liked myself."

Florence Eldridge and her husband, Fredric March, in a scene from Act of Murder *(1948), a controversial film about mercy killing. The couple never achieved a renown or following equal to Alfred Lunt and Lynn Fontanne, but their work was usually of a more serious nature. They were also more natural in their acting than the Lunts and more versatile.*

Florence Eldridge

The Broadway star and film actress was born Florence McKecknie in Brooklyn. Her birthday was September 5, 1901.

After high school, and with no singing or dancing lessons, she got a job in the chorus of *Rock-a-bye Baby* (1918) on Broadway. Also in the chorus were June Walker, Hope Hampton, and Eleanor Boardman.

After an ingenue role and several seasons in stock, Florence made a strong impression on Broadway in *Ambush* (1922). Then she appeared in *Bewitched* (1924), *Young Blood* (1925), and *The Great Gatsby* (1926), in which she played "Daisy."

In 1926 she fell in love with Fredric March, her leading man during a production of *The Swan* at Elitch's Gardens in Denver. March was three years her senior, but Florence was a name on Broadway and was being paid more. They were married in 1927.

Florence Eldridge made it clear that the decision to put March's career first in their marriage was a conscious one and hers alone. She insisted that their individual salaries be added together and divided equally from the time of their marriage.

Paramount signed Fredric to a contract during their Los Angeles run of *The Royal Family* (1928). She made *The Studio Murder Mystery* (1929) with him and then largely gave herself over to being the wife of a major movie star. They became the adoptive parents of Anthony and Penelope.

Some of the pictures she made without March were: *Charming Sinners* (1929), *The Matrimonial Bed* (1930), *The Great Jasper* (1933), *The Story of Temple Drake* (1933), and *A Modern Hero* (1934).

The Marches appeared together in *Les Miserables* (1935) and *Mary of Scotland* (1936). They did not make another movie together until *Another Part of the Forest* (1948). The same year they were reteamed in *Live Today for Tomorrow*. In 1949 they were both in *Christopher Columbus,* with Fredric in the title role and Florence playing Queen Isabella.

Her name never became well known to movie audiences. The film version of their Broadway triumph in Eugene O'Neill's *A Long Day's Journey into Night,* perhaps the capstone of their combined careers, was offered only to March. His widow told Ray Loynd of the *Los Angeles Times* that Fredric declined the part because "he felt uncomfortable doing the movie without me."

In their last joint screen appearance they portrayed Mr. and Mrs. William Jennings Bryant in *Inherit the Wind* (1960).

Broadway saw them costar in *Yr. Obedient Husband* (1937), *The American Way* (1939), *Hope for a Harvest* (1941), *The Skin of Our Teeth* (1942), *Years Ago* (1946), *Now I Lay Me Down to Sleep* (1950), and *The Autumn Garden* (1951).

The Marches had a reputation for being liberals. During the McCarthy era there was some question that they might have been too liberal when the pair donated an ambulance to the Loyalist cause during the Spanish Civil War. (They did the same for Finland several years later, when she was attacked by the Soviet Union.)

The most extreme liberalism was evidenced in the gatherings in their French provincial home on Ridgedale Drive in Beverly Hills. March, in the thirties and forties, ranked alongside Spencer Tracy as the foremost dramatic actor of the screen. Ignoring Hollywood's unspoken tradition, whereby salary bracket determines social acceptability, the couple mixed filmdom's crème de la crème with actors and writers who were not established.

One character actor described their hospitality thusly: "Not only were we invited, they made us feel really welcome. They asked you because they liked you, felt you had something to contribute. Success did not change Freddie and Florence. They remained fellow actors and real human beings."

The Marches lived in Connecticut during the last two decades of Fredric's life. (He died in 1975.) Florence moved to a condominium overlooking the Pacific Ocean. The Santa Barbara Biltmore Hotel was a few minutes' walk from her front door. Her fellow chorine, Eleanor Boardman, who became a silent film

Marty Jackson

Florence Eldridge attended the joint tribute to her late husband, Fredric March, by the Academy of Motion Picture Arts and Sciences and the American Cinematheque, but did not speak. It was held in Beverly Hills on September 21, 1987, less than a year before her death.

star and the second wife of directors King Vidor and Harry D'Arrast, lived less than a mile away.

Understated in her dress as in her acting, the one quality she never projected in any medium was glamor. It seemed her only limitation as an actress.

Florence originated the ageless wife and mother in Thornton Wilder's *The Skin of Our Teeth*, the aging immigrant in *The American Way*, the poignantly irritating wife in Lillian Hellman's *The Autumn Garden*, and the dope-crazed "Mary Tyrone" in O'Neill's *A Long Day's Journey into Night*.

Among their contemporaries, theirs was considered one of the most successful star marriages. She was never competitive with her husband and yet remained his equal, except in fame. The union provided her with her stated goal: "to work with Freddie." Close friends insist she was his most enthusiastic fan.

As one of his fellow actors said of him: "March played with all of them—Jeanne Eagels, Greta Garbo—you name 'em. But he knew he was at his best with Florence."

Florence Eldridge died on August 1, 1988.

57

"Frick and Frack"

Werner Groebli, known as "Mr. Frick," was born on April 21, 1915, in Basel, Switzerland. By 1934 he had become the Junior Skating Champion of Switzerland.

Groebli's next-door neighbor was Hansreudi Mauch, who was born May 4, 1919, in Basel. Like his older friend, Mauch was an avid ice skater.

Groebli and Mauch practiced at the same indoor rink, each taking half of the ice. They began to draw spectators by clowning, trying to outdo each other. The rink's manager, who was booking an ice carnival at St. Moritz, suggested they work out a routine together.

The team debuted professionally at St. Moritz with frappé impersonations of Mussolini and Haile Selassie. From the very beginning the crowds loved them.

They took the names "Zig and Zag" when their parents refused permission to use family names. Comedy on ice was viewed then by many Swiss, particularly the older generation, as ridicule of a serious sport.

From the St. Moritz engagement they were brought to England. By the time they played a command performance at the Royal Opera House in Covent Garden as part of the *Rhapsody on Ice* show, their billing was "Frick and Frack."

Life *magazine proclaimed "Frick and Frack" the "Clown Kings of the Ice," a title that was not appreciated by their employers. Roy Shipstad and Oscar Johnson, who owned the* Ice Follies, *also did a comedy act. In the above photo, "Frack" is seated.*

"Mr. Frick's" specialty, which he calls the "backbend cantilever," was a crowd pleaser for more than forty years.

Groebli took "Frick" from the name of a Swiss border town. "Frack" means *frock* in German.

In 1938 the duo arrived in Hollywood, just at the time Sonja Henie had popularized ice skating. On May 13, 1939, "Frick and Frack" became a featured part of *Ice Follies,* then the leading ice show in the nation.

Their costumes and music changed more than their actual routines over the years, but the fast-paced act of split-second near-misses made audiences gasp and shriek season after season.

Their carefully blueprinted collisions came to an end on August 24, 1954, when "Frack" retired. He had developed a bone condition that precluded any more performing.

An obituary in June 1979 referred to him as "the mustachioed rubber-legged comic of the ice."

Moviegoers saw them in *Silver Skates* (1942) and *Lady, Let's Dance* (1943) with Belita.[9]

Groebli continued with *Ice Follies,* where he was billed as "Mr. Frick and Company," although he never again had a real partner. Ed Sullivan presented him on television as a single. He was enshrined at the World Figure Skating Hall of Fame in Colorado Springs, Colorado, and his name, "Mr. Frick," was once used as a punchline in the comic strip *Peanuts.*

A few were able to duplicate his "back-bend cantilever," which is an upside-down push-up in which he used his legs instead of arms as he glided the length of the ice. "But," he always insisted, "only I can do it and be relaxed. I could eat a pizza while I whirled around the arena." To prove his point he performed reading a newspaper in that position for an entire season.

The career of "The Dean of Ice Comics" came to an abrupt end on December 1, 1979, during another appearance with *Ice Follies.*

Werner "Frick" Groebli, the surviving member of the team "Frick and Frack," photographed in Palm Springs, his winter home.

Marty Jackson

Groebli was moving around the ice at his usual speed of twenty-five miles an hour when he hit a bang-board, doing serious damage to one knee. That last performance was one of more than 15,000 before a live audience.

Groebli and his wife Yvonne, who is also Swiss, have been married since 1954. He makes it clear that they are millionaires due to her business acumen. The childless couple have a summer home in Zurich. Autumns are spent near Lake Tahoe. They winter in Palm Springs.

More than fifty years after his inventiveness on ice met with parental disapproval, he has been acknowledged by a world champion as her inspiration. After winning her title, Debi Thomas told *Time* magazine how she began at the age of five: "I skated for fun; I wasn't skating because I'd watched the Olympics. I started because I'd watched Mr. Frick."

Groebli was present at the ceremonies when Debi Thomas received her gold medal at the 1986 World Championships in Geneva.

Recently, "Mr. Frick" told Palm Springs journalist Herb Pasik: "We brought something new to ice skating. We grew. I continued to improve. I quit on top. No farewell tour. No comeback. I may sound like Muhammad Ali, but in my time I was the greatest."

Pedro Gonzalez-Gonzalez and the late Estelita Rodriguez supported John Wayne in Rio Bravo *(1959), one of many appearances Gonzalez-Gonzalez made with the star. Wayne's production company held an option on Pedro's services for almost twenty years.*

Pedro Gonzalez-Gonzalez

The Latin comedian was born Ramira Gonzalez-Gonzalez on May 24, 1925, in Aquilares, Texas.

He was delivered by a midwife for a fee of $2.00 ($1.50 had he been a girl) in a small tent used as a dressing room. His father, a trumpet player, and his mother, a Spanish dancer, were performers in a traveling show. He was one of nine children, all of whom eventually appeared in the family act, "Las Perlitas."

Realizing her son's comedic sense, his mother directed Pedro with two of his dancing sisters in an act of their own, "Trio Hermanos Del Mar." He was then nine years old.

Pedro Gonzalez-Gonzalez never attended school and is still a functional illiterate.

The seventeen-year-old Pedro married his wife, Lee, in 1942. Lee Aguirre was a fifteen-year-old dancer playing on the same bill at San Antonio's National Theatre when they met. It was the same theatre, then called the Juarez, where his parents were introduced.

In the late forties his parents retired. Pedro eked out a living doing comedy in small theatres catering to Spanish-speaking audiences along the California-Mexico border.

By 1952 Gonzalez-Gonzalez was working at a San Antonio TV station as a stagehand, occasionally making an on-camera appearance. During the early hours of an all-weekend telethon, Pedro got to go on. After doing his act, in which he played a marimba on frying pans, he jitterbugged with Dagmar.[9] Contributions increased by $80,000.

The telethon's host, Walter O'Keefe, recommended Pedro as a guest on *You Bet Your Life.* When he was sent a round-trip ticket to Hollywood, Gonzalez-Gonzalez instead bought a bus ticket and gave the difference to his wife. He was making $28 a week at the time.

His exchanges with Groucho Marx caused a mild sensation when the program was aired. Many *You Bet Your Life* buffs consider that segment to be one of the highlights of the entire series. Its sponsor, the Chrysler-Plymouth dealers, was so pleased with the public's reaction that they sent Pedro a letter, offering him his choice of models as a gift. But, believing their letter to be an advertisement, he threw it away.

The Gonzalez-Gonzalez family had no television set and did not see the show. Pedro had never heard of the program, Groucho, or the Marx Brothers. When a William Morris agent was dispatched to sign him as a client, he refused to quit his job until the agency had given him a $1,000 advance.

"He keep telling me how funny people

think I am," recalls Gonzalez. "People laugh and clap for me all my life. But I still live in two rooms—and I got four kids!"

Their 1934 Model A Ford truck brought the Gonzalezes to Hollywood, where Pedro made his debut in *Wings of the Hawk* (1953).

He is proudest of his part as the merchant ship operator in *The High and the Mighty* (1954). His second favorite role was in *Rio Bravo* (1959), another film in which John Wayne starred and which was produced by his company. Pedro also supported Wayne in *Hondo* (1953), *Ring of Fear* (1954), *The Wings of Eagles* (1957), *McClintock!* (1963), *Hellfighters* (1969), and *Chisum* (1970).

In other movies he supported Mickey Spillane in *Ring of Fear* (1954); Greer Garson in *Strange Lady in Town* (1955); Victor McLaglen in *Bengazi* (1955); Van Johnson in *The Bottom of the Bottle* (1956); Lee Marvin in *I Died a Thousand Times* (1955); Glenn Ford in *The Sheepman* (1958); Karl Malden in *The Adventures of Bullwhip Griffin* (1967); Dean Jones in *The Love Bug* (1959); James Garner in *Support Your Local Gunfighter* (1971); Tab Hunter and the late Divine in *Lust in the Dust* (1985); and Burt Reynolds in *Up Hill All the Way* (1988).

Throughout the fifties and sixties Pedro Gonzalez-Gonzalez appeared on many network TV shows, including *Ozzie & Harriet, Gunsmoke, Perry Mason, The Monkees, Mayberry R.F.D., High Chaparral,* and *I Dream of Jeannie.* He would have been a regular as a gardener on *Peter & Gladys* had the show's costar Cara Williams not objected. Another disappointment in that medium came after he rehearsed a musical number for the *Danny Kaye Show* with the star. Kaye saw to it that Pedro was kept in the background during the actual telecast.

His biggest professional disappointment came when he missed out on a prominent role that would have meant nineteen weeks'

Pedro and Lee Gonzalez-Gonzalez in the den of their Culver City home. They live very close to the studio that was once Metro-Goldwyn-Mayer.

work. Says Gonzalez-Gonzales: "When Edmund Grainger, the producer—the man who insisted he wanted me in this movie—came into the room where we were to sign contracts, I stood up to shake his hand. We'd never met before and he sees that I'm a little guy. You can't blame him. The picture was called *The Tall Men.*"

John Wayne was his favorite actor, his favorite producer, and the person he felt closest to in Hollywood. After the star died, Pedro lost much of his interest in acting.

Of his two daughters, only Yolanda did any acting. Pedro Gonzalez-Gonzalez, Jr., who appeared with his father in *The Young Land* (1959) and *McClintock!* (1963), is now a physician. Of Pedro's seven grandchildren, four are performers. Yolanda Deneen is a dancer. Bonita Deneen has a running part on the TV series *The Five.* Cliff Collins played a leading role in the made-for-TV movie *Gangs* in 1988. Veronica Gonzalez-Collins, who has been on stage with her grandfather at personal appearances, was signed in early 1988 to play the lead in a yet-unnamed feature film.

Pedro and his wife live in a home they bought at the suggestion of Marjorie Main, who lived directly across the street. Pedro used the money he made from making *Ricochet Romance* (1954) with her to purchase the property. He now owns every structure on the block.

Coleen Gray's favorite screen roles are as Tyrone Power's faithful but interfering wife in Nightmare Alley *(1947) and Bing Crosby's love interest in Frank Capra's production of* Riding High *(1950).*

Coleen Gray

The demure leading lady of the screen was born Doris Jensen in Staplehurst, Nebraska. Her birthdate is October 23, 1922.

Doris and her older brother were brought up on a farm near Hutchinson, Minnesota, by Danish parents who were strict Lutherans. Although they were forbidden to go to dances or movies, the children did both, telling their mother and father they were at sporting events. "That was when and why I first learned to lie," recalls the actress fifty years later.

By the time she was in junior high school the teenager had decided on Loretta Young[8] as her favorite movie star. When her seventh-grade teacher asked her class to state their life goals, Doris Jensen stood and said, "I want to be a movie star." After the class dissolved in laughter she learned to keep her ambition to herself.

The boy she dated at Hamline University became her fiancé about the same time he was drafted. After receiving her B.A. degree, she followed him to southern California where his unit was stationed. After they broke up she moved to Los Angeles.

She joined a little-theatre group and appeared in three of their productions before an agent offered to represent her.

Shortly after she was pacted to Twentieth Century-Fox and her name was changed to Coleen Gray, her agent took her to see Howard Hawks. The director tested her for a small but showy role in *Red River* (1948). All of this was done without consulting anyone at her studio. When Hawks and the film's star, John Wayne, decided on her, they were refused. Only after Coleen appealed to production head Darryl F. Zanuck was a loan-out granted. By going over his head the actress earned the enmity of Ben Lyon,[8] the casting director, throughout her seven years under contract.

The screen test that she made at Fox was

written for her by Rod Amateau, a young writer under contract to Fox, who became her husband in 1945.

"Hollywood's Camelot" is what Coleen Gray calls the period in which she was most active. She was directed by Frank Capra, Henry Hathaway, and Stanley Kubrick and was leading lady to Bing Crosby, Ronald Reagan, and William Holden. Yet she does not believe she ever fulfilled the "promise" that was mentioned in many of her reviews.

She appeared on Broadway in *Leaf and Bough* (1949) with Charlton Heston and had running parts on the TV soap operas *Days of Our Lives* and *Bright Promise*. But most of her fan mail is from science fiction enthusiasts who regard her highly because of two cheapies: *The Leech Woman* (1960), in which she played the title role opposite the late Grant Williams,[8] and *The Phantom Planet* (1962) with Anthony Dexter. Another of her pictures that has achieved cult status is *The Killing* (1956). It, too, was made on a low budget. Among her other motion pictures are: *State Fair* (1945), *Fury at Furnace Creek* (1948), *Sand* (1949), *Father Is a Bachelor* (1950), *Riding High* (1950), *Apache Drums* (1951), *Kansas City Confidential* (1952), *Arrow in the Dust* (1954), *Tennessee's Partner* (1955), *Johnny Rocco* (1958), *Hell's Five Hours* (1957), *Town Tamer* (1965), *P.J.* (1968), and *The Late Liz* (1971).

Her daughter, an attorney, is by Amateau, whom she divorced in 1949. After breaking her engagement to producer Stanley Rubin, she married an executive with Lockheed in 1953. Her son, an audio engineer, is by her second husband. In 1979, a year after she was widowed, Coleen married her present husband. The couple are partnered in a network marketing business they conduct from their home in Bel-Air. They usually weekend in Palos Verdes in the house he lived in with his late wife.

Coleen Gray and Monte Montana upon their return from the Memphis Film Festival in August 1987.

Ms. Gray is much more conservative than she was forty years ago when, as a member of the Actors' Lab, she was apt to quote, "The most good for the most people." Ms. Gray is now a Republican.

Her religious views are considerably more liberal than those she was brought up with. She has appeared on television with Oral Roberts, a cleric she greatly admires. Coleen and her husband are active members of their local Presbyterian church.

Coleen Gray feels she was treated well under the studio system. Her only regrets are that she is still confused with Colleen Townsend* and that her name is often misspelled with two *l*s.

Because she and her husband frequently travel, she would not accept a running part on a series or a soap opera. But she would very much like to act more than she has done in recent years.

63

Tito Guizar parlayed his hit song "El Rancho Grande" into something akin to a Mexican ambassadorship in the thirties and forties. He did a nightclub act, guested on many radio shows, and made eleven Hollywood movies.

Tito Guizar

The singer-actor was born in Guadalajara, Mexico. His birthday is April 8, 1908. His original name is Frederico Tito Guizar.

His goal throughout his youth was to sing in opera. Before coming to the United States to continue his classical training, however, he appeared in a Spanish-language western made in Mexico.

"It was an accident," he says today. "I had some free time, I was asked to ride a horse and sing this song. It was a nice song and I was to be paid. Why not?"

In New York City Tito was taken on by the Metropolitan star Tito Schipa as a student and protégé. The great Spanish soprano Lucrezia Bori publicly praised the young Mexican when he concertized at Carnegie Hall. By the time he was signed by RCA Victor Records, his Mexican movie had broken box-office records throughout the Spanish-speaking world.

Tito Guizar came to prominence in the United States in the mid-thirties when the song that became his theme, "El Rancho Grande," was first heard. The tenor, accompanying himself on the guitar, was heard on most of the major network radio variety shows. Frequently he was given a few lines of dialogue, usually an exchange with the program's host. Despite his heavy accent, he projected a very pleasing personality.

His Latin charm and smooth musicianship worked very well for him in such nitery engagements as Ciro's and the Coconut Grove.

Tito Guizar sang in a voice of almost operatic quality, was undeniably good-looking, and had an infectious smile. Except when he played it for comedy, his accent only added to his appeal. But at the time, the thinking among Hollywood producers was that Latin men, with the notable exceptions of Rudolph Valentino, Gilbert Roland, and Ramon Navarro, were unsuitable for starring roles.

Tito Guizar made his Hollywood debut in *Under the Pampas Moon* (1935) playing a gaucho whose horse was stolen. Warner Baxter and Ketti Gallian were the stars. Jack

LaRue,[8] Rita Hayworth (billed as Rita Cansino), and Veloz & Yolanda were other members of the supporting cast.

His next film, *The Big Broadcast of 1938* (1938), starred W.C. Fields, Bob Hope, and Martha Raye.

Other films were: *Tropic Holiday* (1938) with Binnie Barnes;[8] *St. Louis Blues* (1939) with Dorothy Lamour; *Blondie Goes Latin* (1941) with the late Arthur Lake;[8] Penny Singleton, and Ruth Terry;* *The Thrill of Brazil* (1946) with Evelyn Keyes* and Allan Joslyn;[8] and *Mexicana* (1945) with Constance Moore.[8]

In three of his Hollywood films he played the lead, but the scripts somehow managed to keep his leading ladies at a distance. The first, *The Llano Kid* (1939), was a Paramount programmer. Republic Pictures presented Guizar opposite Virginia Bruce in *Brazil* (1944).

The late filmologist Don Miller wrote of Guizar: "It is misleading to evaluate his popularity by what he did in this country. In his own country and throughout South America he was and still is, when he wants to be, one of their superstars."

Tito made many pictures in Mexico that were very successful, but they played in the United States only in ghettos. Yet, when he made personal appearances, such as at Loew's State in New York City and the Million Dollar Theatre in Los Angeles, his fans formed lines that would extend around the block. His featured appearances in the Roy Rogers starrers *On the Old Spanish Trail* (1947) and *The Gay Ranchero* (1948) greatly bolstered the western's box-office appeal in all Spanish-speaking countries.

The Guizars live in the exclusive Lomas de Chapultepec section of Mexico City. They also spend time on their horse ranch sixty miles away. They have owned a large home in the Westwood Hills area of Los Angeles since Tito

Henry Allan Easterling, Out of the Past

The seventy-nine-year-old Tito Guizar photographed at the Memphis Western Film Festival in 1987.

was making American movies, but it is now leased.

When he arrived in 1931 Tito insisted that his wife leave show business. She was a samba dancer under the name Carmen Annette Noriega.

Twenty years later Guizar told an interviewer: "A wife must know who her master is. That way she'll never turn into an old nag. Treat her like a racehorse—riding crop, carrots, and all."

Guizar is the father of two daughters and a son. His son lives in San Antonio, Texas, where he sometimes performs, much in the fashion of his father.

Tito Guizar still makes appearances in Mexico and occasionally tours South American capitals.

Many who remembered Dorothy Gulliver from her silent pictures and early talkies did not recognize her as the same actress who appeared in Faces *(insert), almost thirty years after she disappeared from the screen. Contrary to predictions in 1968, when the John Cassavetes film was released, her highly acclaimed performance did not bring about a comeback or earn an Oscar nomination. It was the last time the public saw her.*

Dorothy Gulliver

The screen actress was born of English parentage on September 6, 1908, in Salt Lake City, Utah.

While in school Dorothy was an avid movie fan. Her favorite star was Marie Prevost.

A scout for Paramount had already shown an interest in her when the teenager won a beauty contest sponsored by Universal Pictures. Her prizes, a trip to Hollywood and a screen test, resulted in her being signed to a stock contract.

Dorothy Gulliver began at Universal in bit parts. It was her role in *The Collegians,* a highly successful series of two-reelers, that put her before the public.

The studio used *The Collegians* to showcase its younger players. George Lewis was her leading man. Virtual unknowns such as Walter Brennan, Andy Devine, and Clark Gable were also seen in the silent shorts.

Fans of the sound serial know Dorothy Gulliver for *The Galloping Ghosts* (1931), in which her leading man was football great turned actor Harold "Red" Grange, *The Phantom of the West* (1931) with Tom Tyler, and *The Last Frontier* (1932) opposite Lon Chaney, Jr. (who was then using the name Creighton Chaney). She also had a small part in *Custer's Last Stand* (1936), which had Rex Lease in the lead for fifteen episodes.

Western film enthusiasts know her for her

roles as leading lady to Jack Hoxie and Hoot Gibson, stars of the twenties and thirties. In the serial *Shadow of the Eagle* (1932) she played opposite the young John Wayne, and in *In Early Arizona* (1938), an oater that starred Bill Elliott, she was the ingenue. Dorothy Gulliver would have been remembered only for these screen appearances had it not been for *Faces* (1968).

She had been retired from acting for more than twenty-five years when she went to a party in the company of her husband, press agent Jack Proctor. During the evening Dorothy sang a song. She thought no more of it until someone asked for her telephone number.

"I was at that stage in life where I knew he didn't want to date me," recalls Ms. Gulliver. "Then John Cassavetes called, and I read, and all at once I was making a movie again. I fully understood the desperate, pathetic woman I played and gave it *everything*."

She was frequently singled out in reviews such as the one by Kevin Thomas in the *Los Angeles Times:* "Most notable is Dorothy Gulliver, playing a dumpy, frowsy housewife markedly direct in her craving for affection."

The momentum of her notices, seconded by the critical and box-office success of *Faces,* was never followed up with personal publicity. Nor were advertisements taken in the trade press at the time, months later, when members of the Motion Picture Academy of Arts and Sciences were considering nominations.

In 1987 the actress, who had been totally inactive professionally since *Faces,* was asked to explain her seeming inaction of twenty years before.

Dorothy Gulliver remarked: "I knew what had to be done and had the means and will to do it. But when you're married to a publicist, he's supposed to do it. He kept telling me that everything was being taken care of. When I finally realized that he had no intention of promoting me for anything it was too

Marty Jackson

Dorothy Gulliver (left), *Dorothy Revier, whose unofficial title during her career in silents and early talkies was "The Queen of Poverty Row," and Judith Wood.[9] The three came together for the first time on December 4, 1986, at "The Night of Far More Than 100 Stars" party.*

late. I didn't care if I ever worked again, but I would love to have been recognized for *Faces*. Just the nomination would have meant the world. But my husband deeply resented me, not just my career. Like a lot of men, he hated all women. He brutalized me physically and emotionally until he died eleven years ago. And yet I did marry him. Why? That's the question I'm still asking myself."

Ms. Gulliver declines to discuss why she left her profession in the late thirties or to discuss the intervening years, except to say that she almost lost a foot in an accident and spent several years recuperating. There was also an early marriage to assistant director Chester De Vito, father of Danny De Vito, which ended in divorce.

In the summer of 1988 Dorothy Gulliver sold her Los Angeles duplex and moved to Valley Center, California. Her new home is on two acres of land and overlooks a vineyard. Her companions are two cats, two dogs, and a retired motion picture art director who has been her friend for over ten years.

She no longer practices her Mormon faith, but believes that "God looks after me very well anyway."

On her eightieth birthday Dorothy proclaimed: "I can't ever remember being this happy before in my life!"

The role of "Georgia," the dance-hall girl, in **The Gold Rush** *(1925) was originally intended for Lita Grey,[8] Chaplin's teenage bride. But when she became pregnant her husband replaced her with Georgia Hale, a "discovery" of Josef von Sternberg.*

Georgia Hale

The leading lady of silent pictures was born Georgette Theodora Hale in St. Joseph, Missouri, on June 24, 1905. Six years later her family moved to Illinois.

In 1922 Georgia Hale was awarded $1,500 in a beauty contest held in Chicago. Despite strong disapproval from her father, the teenager used the money to go to New York City. After she was unsuccessful in trying to get a part on Broadway, she left for Hollywood.

Arriving with only $30, Georgia found work immediately as an extra in silent movies. She can be glimpsed in *By Divine Right* (1924), and she danced in the chorus of *Vanity's Price* (1924). Samuel Goldwyn was sufficiently interested to have Rupert Hughes direct her in a screen test, but he did not sign her. It was during this period that she became acquainted with Josef von Sternberg, who was working as an assistant director.

When von Sternberg and the actor George K. Arthur pooled their talents to make *The Salvation Hunters* (1925), they intended to hire an established actress for the female lead. After it became obvious that they could not afford a "name," Georgia was engaged.

The film made such an impression on Douglas Fairbanks that he bought an interest in it and signed Georgia to play opposite him in *Don Q, Son of Zorro*. His friend Charlie Chaplin prevailed upon him to sell the commitment to him. Chaplin had been taken with her performance as a woman of the streets and cast her as a dance-hall girl in *The Gold Rush* (1925).

Playing opposite Chaplin in that hugely successful comedy made the name *Georgia Hale* world famous. The December 1925 issue of *Photoplay* carried her face on its cover, and it was assumed that she would be with the star-director again in his next vehicle, *The Circus*. The film capital was surprised when Chaplin allowed her contract to expire, but she was immediately pacted by Paramount Pictures.

During her time at Paramount, Georgia played opposite William Collier, Jr., in *The Rainmaker* (1926) and was featured in the prestigious film *The Great Gatsby* (1926), but her voice and diction were thought unsuitable for sound. After *The Last Moment* (1928) she considered herself "all washed up" in pictures.

Chaplin had begun filming *City Lights* with Virginia Cherrill[8] when he had a disagreement with his leading lady. The star-director made a screen test with Georgia Hale playing the blind flower girl while wearing a blond wig. But he did not make the replacement, probably because Ms. Cherrill could have brought legal action.

When Georgia failed to get the part, rumors abounded that her relationship with the star was finished and that she might sue him. At the Hollywood premier of *City Lights* in 1930, Charlie Chaplin's date was Georgia Hale.

Georgia and Charlie Chaplin saw each other frequently until the early thirties. She always maintained it was she who introduced him to tennis, one of his great enthusiasms.

For a while she and her sister ran a dance studio in Hollywood. Then Georgia began buying and selling real estate. According to her longtime friend, the widow of the late actor Jay Jostyn, she died "quite a wealthy woman." Most of her estate went to the man who had been her companion since they met at a dance in 1969. Although they lived together for more than fifteen years, it was not until shortly before her death in 1985 that he knew of her career.

"Twice we saw *The Gold Rush* together," he admitted in 1986, "but Georgia told me it was her sister in that picture. She'd keep saying, 'He's a genius!' throughout the screening. She really loved Chaplin, admired him and respected his great gifts."

It was during the filming of *The Gold Rush* that Georgia Hale embraced Christian Science. When she met with Chaplin in 1972 for the first time in many years, her gift to him

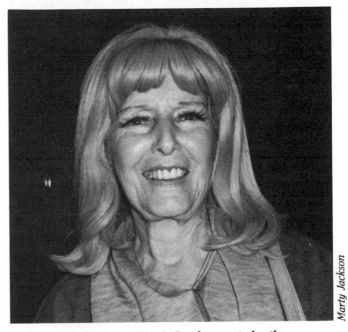

Georgia Hale leaving a Minnie Pearl concert shortly before she died on June 7, 1985.

was a copy of *Science and Health with a Key to the Scriptures,* the writings of the religion's founder. After thanking her he said, "I remember you going on about this long ago. I should have paid more attention because, looking at you, I'm prepared to believe there's something to it."

Georgia Hale granted only one interview after she stopped making movies. She agreed to appear on *The Unseen Chaplin,* a three-part TV special seen on PBS stations, because it had the approval of Chaplin's family. She confined her remarks to her professional relationship with the filmmaker. It was the only time the public saw her in more than fifty years.

After her retirement she steadfastly refused to sign autographs or correspond with fans, explaining to the few who spoke with her, "I am no longer the person you seek."

The four-unit dwelling in which she died in 1985 was one of several Hollywood properties that she owned. It is located on the same street as the studio in which she made *The Gold Rush.*

Signe Hasso was teamed with the late James Craig in M-G-M's Dangerous Partners *(1945). Craig had been contracted to the studio as a replacement for Clark Gable, who served in the army during World War II.*

Signe Hasso

The leading lady of movies and stage was born on August 15, 1915, in Stockholm. Her original name is Signe Larsson. She was not yet school-age when her father died, leaving his family penniless. Her mother, who was a serious but unsuccessful painter, supported them by selling hot cakes from a street stall.

She made a great hit at Stockholm's Royal Dramatic Theatre at age eleven, taking over at the last minute when another child became ill. She remained with the company, winning a prestigious acting prize when she was sixteen.

In 1936 her name was changed to Signe Hasso (pronounced Seen-yah Hah-so) when she married a theatre director-inventor named Harry Hasso.

She was in her early twenties when she received the Swedish equivalent of the Oscar, the "Guld Bagge," for her appearance in *Kaviar* (1938). It was the first time a woman had been so honored. The same year her acting on stage brought another award.

After their son was born in 1937 Signe was directed by her husband in a Swedish-German production released in Germany as *Geld Fallt vom Himmel* (1938).

Signe Hasso came to Hollywood with a reputation in her native land equal to that of Ingrid Bergman. But while Ms. Bergman came under the expert auspices of David O. Selznick, Signe was under contract to RKO, a studio in a state of flux that had no assignment for her.

She went instead to Broadway, where she debuted in *Golden Wings* (1941). The play, though a flop, brought her a review from George Jean Nathan, the dean of American theatre critics, that proclaimed Signe "the most attractive new foreign actress in America."

Her first Hollywood film was *Journey for Margaret* (1942) in a small role. In *Assignment in Brittany* (1943) she betrayed Jean-Pierre Aumont. Ernst Lubitsch directed her flirtation with Don Ameche in *Heaven Can Wait* (1943). Cecil B. De Mille guided Signe and Gary Cooper in *The Story of Dr. Wassell* (1944). Then she played with Spencer Tracy in *The Seventh Cross* (1944). She sang and danced in *A Scandal in Paris* (1946) and played an officer in the military in the Bob Hope starrer *Where There's Life* (1947). In *A*

Double Life (1948) she played "Desdemona" to Ronald Colman's "Othello." In *Crisis* (1950) she had key scenes with Cary Grant.

She played on Broadway opposite Melvyn Douglas in *Glad Tidings* (1951), and the two were paired again in the televersion of *Reunion in Vienna*.

Ms. Hasso has written novels, short stories, and song lyrics. She has appeared in a one-woman show, in summer stock, and Off-Broadway. She was leading lady to Maurice Evans during his revival of Shaw's *The Apple Cart* (1956). Two years later she toured in *Mary Stuart* with Eva Le Gallienne, a production that was filmed for TV's *Play of the Week*.

Signe took over the role in *Cabaret* that had been originated by Lotte Lenya on Broadway and toured in the national company. She occasionally appears in plays on the Stockholm stage, always with star billing. In the United States she is seen on TV at least once each season in such programs as *Trapper John, M.D.* and *Murder, She Wrote*.

Signe Hasso has enjoyed a wide range of roles on screen and stage but never achieved in the United States the status her admirers feel she deserves.

Her first marriage ended in divorce after eight years. She was widowed after four years with her second husband. Her son was killed in an auto collision when he was twenty-two years old.

Her two-bedroom apartment in the Park-La Brea complex was described by Mark Mac-Namara in *Los Angeles* magazine thusly: "Heavy carpets, dark colors, drapes, Bergman atmosphere: a picture of black faith healer and spiritualist Ruthi Thompson, paintings by Signe's son Henry; a letter from J. Edgar Hoover congratulating Signe for her portrayal of the spy master in *The House on 92nd Street*."

Director Curtis Harrington spoke of her

James Craig made an occasional appearance on television during the seventies, but the major portion of his income was from real estate commissions. Divorced for the third time, the actor was living in Orange County, California, when he died on July 4, 1985.

Signe Hasso recently during the intermission of a play in Los Angeles.

recently: "Signe is living proof that you can be an exceptionally gifted and versatile actress for all these years in Hollywood and yet not become a star. To add to the irony of it all, she's *still* beautiful."

71

Paul Henreid is best known for his portrayals of Ingrid Bergman's husband in Casablanca *and the lover of Bette Davis in* Now, Voyager. *Both films were released in 1942.*

Paul Henreid

The suave star of the forties was born in Trieste, Italy, but raised in Vienna. His birthdate is January 10, 1908. He was baptized Paul George Julius Hernried Ritter von Wasel-Waldingau.

His father, a banker, left a sizable estate when he died in 1916. But, through mismanagement and the inflation of the twenties, the family suffered serious reversals in fortune. Paul attended the elite Maria Theresianische Akademie on a special scholarship because his father had been a friend and financial counselor to Emperor Franz Josef.

By the time of graduation he was thoroughly stagestruck but took a position with a publishing firm to help support his mother and younger brother. His evenings were spent studying acting. It was in a production by his night school that Paul was seen and "discovered" by Max Reinhardt, Europe's leading impresario.

Viennese critics singled out Paul von Hernried in a Reinhardt production of *Faust.* That play brought him his leading role in *Hohe Schule* (1935), a film that was a great success in central Europe. On the strength of that picture he was invited to Berlin, where a lucrative contract with UFA was offered. He declined, citing the rider whereby the signee swore allegiance to Nazism. He was immediately placed on a blacklist that made him unemployable in films made on the continent.

London first saw him in the musical play *Café Chantant* (1936). After the final curtain each evening he sang at the Ritz Cabaret. *Victoria Regina,* in which Paul played the Prince Albert role, was a major success and brought about a change in English law, thereafter permitting the portrayal of royalty on stage.

He had a role in *Goodbye, Mr. Chips* (1939) and *Night Train* (1940), a sleeper hit in the United States. Both films were made in England.

He was brought to New York, expecting to re-create his role in *Jersey Lily,* a play he did at a London theatre club in early 1940. The production never materialized. Instead, he played Prince Albert again, this time to Helen Hayes's Queen Victoria on network radio. Then he made his Broadway debut, drawing critics' praise in Elmer Rice's *Flight to the West* (1940).

He came to Hollywood assured of star billing and a substantial salary. His first film was *Joan of Paris* (1942), in which he played a French aviator opposite Michele Morgan.

In *In Our Time* (1944) he was a Polish count; in *Between Two Worlds* (1944), a neurotic French concert pianist. He was also a Dutch resistance leader in *The Conspirators* (1944), a pirate in *The Spanish Main* (1945), and a jealous cellist in *Deception* (1946). In *Song of Love* (1947) he portrayed composer Robert Schumann.

In 1946 the *Harvard Lampoon* named Paul Henreid the year's "most miscast" actor in *Of Human Bondage,* a picture it listed on the magazine's "worst" list.

His image of the continental lover was firmly established after playing with Katharine Hepburn, Hedy Lamarr, Ingrid Bergman, and Bette Davis (twice). His portrayal of a heavy in *Rope of Sand* (1949) gave him a macho reputation as well.

Casablanca (1942) was his first assignment under a contract with Warner Brothers. It has proven to be one of the most popular movies ever made. He is pleased by its success, but considers *Casablanca* to be merely entertainment and not a serious film. Asked about his role in it, he has responded: "Whoever heard of a resistance fighter running around in a white suit?"

Warner Brothers then cast him in *Now, Voyager* (1942) as an architect who falls in love with Bette Davis during a South American cruise. In its most famous scene he puts two cigarettes in his mouth, lights both, and gives one to Davis. The gesture created a minor sensation at the time and started a fad among couples. Ms. Davis has stated that the idea was hers. Possibly she remembers the bit from *The Rich Are Always with Us* (1932), in which George Brent does the same for Ruth Chatterton. (Bette Davis had a small role in that feature.)

Henreid was one of the group of stars who flew to Washington, D.C., to protest the House Unamerican Activities Committee's hearings. Unlike most of the others, he was

Marty Jackson

Paul Henreid exiting the Hollywood Bowl recently after attending An Evening with Victor Borge.

not under the protective auspices of a major studio. Soon afterward it became apparent that his acting career had suddenly come to a complete halt.

As early as 1948 Paul had produced motion pictures. His first credit was *Hollow Triumph,* in which he costarred with Joan Bennett.[10] He worked throughout the blacklist years, mostly as a director. *For Men Only* (1952), *A Woman's Devotion* (1957), *Dead Ringer* (1964) with Bette Davis, *Blues for Lovers* (1966), and *The Last Man to Die* (1968) are some of the features he directed.

His directorial credits on television include: *Alfred Hitchcock Presents, Thriller, Maverick,* and *Bracken's World.*

He acted again in movies and on TV after the blacklist became less effective. Roles in *The Four Horsemen of the Apocalypse* (1962) and *The Madwoman of Chaillot* (1969) might have reactivated his acting career. Both were prestigious, but neither was a success critically or financially.

In 1936 Paul married Lisl, a well-established Viennese couturiere who continued in her career even after he was a Hollywood star. Mimi, one of their two daughters, won three collegiate tennis championships. The Henreids' home is at the end of a dead-end road in the Sunset Mesa area of Pacific Palisades.

His autobiography, *Ladies Man,* was published in 1984.

Irene Hervey wins James Stewart from Marlene Dietrich in Destry Rides Again *(1939). She was once described in Jack O'Brian's nationally syndicated column as having "a beautiful combination of delicately, naturally aristocratic poise and ease."*

Irene Hervey

The dimpled screen beauty was born Irene Herwick on July 11 in Los Angeles. Her father was a sign painter.

Irene was in her late teens when she married a musician. When they divorced after four years she found herself with the responsibility of raising and supporting their baby girl.

A family friend introduced her to a casting director at M-G-M, who suggested she return when she was prepared to do a scene for him.

At the suggestion of her mother, a Christian Science practitioner, Irene went for coaching to Emma Dunn, a character actress who was a patient of Mrs. Herwick.

Irene was screen-tested and put into M-G-M's training program. After eight months on the lot, but without salary, she informed Louis B. Mayer that she would have to leave for a paying job. He immediately cast her as Franchot Tone's wife in *Stranger's Return* (1933) under King Vidor's direction. She was also pacted at $50 a week.

During the four years she spent under that M-G-M contract, Irene played on the screen in the feature *Hollywood Party* (1933) with Laurel & Hardy, and made one *Crime Does Not Pay* short and two shorts for Pete Smith. She was loaned out to Fox Films, Monogram Pictures, United Artists, Columbia, and Paramount. She also became engaged to Robert Taylor, her studio's most promising young male star.

M-G-M and the actor's mother disapproved of Taylor's marrying anyone at that point. Irene remembers that her fiancé's "impossible jealousy" also contributed to their breakup.

Shortly afterward she went to a party at the home of director Raoul Walsh in the company of Betty Furness and Caesar "Butch" Romero. By the end of the evening Irene and Allan Jones had become "entranced with each other."

In 1936, the year she married Jones, the actress, discouraged by the roles she was assigned, asked for her release from M-G-M.

Not long afterward she signed with Universal Pictures, where her husband was also under contract.

The couple was well publicized by Universal and costarred in *The Boys from Syracuse* (1940). Irene made as many as seven features a year, but most were programmers. She never fulfilled the expectations of some critics and fans, who saw in her skills and qualities similar to those of Myrna Loy. Even teaming her with Loy's "screen husband," William Powell, in *Mr. Peabody and the Mermaid* (1948) failed to ignite her career.

Yet when she married Jones, the actress stated that she had no ambitions to become a star and that her family would come "first and foremost." In 1987, fifty years later and thirty years after Irene and Allan were divorced, she assured an interviewer that she had no regrets about those priorities.

Two of the best-known of Irene Hervey's more than sixty movies are *The Count of Monte Cristo* (1934) with Robert Donat and Leon Ames,[8] and *East Side of Heaven* (1939) with Bing Crosby and Baby Sandy.[8]

Among the others were: *Three on a Honeymoon* with Sally Eilers[8] (1934); *The Winning Ticket* (1935) with Leslie Fenton;* *Along Came Love* (1936) with Charles Starrett; *The Lady Fights Back* (1938) with the late Kent Taylor;* *Say It in French* (1938) with Mary Carlisle;[10] *Missing Evidence* (1939) with Chick Chandler, *Three Cheers for the Irish* (1940) with Dennis Morgan,[8] Priscilla Lane, and Virginia Grey; *Mr. Dynamite* (1941) with Ann Gillis; *Mickey* (1948) with Rose Hobart[10] and Skip Homeier;* *Chicago Deadline* (1949) with Alan Ladd, Arthur Kennedy,[9] and John Beal;[9] and *A Cry in the Night* (1956) with Edmund O'Brien.[9] Her last two films were *Cactus Flower* (1969) and *Play Misty for Me* (1971).

She appeared on the live TV dramas presented on *Studio One, Playhouse 90,* and

Kim Jones

Irene Hervey and her son Jack Jones recently during a cruise of the Caribbean Sea aboard the S. S. Norway.

Matinee Theatre and guested on segments of *Perry Mason, Burke's Law,* and *Ironside.* In the mid-sixties Ms. Hervey played a running part on the soap *The Young Marrieds* and was nominated for an Emmy for her performance on an episode of *My Three Sons.*

The day after their divorce, Allan Jones married the heiress to the Florsheim shoe fortune. He predicted that Irene, too, would soon remarry. She felt the same.

In 1987 Ms. Hervey explained: "To my surprise I discovered solitude, something I had never experienced. I found it very much to my liking. And my children are very close, both in physical distance and in the even more important sense. I am greatly blessed and very grateful."

Joy Hodges made Follow the Fleet *(1936) at RKO with Rodgers and Astaire and then went to Broadway where she appeared in* I'd Rather Be Right *(1937), a musical spoof of the New Deal.*

Joy Hodges

Ronald Reagan's first link to Hollywood was born Eloise Hodges in Des Moines, Iowa. Her birthdate is January 29, 1915.

Her parents, convinced that she was talented, gave her lessons in singing and dancing from a very early age. She appeared in school plays and sold sheet music, which she played and sang, in a dime store.

She was one of the "Bluebird Twins," vocalists heard over radio station WHO in Des Moines. Winning a talent contest resulted in bookings in several nightclubs. After singing at the Chez Paree in Chicago, she joined Carol Lofner, a one-time partner of Phil Harris, as singer with his dance band.

After a short time with Lofner, she joined Jimmy Grier's band. Because of a short she made with Grier, RKO put her under contract. The only movie of note Joy made during her six months at the studio was *Follow the Fleet* (1936).

From Hollywood she returned to Chicago to fill in for Harriet Hillard, who had become pregnant with David Nelson. She sang with Ozzie Nelson's band at the Palmer House until Jimmy Grier hired her back as his vocalist on Joe Penner's radio show.

George S. Kaufman and Richard Rodgers saw Joy perform in a show at the Pan Pacific Auditorium, a benefit produced by Bing Crosby. The team immediately agreed that she was right for a leading role in their next show.

The part was "Miss Jones" in *I'd Rather Be Right* (1937), a Broadway musical that starred George M. Cohan. The hit song, "Have You Met Miss Jones?" was introduced by Joy and her leading man, Austin Marshall.

Her friend Mary Martin always introduces her as "the girl who got the parts I wanted." Ms. Martin auditioned for *I'd Rather Be Right* and was screen-tested for *Merry-Go-Round of 1938* (1937), a movie that Joy did with Bert Lahr.

Her other Broadway credits are: *Dream with Music* (1944), in which she was a replacement for Marilyn Maxwell during the musical's out-of-town tryouts; *The Odds on Mrs. Oakley* (1944); the Eddie Cantor production *Nellie Bly* (1946); and *Jo* (1964), a musical version of *Little Women* (1964) in which Joy played "Marmee."

Her screen credits include: *Personal Secretary* (1938), in which she shared billing with William Gargan; *Service de Luxe* (1938); *They Asked for It* (1939), in which she costarred with Michael Whalen; and two Baby Sandy[8] features.

Early in her career the singer-actress married an editor of the *Omaha World-Herald*. After their divorce she was married to a radio-TV critic. They were divorced after eight years.

Joy's third husband, Eugene Schiess, was an advertising executive. When they married in 1956 she decided to concentrate on her domestic life. She does not rule out performing again, but it would have to be a role that was "irresistible" to her. The only one in recent years was the part in *No, No, Nanette* that Ruby Keeler originated. Joy replaced Ruby in the Broadway production in 1972.

She recently explained the slackening of interest in her profession: "It was my parents' idea to begin with. Part of me enjoyed the applause. Another side resented that I wasn't with other kids. And as an adult, everything just fell into my lap. But, understand that I had a wonderful time doing everything I've done. It's just that I am perfectly happy away from the stage and cameras."

Ms. Hodges took her first name from Leatrice Joy,[8] a fellow Christian Scientist. Ginger Rogers, her close friend since they made *Follow the Fleet,* is a member of the same religion.

Joy Hodges and Ronald Reagan first met when he interviewed her over WHO, where he was employed as a broadcaster. He opened the program by asking her how it felt to be in

In 1988 Joy Hodges and her husband sold their home in Katonah, New York, and retired to Cathedral City, California.

Marty Jackson

the movies. She replied, "Perhaps someday you'll know that for yourself." He confessed after the show that he had thought about screen acting as a career. She suggested he look her up if he ever came to Hollywood.

A few months later Reagan came to see her between shows at the Biltmore Bowl where she was singing. Asked for help, Joy set up an appointment with her agent for the following day. In preparation for the subsequent Warner Brothers screen test, she went over Reagan's lines with him and gave him a few pointers about the camera. Perhaps the most important advice she gave him, which was seconded by their agent, was to take off his eyeglasses and never wear them at the studio.

They have remained in touch over the years, seeing each other last when the president took Joy and her husband on a tour of the White House in 1983.

Said Joy Hodges in February 1988: "I suppose that was the most important thing I did throughout my career, and yet we never actually worked together. We didn't even date. Why, he wasn't even a fellow Republican then! It just proves the far-reaching effects of kindness to others."

John Hubbard had high regard for Carole Landis, his costar in three Hal Roach features made during 1940 and 1941. She was separated from her fourth husband and having an affair with Rex Harrison when she committed suicide in 1948 at the age of twenty-nine.

John Hubbard

The leading man of the forties was born on April 14, 1923, in East Chicago, Illinois. From an early age everything about performing interested him. He sang in the church choir and the school chorale and acted in plays produced locally. During high school he ushered in the town's presentation house, but the shows on its stage interested him much more than the movies on its screen.

Hubbard had spent more than two years studying at the famed Goodman Theatre in Chicago when Carl Laemmle, Sr., the founder of Universal Pictures, offered him a contract. Wanting to complete the four-year course, Jack declined. By graduation in 1937

he had been signed by Paramount Pictures.

He made his screen debut under Cecil B. de Mille's direction in *The Buccaneer* (1938). Twenty years later he was to play another part in its remake.

After Jack Hubbard, as he was known to friends, married his high-school sweetheart, his studio lost interest in him, and his contract was sold to M-G-M. At his new studio producer Mervyn LeRoy changed his name to Anthony Allan and cast him in *Dramatic School* (1938). The actor believes that Luise Rainer vehicle to have been his "first real break in Hollywood."

His assignments on the Culver City lot after it, however, were small roles in an "Andy Hardy" feature, the first of the "Maisie" series, and *Fast and Loose* (1939), a murder mystery.

Hubbard agreed to a four-film pact with Hal Roach because the producer promised he would be directed by Norman Z. McLeod or Leo McCarey, or both. But Roach was the director on all four films: *The Housekeeper's Daughter* (1939), *One Million B.C.* (1940), *Turnabout* (1940), and *Road Show* (1941).

In John Hubbard's opinion he did his best work in *Whispering Footsteps* (1943), a low-budget feature even by the standards of Republic Pictures, where it was made. In his book *"B" Movies,* the late Don Miller called the film "extraordinary" and singled out Hubbard's understated performance for praise.

Some of his other screen credits are: *The Big Broadcast of 1938* (1938); *Our Wife* (1941) with Ruth Hussey;* *The Mummy's Tomb* (1942); *Youth on Parade* (1943) with Martha O'Driscoll; and *Up in Mabel's Room* (1944).

After serving as a sergeant in the U.S. Infantry in Italy, Hubbard returned to find fewer and smaller roles in pictures. *Linda Be Good* (1947) with Elyse Knox;* *Mexican*

Hayride (1949) with Abbott & Costello; and *An Old-Fashioned Girl* (1949) with Gloria Jean[8] and Frances Rafferty[10] were among them.

He was the star of another stage farce, *Mary Had a Little,* which he took across Australia and which then had a respectable run on London's West End.

In the early fifties John began selling automobiles between acting jobs. Subsequently, he became manager of a large restaurant, a position he held until he began experiencing back problems in recent years.

Hubbard was a regular on *The Mickey Rooney Show,* which ran on NBC-TV during the 1954–55 season, and he played the title role in *Don't Call Me Charlie* over the same network in 1962–63. He also appeared in the features *Fate Is the Hunter* (1964) with Nancy Kwan, *Duel at Diablo* (1966), and *Herbie Rides Again* (1973).

Probably his most important film was *The Bullfighter and the Lady* (1951), considered by many to be the best of the genre. He was originally slated for the leading role, but financing of the independent production took several years, and Robert Stack, a young actor, replaced him as the matador. In preparation for the role he never got to play, John became friendly with the legendary Manolete, whose photograph hangs on the wall of his living room.

The only other evidence of his career on view in his home is a coffee mug inscribed "To Hub from Duke"—a gift from his "drinking buddy," John Wayne—and two photos of himself.

No one in the family—which includes two daughters, one son, eight grandchildren, and one great-grandchild—is in the entertainment business, and John was out of touch with everyone he ever worked with.

Forty years after it passed him by, the actor recalled what he thinks was his one real

Dick Lynch

John Hubbard in the den of his condominium in Camarillo, California, beside portraits taken while he was making One Million B.C. *(1940).*

chance for screen stardom: "Claudette Colbert and I both had a one-feature commitment to Columbia Pictures. Harry Cohn screened *Turnabout* for her and she approved me to play opposite her in what was supposed to have been a light comedy. But after she turned down one script after another, Cohn gave up on her. But I fulfilled my contract in support of Fred Astaire and Rita Hayworth in *You'll Never Get Rich* (1941)."

In retrospect, he felt his career would have been longer and more rewarding had he and his wife socialized more: "It occurred to me right from the start that we should get out and around more, but neither of us felt the need really. But professionally, I needed to be seen here and there with so and so. Perhaps I've paid the price for remaining in love with my wife and spending as much time as I could with her and our kids. If that's the case, all I can say is, 'It was worth it!'"

John Hubbard died on November 6, 1988, in Camarillo, California.

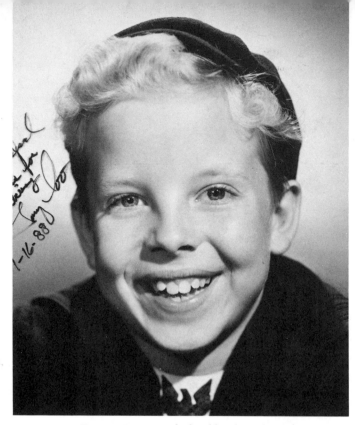

Tommy Ivo was slight, blond, and looked younger than he really was. He usually was cast as a wimpy, delicate, disabled, or downright dying child.

Tommy Ivo

The child actor of the forties and fifties was born of German and Danish parentage in Denver, Colorado. His birthdate is April 18, 1936.

His family moved to Los Angeles in 1943, hoping the milder climate would alleviate Mrs. Ivo's arthritis.

Tommy continued his weekly tap-dance lessons and happily performed whenever asked. Neither he nor his parents, however, gave any thought to a performing career.

A friend of the Ivos heard that a producer was having difficulty finding a boy who could tap dance to play in a musical. Tommy auditioned and was signed to play the son of a

pair of vaudevillians, Constance Moore and Dennis O'Keefe, in *Earl Carroll Vanities* (1945). It was the only time he ever danced on the screen and one of the few times he appeared in such an upbeat film.

Casting people saw in Tommy a pathetic quality and hired him over and over again for roles in tear jerkers.

The most memorable of his more than five dozen appearances in features are as the seriously ill son of Irene Dunne[8] in *I Remember Mama* (1948) and in *Plymouth Adventure* (1952). In the latter Tommy portrayed the little boy who dies just before the Mayflower arrives in the New World.

In 1988 Ivo commented on his screen image: "Boy, was I typed! For a while I played nothing but orphans. And when I had parents, I also had some terrible disease or got hit by a car. If I wasn't sickly, then I'd be a sissy. I'm not complaining because I enjoyed being an actor. I must have been a fairly good one because I had parents, good health, and liked sports."

Among his other screen credits are: *Father Is a Bachelor* (1950); *Operation Haylift* (1950); one of the "Bomba, The Jungle Boy" series; *The Lost Volcano* (1950), which starred Johnny Sheffield; *The Whirlwind* (1951); *Snake River Desperadoes* (1951); *Belles on Their Toes* (1952); *The Rough Tough West* (1952); *You're Never Too Young* (1955); *Beast of Budapest* (1958); *Life Begins at Seventeen* (1958); *The Ghost of Dragstrip Hollow* (1959); and *The Cat Burglar* (1961).

The role that might have hyped his career instead became his biggest disappointment. Tommy Ivo was signed to play the lead in *The Window* and was eagerly looking forward to going to New York City, where the film was to be made. His mother was packing their bags when his agent was advised that Tommy would be paid in full, but that he had been dropped from the cast. He was replaced by

Bobby Driscoll, who won an Oscar and became a star with that movie.

Tommy was a semiregular on the *Donna Reed Show* and remembers the star and her husband, who produced the TV show, as being the most difficult to please. The late Edmund O'Brien,[9] whom he supported in a teleplay on *Climax,* he recalls as the most insensitive of the many stars he worked with.

One of the few reminders of his acting career to be found in his home is a huge poster from *The Treasure of Lost Canyon* (1952), which hangs over his bed. William Powell, whom he supported in the picture, was one of the three stars he most enjoyed working with. The late Charles Starrett[8] was another. Tommy played with him in a number of his "Durango Kid" series, his favorite being one in which he wore an all-black outfit exactly like Starrett's.

He rates Boris Karloff, along with Powell and Starrett, as being very nice to work with. In 1946 they appeared together on stage in Los Angeles in *On Borrowed Time.* Margaret Hamilton[10] and Beulah Bondi[8] were also in the cast. Ivo particularly liked performing before a live audience. That play, however, was the only time he had the opportunity.

On *Margie,* an ABC-TV sit-com of the 1961–62 season, he played "Heywood Botts," klutzy boyfriend of Cynthia Pepper, who had the title role. When he was not on the set of the series, Ivo spent his time tinkering with racing cars.

As soon as he achieved his first minor success in drag racing he realized he had to withdraw from acting. Contracts with insurance companies prevented studios from engaging actors who participate in so dangerous an activity. Also, he was serious about racing as a profession and knew it would require all of his time.

During the next twenty years, which Tommy Ivo spent on the international racing

Tom Ivo beside a picture of him from his first movie, **Earl Carroll Vanities** *(1945), in 1988.*

Marty Jackson

circuit, he held the world's speed record eleven times. He claims that he was almost killed about as often.

His second career came to an end in May 1982 when, while he was driving at top speed, his engine exploded. He suffered a broken back, which when healed left him with a "yellow streak right down it."

Ivo has been married to and divorced from the same woman twice. They share custody of a Lhasa apso named "Theodora."

Tom, as he is now called, lives in a home he recently designed and had built in Burbank, California. It is directly behind his widowed mother's house, which was purchased with his earnings when he was twelve years old.

Tom considers himself semiretired, although he recently purchased a partnership in a franchise for Bekins moving vans. He has been on several world tours and intends to do more traveling.

In his last movie, *Heart Like a Wheel* (1982), he was not seen. Ivo drove the racing car as the double for Bonnie Bedelia, who was playing Shirley Muldowney, the pioneer female driver. Muldowney is a lifelong friend of his.

Dean Jagger was in the original Broadway production of Tobacco Road *(1933) and had the starring role in* Brigham Young—Frontiersman *(1940) on screen, but he is best known as a character actor. On TV he played opposite James Franciscus in* Mr. Novak, *a popular series of the sixties.*

Dean Jagger

The Oscar- and Emmy-winning actor was born into a farm family in Columbus Grove, Ohio. His birthdate is November 7, 1903.

His first profession was as a teacher in a rural school. After several semesters he left to pursue an acting career.

Jagger studied with the Lyceum Arts Conservatory in Chicago, toured the Chautauqua circuit, and joined the W. H. Wright Stock Company in Grand Rapids, Michigan, replacing Spencer Tracy. He first came to Hollywood with Irene Rich in a vaudeville sketch.

His "break," *Tobacco Road* (1933), was also his Broadway debut. Then he did *They Shall Not Die* (1934), a play based on the Scottsboro case, with Ruth Gordon. His films were interspersed with other New York stage productions such as *Missouri Legend* (1938) with Dorothy Gish, *The Brown Danube* (1939), *The Unconquered* (1940), and *Doctor Social* (1948).

Of his screen debut, *The Woman from Hell* (1929), he has remarked, "a shame she ever left." It was followed by roles as a cowboy, an Egyptian in *Sign of the Cross* (1932), and a zombie in *Revolt of the Zombies* (1936). Some of his early credits are: *You Belong to Me* (1934), *Car 99* (1935), *Pepper* (1936), and *Dangerous Number* (1937).

It was being cast in the title role of *Brigham Young—Frontiersman* (1940) that established him with moviegoers. After the success of that big-budget production he made mostly A pictures: *Western Union* (1941), *The North Star* (1943), *A Yank in London* (1946) opposite the late Anna Neagle,[9] *Sister Kenny,* (1946) and *Sierra* (1950).

His favorite among the more than 120 features he has appeared in is *Twelve O'Clock High* (1950). For his portrayal of an aging military officer he won an Academy Award as Best Supporting Actor.

The Oscar brought featured roles in important, frequently prestigious, movies: *My Son John* (1952); *It Grows on Trees* (1952), the swan song of Irene Dunne;[8] *The Robe*

(1953); *Executive Suite* (1954); *White Christmas* (1954); *Bad Day at Black Rock* (1955); *The Great Man* (1957); *The Nun's Story* (1959); *Elmer Gantry* (1960); and *Parrish* (1961).

Some of his other screen credits include: *It's a Dog's Life* (1955); *Rawhide* (1951); *The Denver and the Rio Grande* (1952); *The Eternal Sea* (1955); *On the Threshold of Space* (1956); *Three Brave Men* (1957); *Bernardine* (1957); *The Proud Rebel* (1958) with Alan Ladd and David Ladd, the Elvis Presley starrer *King Creole* (1958); *Cash McCall* (1960); *Jumbo* (1960); *First to Fight* (1967) with Bobby Troup;* *Day of the Evil Gun* (1968) with Arthur Kennedy;[9] *Firecreek* (1968) with James Stewart; *Smith!* (1969); *Tiger by the Tail* (1970); *Kremlin Letter* (1970); *Vanishing Point* (1971); *So Sad About Gloria* (1975); *End of the World* (1977); and *The Game of Death* (1978).

Jagger received wide exposure and drew two Emmy nominations for his role of a high school principal in *Mr. Novak*, the series that ran on NBC-TV during the 1963–64 and 1964–65 seasons. The title role was played by James Franciscus, whom Dean recently described as "a real pain in the ass." When Dean left the program during its second season on the air, it was announced that he was suffering from an ulcer.

The Emmy he won was for Individual Achievement in Religious Programming, for a show of the 1979–80 season entitled *Independence and '76, This Is the Life*.

His last notable role was in *Gideon's Trumpet*. On that TV docudrama of 1980, Dean portrayed a United States Supreme Court Justice.

According to press reports in 1943, the first Mrs. Dean Jagger left him for another man after eighteen years of marriage. When he wed for the second time in 1947 the ceremony had to be performed out of state: His

Marty Jackson

Dean Jagger keeps his Oscar (above) in the bedroom and his Emmy in the den of the Santa Monica condominium he shares with his third wife.

fiancée's Chinese background precluded their obtaining a wedding license at that time in California. They separated for a time in 1966 and were divorced in 1967.

He married his present wife, a former ballerina, in 1968. Until 1987 they lived in a large house near the Pacific Ocean in Santa Monica. They have since moved to an apartment nearby. Many of Jagger's paintings hang on their walls. He works mostly in oil.

Dean Jagger's health does not permit him to travel or accept roles that might prove taxing. A rare exception was his portrayal of a hospital patient on *St. Elsewhere* in 1986. He played a man in very much the same condition as himself, determined to live as long and as fully as possible.

Twentieth Century-Fox produced seventeen "Jones Family" features between 1935 and 1940. The cast (from left to right) were: June Carlson as "Lucy," Spring Byington as "Mrs. Jones," George Ernest as "Roger," Jed Prouty playing the small-town pharmacist "John Jones," Billy Mahan as the youngest son "Bobby" (foreground), *Ken Howell as the oldest son "Jack," and Florence Roberts in the role of "Granny Jones."*

"The Jones Family"

The programmers known as the "Jones Family" series are sometimes mistakenly referred to as Twentieth Century-Fox's answer to "Andy Hardy." M-G-M did not produce the first "Hardy Family" picture until 1937. *Every Saturday Night,* the movie that introduced the "Joneses" to the public, was released in 1936.

The daughter, "Lucy," was played by June Carlson, a native of Los Angeles. Her birthday is April 16.

June was picked from a class of tap and toe dancers by a scout for Twentieth Century-Fox. Although she appeared in westerns and Jane Withers starrers, she claims that "my career really began and ended as 'Lucy Jones.'" She found very few parts after the series ended.

In 1945 June married and retired to raise two sons and a daughter. She is now a divorcée and a grandmother of five girls. Jane Withers is the only one from her past with whom she is in contact.

June works as the manager of the cosmetics department in a store in El Toro, California. She shares a house in Irvine with a male friend, explaining: "It's very friendly between us, but nothing romantic, just two people coping with high rents."

The father, "John Jones," was portrayed by Jed Prouty. The actor was a well-established name in theatre and vaudeville who had been making movies since 1921. Although he appeared in A features such as *The Broadway Melody* (1929), *Music in the Air* (1934), and *100 Men and a Girl* (1937), it is for the "Jones Family" films that he is best remembered.

Jed Prouty died at the age of seventy-seven on May 10, 1956.

Before playing the mother of the "Jones" brood, Spring Byington was well known to movie audiences for her role of "Marmee" in *Little Women* (1933). She went on to stardom on radio and TV in the title role of *December Bride.*

Spring Byington died on September 8, 1971, at the age of seventy-seven.

"Grandmother Jones" was played by Florence Roberts, who had appeared on stage under David Belasco's auspices in *Zaza* and *Camille* during the early part of the century. After Mack Sennett induced her to enter pictures, she made more than one hundred.

Florence Roberts had just returned from a cruise when she died on June 6, 1940, at the age of seventy-nine.

George Ernest, who played the middle son, was born in Pittsfield, Massachusetts, on November 20, 1921.

His mother began taking George to casting offices after he was pronounced "cute" by Syd Grauman. (The impresario was a regular patron of George's father's Hollywood restaurant.)

Before the "Jones" films George had been in four "Our Gang" shorts and Cecil B. de Mille's *The Plainsman* (1936). *20,000 Men a Year* (1939) was one of his feature credits. He also appeared as one of the sons in *Four Sons* (1940).

He spent World War II under John Ford's command in the OSS, serving in North Africa, Scandinavia, and Italy. George then joined McDonnell Douglas Corp. He retired recently after thirty years with the company but is still retained as a consultant.

George gave Jane Withers her first screen kiss in *Boy Friend* (1939), but he is in touch only with Marsha Mae Jones from his career.

He and his wife are the parents of two sons. They live in Cypress, California, under his original name, George Hjorth.

Billy Mahan took the part of the youngest, "Bobby Jones." He was born on July 9, 1930, in Port Townsend, Washington.

He did very little film acting after the last "Jones" picture, *Young As You Feel* (1940), but he has remained in the industry as an editor and writer.

In 1933 he commented: "If I had to do it over again, I wouldn't. On the Fox lot we were looked at as players in B pictures. But at public school I was taunted as 'the movie

George Ernest and his wife entertained June Carlson (shown here with George) at dinner in their home on May 28, 1988. "Lucy" and "Roger Jones" had not seen each other in more than forty-three years.

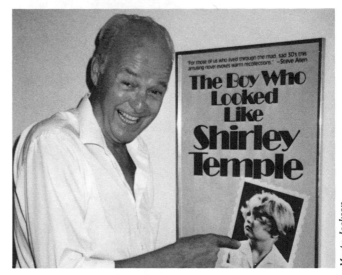

Billy Mahan, who played "Bobby Jones," is a resident of Canoga Park, California, and the author of the autobiographical novel, The Boy Who Looked Like Shirley Temple.

star.' I was in fights all the time."

At approximately twenty years of age, Mahan was working on his boat when he ran into Kenneth Howell, who had played his older brother, at a marina. Billy had heard that Howell had made a career in the U.S. Navy or Coast Guard but had no opportunity to ask. When Billy recognized him and introduced himself, Howell "made it clear that his career was a closed chapter in his life. He cut me dead."

85

Walter Woolf King considered the making of A Night at the Opera *with the Marx Brothers and* Ginger *(above)* with Jane Withers *(right) and Jackie Searle [10] to be "my most pleasant experiences in Hollywood."*

Walter Woolf King

The leading man, singer, and character actor was born in San Francisco on November 2, 1899. His father, a wholesale whiskey salesman, moved his wife and son to Salt Lake City in 1906.

Walter began singing in the choir of the Mormon Church at a very early age. After his father died in 1912, the teenager was forced to leave school. He moved with his mother into a rooming house run by the mother of Charles Le Maire. The boys were close in age and soon became partners in a vaudeville act. Le Maire accompanied his friend's vocalizing on the piano.

The team broke up shortly after they won first prize in an amateur contest at Salt Lake City's Pantages Theatre. Le Maire went on to win three Academy Awards for best costume design. Walter toured the Chautauqua circuit and played in stock companies before appearing on Broadway.

His break came when Reginald Denny, the star of *The Passing Show of 1919*, was taken ill and Walter appeared in his stead. The producers, the Shubert brothers, liked him sufficiently to cast him as the lead in their next show, *The Florodora Girl* (1920). Under their auspices he headed the cast of *The Last Waltz* (1920) and appeared in *The Lady in Ermine* (1922), *The Passing Show of 1923*, *The Dream Girl* (1924), *Artists and Models* (1925), *Countess Maritza* (1926), *The Red Robe* (1928), and *The Duchess of Chicago* (1929) on Broadway. He was well known to theatregoers by this time under his original name, Walter Woolf.

Warner Brothers brought Walter to Hollywood with a three-year, one-movie-per-annum contract. After his first picture, the talkie musical *Golden Dawn* (1930) with Vivienne Segal,[8] failed at the box office, his studio claimed his singing voice was unsuitable for sound films. An out-of-court settlement in his favor was reached, but his reputation was still in question.

Making a great hit in *Music in the Air*, which he did in Los Angeles in 1933 with Vivienne Segal, brought offers from Paramount

Jane Withers ties with Caesar Romero for being the most frequently seen celebrity at Hollywood parties, openings, reunions, screenings, and gatherings of all and any kind. As longtime filmdom journalist and biographer Doug Warren has said of Jane: "If you place a potato chip on your windowsill, she will attend."

Walter Woolf King in the den of his Beverly Hills home shortly before he died on October 24, 1984.

and Fox. He was signed by the latter at better terms than were offered by Paramount, but he had to agree to change his name. Winfield Sheehan, the production chief, thought "Walter Woolf" was "un-American and unromantic."

"Walter King" was his billing in *One More Spring* (1935) with Warner Baxter and Janet Gaynor, *Spring Tonic* (1935) with Lew Ayers and Claire Trevor, and *A Night at the Opera* (1935). In the latter he played an opera singer and the film's heavy to the mayhem of the Marx Brothers.

In 1935, when he returned to Broadway in *May Wine,* the theatre marquee read "Sigmund Romberg's new musical *May Wine,* starring Walter Slezak and Walter Woolf King." It was the name he used for the remainder of his life.

He returned to Hollywood for *Call It a Day* (1937). After that came the Laurel & Hardy feature *Swiss Miss* (1938), *Big Town Czar* (1939) with Tom Brown,[10]* *Balalaika* (1939) with Nelson Eddy and Ilona Massey, and *Go West* (1941), another Marx Brothers starrer.

Walter appeared as both announcer and vocalist on Eddie Cantor's radio show. He played many roles, usually comic heavies, with George Burns and Gracie Allen on radio and later on their TV series.

In the mid-forties King gave up perform-

ing to become a talent representative. Humphrey Bogart, John Payne, and Lee J. Cobb were among his clients. When he left the profession after ten years, he had developed an ulcer.

He was quoted at the time he resigned from the Sam Jaffe Agency as stating: "There was too much hand-holding involved. Actors want their agents to be around and available at all times. It was very difficult getting them to listen to reason, and their egos had to be fed constantly. You might say that I had miscast myself."

Walter Woolf King went from being an agent to playing one in *Tonight We Sing* (1953). He worked sporadically thereafter in pictures.

Walter Woolf King's wife of more than forty years died in 1980. A few years later he encountered Della Lind, the leading lady to Laurel & Hardy in *Swiss Miss,* at a Sons of the Desert meeting. They had not met since the making of the picture, but began entertaining each other at dinners and musicals in their homes. When, in October 1984, Ms. Lind telephoned to say how much she had enjoyed a recent date, King's housekeeper answered. She was informed that the man she had been referring to as her "new-old friend" had died of a heart attack a few hours before.

June Knight introduced Cole Porter's "Begin the Beguine" and "Just One of Those Things" in the Broadway musical Jubilee (1935). *Three years later, had she not left the cast of* Leave It to Me! *during rehearsals, June would have been the first to perform another Porter song that became a standard. Mary Martin, who replaced her, stopped the show and was catapulted to stardom singing "My Heart Belongs to Daddy."*

June Knight

The Broadway leading lady was born in Los Angeles on January 22, 1913. Her original name was Margaret Rose Vallikett. She was the only daughter of the proprietors of a restaurant in Glendale.

After she survived childhood bouts of polio and tuberculosis, the family physician advised she be given physical therapy. Her parents enrolled her in classes given by Ernest Belcher, a renowned dance instructor and the father of Marge Champion.*

A scout picked her to appear in the prologue of the Million Dollar Theatre, where the Valentino starrer *Son of the Sheik* (1926) was the screen fare. After that engagement the teenager, who had taken the name Marie Valli, went on a tour of presentation houses as one of Fanchon and Marco's "Gingham Girls."

She worked as stand-in for Loretta Young in an early talkie and danced in the first color film musical, *On with the Show* (1929). The same year she was in the chorus of *Fifty Million Frenchmen* on Broadway.

It is she, not Greta Garbo, who dances in *Mata Hari* (1932). Garbo approved of the girl in her stead and was present when she was being fitted for her costume.

More than fifty years after making *Mata Hari*, June Knight laughed about the star's keen interest in how the dress fit: "She'd feel a little here and then a little there and so forth. It felt strange and yet somehow familiar, the kind of thing boys were always trying. I didn't really mind it at the time because I was so young and dumb. I didn't figure out what she was doing until it was over."

Her break came shortly after she partnered with Jack Holland in a dance act. The girl she replaced had completely retired and did not object to her assuming the name "June Knight."

Florenz Ziegfeld hired the pair to dance in *Hot Cha!* (1932) but also gave June a song by herself. He was planning to star her in his next production when he died.

She immediately went into *Take a Chance*

(1932) and repeated her singing role in the screen version, which was released in 1933.

Among June Knight's other movies are: *Wake Up and Dream* (1934); *Broadway Melody of 1936* (1935), in which she sang "I Got a Feelin' You're Foolin'" to and with Robert Taylor; *The House Across the Bay* (1940); and *Break the News* (1941) opposite Jack Buchanan and Maurice Chevalier.

June Knight seemed the quintessential "Broadway Baby." Her name appeared frequently in newspaper columns, where she was invariably described as "mink-coated" or "orchid-bedecked." She was expected to marry prize fighter-actor Max Baer, but June denied they were ever engaged. In 1934 her break with her socialite-stockbroker husband came after only twelve days of marriage and made front pages nationwide. She always wore the 1¼-carat yellow diamond given her by publisher Walter Annenberg, another of her "serious beaus."

In *And On We Go* (1937), which was produced by David Wolper, she sang "I'm Laying Away a Buck," but the show soon folded.

June had just married a Texas oilman when she went into rehearsals for *Leave It to Me!* (1938). Her husband had no objections to her continuing to perform, but not in that show. He objected to the risqué lyrics in "My Heart Belongs to Daddy" and to the fact that she was to sing it wearing only a fur "chubby." Cole Porter had written the song with June in mind but granted her a release from her contract.

Ms. Knight recently admitted that leaving the part that made Mary Martin a star overnight was "probably a big mistake," but at the time she had no misgivings. She and her husband left at once for a motor trip to Texas in her wedding present, a four-door, 12-cylinder Lincoln. Her second thoughts about her career came after he beat her up. They were divorced in 1943.

June Knight posed in her Studio City, California, home wearing the same maribou hat and aquamarine jewelry she had on when the early still was taken, sometime in the mid-forties. She died after a lengthy illness shortly after this photograph was taken.

Wayne Clark

Her comeback was to be *Dream with Music* (1944), but she left the show before its early closing on Broadway. Her next appearance was in the Mike Todd presentation *The Would-Be Gentleman* (1946), which had Gene Barry in the cast. June's swan song was opposite Bobby Clark in *Sweethearts* (1947).

In 1949 she married Carl Browne Squier, a vice-president of Lockheed Aircraft and the thirteenth person to hold a pilot's license in the United States. In 1969, two years after her second husband died, she married one of their close friends, a widower and an aviation executive named Jack Beuhler.

In an interview June Knight gave a month before her death she described Nancy Walker, who lived several doors away, as "a lovely person and a good neighbor." The house directly across from hers was owned by Erik Estrada, who impressed her as "the type that has never owned anything before now but thinks the whole block belongs to him."

June Knight died on June 16, 1987.

"The Male Cass Daley"[8] *was Gil Lamb's unofficial title. He and the late comedienne both did physical comedy and made three pictures together for Paramount during the forties.*

Gil Lamb

The lanky comic and mime was born on June 14, 1904, in Minneapolis, Minnesota.

Lamb had been playing saxophone, clarinet, and oboe since he entered high school. He left the University of Minnesota during his sophomore year to join a dance band. His clowning soon caught the attention of professionals, who suggested he work out routines for himself. His long face seemed as flexible as his lanky frame.

After dancing on stage with Patti Moore, he took lessons, six hours a day, six days a week, in front of a mirror. His skills as a pantomimist were learned from the Australian performer Fred Ferry Corwey.

By the early thirties he was paired with a young woman in a knockabout comedy act that played vaudeville houses. He toured Europe as a single, doing a send-up of Sally Rand's world-famous fan dance. When he played Berlin, Adolf Hitler was in the audience. King Gustav of Sweden was so amused that he engaged Gil to perform at a private party at his villa in Nice.

Upon his return to the United States, Gil had a featured spot in *The Show Is On* (1936), a Broadway revue that starred Bea Lillie, Bert Lahr, and Mitzi Mayfair. He emceed shows in presentation houses, gradually developing a routine that he did in front of the curtain.

Lamb was part of the *Follies Bergere* show that played Hollywood's El Capitan Theatre. By then his act had evolved to the one for which he is now best known. In it he appears to be alone. After playing a few bars on the harmonica, he pretends to swallow it. A colleague behind the curtain then plays various pitches on the instrument, to which Lamb reacts with physical and facial contortions.

Al Jolson liked his act so much he hired him for his Broadway vehicle *Hold On to Your Hats* (1940). Buddy DeSylva, who was then head of production at Paramount Pictures, saw the show during its Chicago run and put the comedian under contract at $1,000 a week.

In *The Fleet's In* (1942), moviegoers were as amused as live audiences had been over his harmonica routine. Dorothy Lamour and

William Holden were the nominal stars, but the picture, which was a top grosser, marked the screen debuts of Cass Daley,[8] and Betty Hutton.

In his next film for Paramount, *Riding High* (1943), Gil was a sheriff taking a correspondence course in clarinet playing. His big number ended with furniture and musical instruments being smashed and Lamb being thrown into a collapsing piano.

After Claudette Colbert saw Gil entertain a group of G.I.s, she asked that he be cast as her very proper suitor in *Practically Yours* (1944). Fred MacMurray was the male star. The comedy was a disappointment, both critically and at the box office.

In *Rainbow Island* (1944) he was again teamed with Eddie Bracken, whom he refers to as "that mean little bastard." It was filmed in Technicolor and gave Lamb a chance to display his comedic dancing, but it was not a success.

His other screen credits include: *Star Spangled Rhythm* (1942); *Hit Parade of 1947* (1947) with Constance Moore;[8] and *Her Wonderful Lie* (1950) with the late Jan Kiepura and Marta Eggerth.*

He proved his skills were not only visual during a featured spot for twenty weeks on Rudy Vallee's radio program.

The role that Gil Lamb always felt he was meant to play was "Ichabod Crane." He was deeply disappointed when *Sleepy Hollow,* the Broadway musical in which he starred, closed after a short run in 1948.

Even at the height of his career Gil was involved in other businesses as well. He owned a manufacturing company during the forties. The restaurant in which he was partnered was in the same block on Broadway as the Palace Theatre.

Lamb appeared on TV shows and in commercials sporadically until recent years, when he and his wife moved to Palm Springs.

Ronnie Britton

Gil Lamb posed for a fan in the lobby of the Hollywood Roosevelt Hotel. The gangly comedian accompanies his wife, a real estate broker, on frequent business trips. They live in Palm Springs with their Lhasa apso.

His only child, a son whom he adopted, is a career U.S. Marine. They have not communicated for several years.

In his early eighties Gil was smoking heavily and gambling frequently in Las Vegas, where he usually plays craps.

Asked about the comic George West, whose act includes a bit with a harmonica very reminiscent of Lamb's, he said: "He never asked me if he could do my stuff, nor does he acknowledge me in the act. People tell me I should be flattered. I am *not* flattered. I am incensed."

Ann Little had been making films in Los Angeles since 1911, years before Hollywood became the movie capital of the world. She appeared in Cecil B. de Mille's The Squaw Man *(1913), the production that triggered the influx of East-coast film makers into California.*

Ann Little

The star of the silents, who went on to run Hollywood's Chateau Marmont, was born Mary H. Brooks in what is now Mount Shasta, California. Her birthday was February 7, 1891.

Because she was reluctant to be interviewed or even to discuss her first career with friends, little is known of her background, except that she was an only child.

Using the name Anna Little, she acted first on stage. In the book *Best Plays of 1894–1899* she is listed as a member of the cast of *Always on Time,* which was performed in New York City in November 1897. By 1909 she was playing a Gibson girl in *The Tenderfoot,* a presentation at San Francisco's Princess Theatre.

She once stated that she got her first movie role when a casting agent thought she looked Indian. Playing the title role in *A Young Squaw's Bravery* (1911) and a similar role in *The Indian Massacre* (1912), both two-reelers, led to many such parts. In *The Squaw Man* (1913), a film frequently referred to (erroneously) as the first western feature made in Hollywood, she again played a young Indian woman. She had become so identified with such parts that a tribe of Sioux made her a "blood sister."

She headed the cast of two-reelers and features for such early studios as Bison, Kalem, and Gold Seal. Her specialty, besides her portrayals of Indians, was women of the early West. She was an excellent horsewoman and required a stunt man in her stead only for the most dangerous scenes.

Within a few years her screen credit read "Ann Little," the name she was to use for the rest of her life.

In most of her pictures Ann Little had the lead. She played opposite numerous leading men, including Jack Hoxie, J. Warren Kerrigan, William S. Hart, William Farnum, Harold Lockwood, Charles Ray, and Herbert Rawlinson. She made more than a dozen pictures with Frank Borzage, who eventually became a director, as her leading man. Then she made ten films for Paramount Pictures as Wallace Reid's leading lady.

In 1923, a year after Reid died as a result of morphine and alcohol addiction, Ann headed the cast of *The Greatest Menace,* an exploitation feature on narcotics. It was also Little's last year before the cameras. *Secret Service Saunders* was not released until 1925, but was made in 1923 shortly after another serial, *The Eagle's Talons* (1923), with Fred Thompson and Ann.

Because most of her screen work had been in action and out-of-doors pictures, she was frequently away on location. When her mother was diagnosed as having cancer, Ann decided to work at various jobs in production so she could remain close to Mrs. Brooks.

Ann and her mother were Christian Scientists. Once they were satisfied that Mrs. Brooks's health had been restored, Ann began acting again, but only in local plays. She was appearing as a member of the Henry Duffy Players when she was given the position of manager of the recently constructed Chateau Marmont.

In 1931 Albert E. Smith, a cofounder of Vitagraph Studios, bought the building at the beginning of the Sunset Strip. Shortly after Ms. Little and her mother took up residence, the apartment house became a hotel and changed its decor to what has been known ever since as "the Marmont look," or "early Inquisition," as it is sometimes called. She presided over the Chateau Marmont for more than a decade, the same years during which it gained an international reputation for luxury, service, and discretion. With Roy D'Arcy, arch villain of the silents, as her assistant, Ann oversaw the tenancies of Humphrey Bogart, Orson Welles, Hedy Lamarr, Errol Flynn, Howard Hughes, Mickey Cohen, John Wayne, and the Ritz Brothers.[9] She provided Billy Wilder's first home in Hollywood and Jean Harlow's honeymoon hideaway for her second marriage.

In 1945, four years after the death of her mother, Ann Little began what she always referred to as her "third career." She became a Christian Science practitioner, her profession until her death on May 21, 1984.

Dorothy Stanhope

When this last photograph of Ann Little was taken, she had been a Christian Science practitioner for more than thirty years.

She remained in touch with only two of her contemporaries, Dorothy Davenport Reid,[10] widow of Wallace Reid, and Jean Paige, silent-screen actress and widow of Albert E. Smith.

Ann and Jean Paige were longtime neighbors in the residential community of Park-La Brea Towers in Los Angeles.

She admitted to having been married twice during the twenties, dismissing both unions as "mistakes that were soon realized as such." She denied the rumor that one of her husbands was Allan Forrest, a prominent player in silents.

She believed that her effectiveness as a practitioner of Christian Science would be compromised by any publicity concerning her acting career and firmly resisted efforts to draw her into discussions of her work in silents.

Once, when pressed about the films themselves, she remarked: "My pictures, like almost all movies, were produced for the sole purpose of making money. They did not inform audiences, nor did they uplift them."

Eric Linden and Cecilia Parker[8] were a popular screen love team during the thirties. One of the pictures they made together, A Family Affair *(1937), was the first of the "Andy Hardy" series. That film brought Ms. Parker the part of "Marian Hardy," which she was to play in eleven subsequent movies.*

Eric Linden

The movie star of the early talkies was born in New York City on September 15, 1909. His father, who had acted in his native Sweden, eventually abandoned his wife and four children.

Eric appeared in several plays during high school and then took courses in writing at Columbia University. He supported himself and contributed to his family by part-time jobs. He was ushering at the Roxy Theatre when an introduction was arranged for him with Cheryl Crawford, who was then an official with the Theatre Guild.

Eric spent several seasons under the auspices of the tony Theatre Guild, but none of the stage roles he did brought him recognition. He had six changes of costumes and characters in their production of *Marco's Millions* (1928) and acted as assistant stage manager for the original run of *Strange Interlude* (1928), both by Eugene O'Neill.

He was playing the title role on radio's *The Adventures of Dick Trever* when asked to test for *Are These Our Children?* (1931). Wesley Ruggles chose Eric and directed him as the young man sentenced to die in the electric chair.

When he was first brought to Hollywood, the studio began to publicize him with typical filmdom exaggeration as "the big sensation of the Theatre Guild." But, when his reviews for *Are These Our Children?* were raves and were seconded by a strong reaction from the public, his title was changed to "the Cinderella boy of the screen." That was soon replaced by "the tragic boy actor of films," after he appeared in a succession of sympathetic roles.

Eric was thought to have a vulnerable quality that brought out the maternal instincts in female moviegoers. "Women's pictures" were the rage at the time, and Eric was cast in a succession of them.

He played opposite Helen Twelvetrees in one of her popular weepers, *Young Bride* (1932); was made a widower by Loretta Young[8] in *Life Begins* (1932); and played Lionel Barrymore's debauched son in *Sweepings* (1933). He remade the silent tearjerker *The Goose Woman* under the title *The Past of Mary Holmes* (1933). *No Other Woman* (1933), with Irene Dunne,[8] was in a similar mold. In *The Silver Chord* (1933) he portrayed a young man dominated by his mother.

After Frances Dee, who had dated him, married Joel McCrea, Linden spent much of 1934 touring Europe. Hollywood gossip had it that the young actor had walked out on his picture commitments and was traveling in hopes of getting over a broken heart. Others believed he was more disappointed by losing

Cecilia Parker is married to former actor Richard Baldwin, who is a retired realtor. The couple, who are great-grandparents, live in Ventura, California.

Eric Linden had just celebrated his seventy-eighth birthday when he posed for this photograph in the doorway of his home in the hills of South Laguna, California.

the part that had been promised to him in *Little Women* to Douglas Montgomery.

Playing the leading role in M-G-M's *Ah! Wilderness* (1935) was expected to revitalize his career. The screen version of Eugene O'Neill's play was a success, but Eric never again appeared in a prestigious film. It did pair him for the first time with Cecilia Parker, who was to be his leading lady in five subsequent movies. They were sweethearts, off the screen as well as on, but the romance ended abruptly. Fifty years after she and Eric broke up, Cecilia Parker was asked the reason. "I never knew," she replied. "He never told me."

Although they had not been in touch in more than thirty years, Ms. Parker was aware that Linden had been divorced in 1985.

Between screen assignments the young actor appeared on Broadway for a month-long run of George Abbott's *Ladies Man* (1934). Eric replaced Luther Adler in the lead of *Golden Boy* in London opposite Bernice Claire.[9] In the fall of 1940 he headed the cast of a *Golden Boy* tour that played in more than seventy North American cities.

Although he never again acted on Broadway, Eric Linden continued to appear on stage throughout the forties opposite such stars as Fritzi Scheff, Diana Barrymore, and Claire Luce.

Among the thirty-three movies he made

were: *The Crowd Roars* (1932) with James Cagney; *The Age of Consent* (1932); *Flying Devils* (1933); *I Give My Love* (1934) with the late Wynne Gibson; *Ladies Crave Excitement* (1935); *Old Hutch* (1936); *Good Old Soak* (1937); and *Romance of the Limberlost* (1938) with Jean Parker.[8]

The screen career that had such an auspicious beginning ended a decade later with *Animals Within* (1941), a quickie with Ann Doran[9] at PRC studios. Prior to that he had a minuscule part as a wounded soldier in *Gone With the Wind* (1939) and a supporting role in the Irene Dare* vehicle *Everything's on Ice* (1939).

When he married a nonprofessional in 1955, the public had not heard his name in almost two years. Linden had taken a job inspecting roads in Orange County, California. The couple, who settled in South Laguna, became parents of two daughters and a son. One daughter and the son still live with Eric.

In late 1987 Eric Linden spoke of his reason for leaving his original profession: "I never set out to be an actor. I always wanted to write for the stage, but when you're young and are offered acting jobs, you take them. It was enjoyable only if the parts were really good ones. I had a few of those. The others— most of them—were agony. After World War II I tried playwriting. Had that panned out, I'd probably still be at it."

Carol Hughes was Bob Livingston's leading lady in Ghost Town Gold *(1937), one of* The Three Mesquiteer *series he made at Republic Pictures. She is best known to fans as "Dale Arden" in* Flash Gordon Conquers the Universe *(1940).*

Bob Livingston

The screen actor who became a western star was born in Quincey, Illinois, on December 9, 1908. His original name was Robert Randall.

Both of his parents were writers. His father, whose *Say, Bill* column was a popular one in newspapers during World War I, was also an editor for the Associated Press.

The Randalls moved to Glendale, California, when Bob was twelve years old. During his teens he worked as a merchant seaman and lumberjack. He also worked as a reporter briefly before deciding to act.

By 1929 he was appearing regularly in *The Collegians* series under the name Robert Livingston. Under an M-G-M contract he played supporting roles in such programmers as *The Band Plays On* (1934), *West Point of the Air* (1935), *Mutiny on the Bounty* (1935), and *Absolute Quiet* (1936).

Moviegoers saw him play light comedy and romantic and character roles before, during, and after his years as a B western star. He was in *Federal Man-Hunt* (1939), *Pistol Packin' Mama* (1943), *Storm Over Lisbon* (1944), *Lake Placid Serenade* (1944), and *Brazil* (1944). But he was a star only to Saturday matinee audiences.

He was "Zorro" in *The Bold Caballero* (1936), Republic Pictures' first color feature, and the hero of *The Vigilantes Are Coming* (1936), a serial. His greatest exposure came as one of "The Three Mesquiteers," a popular series of twenty-nine low-budget "horse operas" made between 1936 and 1941. He was replaced by John Wayne for a few of the features but returned to the "Stony Brooke" role when Wayne became a major star upon the release of *Stagecoach*. Livingston was the legendary masked man in the serial *The Lone Ranger Rides Again* (1939) and then made nine six-reelers for PRC Studios as "The Lone Rider." He also appeared as the heavy in several Gene Autry and Tim Holt oaters.

Bob Livingston was disdainful of his westerns and made no effort to disguise his attitude on the set. Yet his true feelings never came through on the screen. Not only was he one of the most handsome sagebrush heroes of the time, he was probably the best actor among them. He also managed to convey a pleasing sense of humor, a quality not usually apparent in western stars.

In 1984 a western enthusiast called on Livingston in his Tarzana apartment when his son was absent. He told the fan the same thing he has told others over the years; that his career as a screen cowboy meant nothing to him.

"I made westerns," said Livingston, "but there was nothing in my contract that said I had to look at them."

He made it clear, however, that it was the B western that he held in contempt, not his work in them, which he rated as "the best of my day."

The actor's older brother was known to moviegoers as Jack Randall,* the singing star of screen westerns.

Livingston's son lived with his father and usually shielded him from fans and professionals. His mother, Margret, was the daughter of Hal Roach, Sr. She was one of Livingston's five wives.

He had been invited numerous times to western film festivals, but asked a fee no promoter ever met. When he appeared in 1987 to accept the Golden Boot Award, which was presented to him by Gene Autry,[8] it was a very rare occasion. Livingston accepted the statuette but did not stand or speak. He was in a wheelchair and was breathing with the aid of a respirator.

He did not correct those who addressed him as Bob or Robert Livingston, but he always lived under the name Randall.

The western star died on March 7, 1988.

Carol Hughes was with her two daughters at the funeral of her husband, Frank Faylen.[8] The character actor was buried in the San Fernando Mission Cemetery in August 1985.

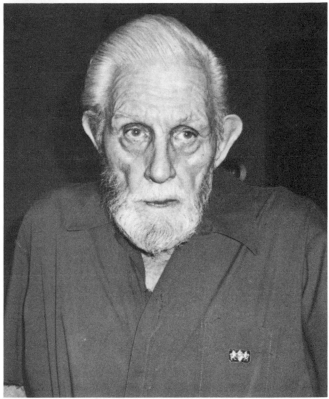

Widower Bob Livingston shared an apartment in Tarzana, California, with his son by the daughter of Hal Roach, Sr.

The episode of The Danny Thomas Show *telecast on October 20, 1958, revolved around the first wedding anniversary of "Clancy" and "Danny." Marjorie Lord is best known for having played the star's second wife from 1957 to 1971, the conclusion of the series.*

Marjorie Lord

The actress best known for playing the wife of Danny Thomas on TV was born Marjorie Wollenberg in San Francisco. Her birthdate is July 26, 1918.

Even before her family moved to New York City when she was fifteen, Marjorie had decided to be an actress. Mrs. Wollenberg, an avid playgoer, encouraged her ambition and enrolled her daughter at the American Academy of Dramatic Arts.

She had been studying acting only a few weeks when she replaced the actress who originated the ingenue role in *The Old Maid,* a Broadway hit of 1935. With the approval of the play's star, Judith Anderson, Marjorie toured with it as well.

After Pandro S. Berman saw her in *The Old Maid,* the producer announced that Marjorie Lord would make her movie debut in *Stage Door.* It was a keenly felt disappointment when Andrea Leeds was subsequently cast in the part Marjorie had been promised.

Fifty years later she talked about that experience: "They told me I photographed too young, and I thought my heart would break. Then Andrea got an Oscar nomination for that performance and I thought it would break again. But she was just enough older than me to have the life experience that role called for. Then, I thought that quality could be acted, but I was wrong. I photographed too young because I was too young."

Another screen part that might have changed her career went to Laraine Day in the "Dr. Kildare" series.

Marjorie had played in more than five hundred performances of *Springtime for Henry,* the Edward Everett Horton vehicle, when their company came to Los Angeles in 1942. Within days she had a contract with Universal Pictures which lasted for a year. She was then pacted by James Cagney and played with him in *Johnny Come Lately* (1943).

Marjorie Lord worked intermittently in movies beginning with her debut in *Border Café* (1937) with John Beal.[9] When she had no film assignments she acted on Broadway. She met John Archer, her first husband, when they assumed the roles of the original cast members of the hit *The Male Animal.* They were married in 1941.

She was in the original cast of the Broadway productions of *Signature* (1945), *Little Brown Jug* (1946), and *The Girl in the Freudian Slip* (1967). When Kitty Carlisle left the lead role in *Anniversary Waltz,* Marjorie took over in 1954.

Among her other motion picture roles were: *Forty Naughty Girls* (1937), *Escape from Hong Kong* (1942), *Sherlock Holmes in Washington* (1942), *Flesh and Fantasy* (1943), *New Orleans* (1947), *Riding High* (1950) with Bing Crosby, and *Port of Hell* (1954). She played Bob Hope's wife in *Boy, Did I Get a Wrong Number!* (1966).

In 1953, two years after the Archers separated, they were divorced. Their children, Gregg, who is now an airline pilot, and Anne, remained with their mother.

In 1958 she became the wife of Randolph Hale, an heir to the Hale Bros. department stores and a legitimate theatre producer. She appeared in plays with Howard Duff and Fernando Lamas at San Francisco's Alcazar Theatre under Hale's auspices. After his death in 1974 she continued on the stage, her favorite medium, both as an actress and a director.

Her greatest exposure came by playing the wife of Danny Thomas on his long-running TV series. Ms. Lord played the role from 1957 to 1971. Jean Hagen, who had the role of Thomas's wife when the program premiered in 1953, left the cast after three seasons. After a brief "widowhood" Thomas took Marjorie as his second TV wife. For years after production ceased in 1971, the sitcoms played in syndication throughout the world.

The Thomas show so strongly typecast Lord that work on television was virtually impossible until recently. However, the name she made and the image she forged on TV made her a reliable box-office draw on the dinner-theatre circuit.

The actress refers to Harry Volk, the investment banker she married in 1977, as "the

From her terrace in the Truesdale Estates Marjorie Lord is able to wave to Danny Thomas, who built his "Lebanese modern" home on an opposite hill.

Marty Jackson

real star of our house." Her third husband was unaware of her career when they met and does not encourage her to seek or accept acting assignments. One recent exception was a role on *Falcon Crest* in which she would have played the mother of Anne Archer, her own daughter. Both Volk and Marjorie would have liked her to have gotten the part, which was eventually played by Celeste Holm.

Asked if she missed her profession Marjorie Lord replied: "Acting helped me overcome the terrible shyness I had when I was young. It also kept me from confronting the real me, a person I suspected was not very likable. But I know her now and she's quite a nice lady. I think I just outgrew the need for that sort of approval."

Mrs. Volk is an active board member of the Joffrey Ballet. She is very flattered to be on the board because, she says, "Harry never gave them a penny, so they must like me."

She is a member of the First Church of Christ, Scientist in Beverly Hills.

Blues singer Ethel Waters and Fred Lowery headed the bill at Loew's State Theatre, a Broadway presentation house, in 1945. The on-screen attraction was an Esther Williams musical, Thrill of Romance.

Fred Lowery

The Blind Whistler was born on November 9, 1909, in Palestine, Texas.

Within the first few years of his life Fred Lowery lost both of his parents and 98 percent of his eyesight. Complications from scarlet fever and misguided treatment rendered the eighteen-month-old boy legally blind. He could, however, see some color with his left eye.

He learned to whistle while on his grandparents' farm, where he spent his early years.

At the State School for the Blind he was told that because he was unable to read music, becoming a professional musician was out of the question. But he listened to recordings and to music on the radio and developed a memory that was to astound musicians all his life.

Ernest Nichols, a blind vaudevillian who did bird calls, coaxed Fred on stage during a performance at the school. Up until that moment his fellow students and faculty knew him chiefly as the school's leading athlete. There was a burst of applause when he finished. Nichols was amazed that Lowery's "William Tell Overture" was note perfect and encouraged him to turn professional.

More than fifty years later Lowery recalled that day: "I left the stage a different person. In today's language, I had found my identity."

From the school he went to the Texas Senate as a page from 1929–1931. Publicized as the "blind and whistling page," Fred began performing over radio station WFAA in Dallas on Early Birds, a popular show of the time.

Fred Lowery went to New York City in 1934 with his savings of $200 but without a single professional contact. After a few months he got his break when Rudy Vallee, who prided himself on the discovery of talent, presented him on network radio. His rendition of "The World Is Waiting for the Sunrise" proved the highlight of the show. Walter Winchell was in the audience and praised Fred in print and on his network radio program. Winchell's nationally syndicated column, for many years the most influential in the nation, carried plugs for Lowery throughout both their careers.

The wealthy art patroness, Clara Belle Walsh, took him personally to Vincent Lopez, one of the most prominent orchestra leaders of the thirties. For the next four years Fred was heard from coast to coast whistling on Lopez's radio program.

In 1938 Lowery was contracted by the late Horace Heidt,[8] who presented him on his popular radio show, in personal appearances for eight years, and in the feature film *Pot of Gold* (1941).

During his time with Heidt, Fred began working with singer Dorothy Rae. After Heidt disbanded in 1953, Lowery and the vocalist appeared together for several years.

As Harry James once pointed out, Fred had two strikes against him: Along with his blindness, there was very little demand for whistlers. Yet Lowery performed before President Franklin Delano Roosevelt, in Carnegie Hall, and at the Palace Theatre. He hosted his own radio talk show, and in the fifties he was the emcee of a nightclub in Indianapolis for five years. For many years *NBC News* ended their Christmas Eve broadcast with Fred Lowery's rendition of "Silent Night."

During the late thirties his rendition of "Indian Love Call" sold more than two million phonograph records. His other big seller was actually a cover record of the theme from the hit movie *The High and the Mighty* which he did with the LeRoy Holmes orchestra. It is Muzzie Marcelino's whistling in the picture.

The famed baritone John Charles Thomas was one of Fred's fans, as was blind pianist Alec Templeton. Fritz Kreisler honored him with a special arrangement of his composition "Caprice Viennois, Opus 2."

In 1940 Fred married Gracie Johnston whom he liked to refer to as "my seeing-eye wife." Their son, Fred, Jr., or "Scooter," is a photographer.

In the last years of his life he broke his arm, survived a heart attack, and became diabetic. When asked about retirement, however, he would insist that he was "still

Fred Lowery, Jr.

Lowery whistled the "Star Spangled Banner" at home games of the Texas Rangers until he died in 1984.

puckering up" and refer to his bookings, which ran through 1985. After *Whistling in the Dark,* the autobiography he wrote with John McDowell, was published in 1983, he went on tour to promote the book.

At one point during the heyday of his career Lowery remarked: "Whistling is an off-the-wall kind of talent on which to base a life. No college of music offers a major in whistling. It is, however, a sort of magical gift, and there is always a place in the world for magic."

In one of his last interviews he lamented: "People don't whistle much anymore. I guess it's a sign of the times. Whistling is a carefree, happy thing. And these aren't carefree, happy times. Everybody's uptight about something."

The world's foremost whistling virtuoso died on December 11, 1984, in Jacksonville, Texas.

In Claire Luce's one Hollywood film, Up the River *(1930), her role was not a glamorous one, and she was overshadowed by Humphrey Bogart and Spencer Tracy. On stage she costarred with Fred Astaire in the Cole Porter musical* Gay Divorce *on Broadway and in the West End. A few years later New York audiences saw her in the original production of the John Steinbeck drama* Of Mice and Men, *which she later took to London.*

Claire Luce

The international stage star was born aboard a train that was passing through Syracuse, New York, on October 15, 1903.

In her teens she studied dance at the Denishawn School in New York City. She made her professional debut as a member of the chorus in Sol Hurok's Russian Opera Company in 1921.

As a schoolgirl she watched Marilyn Miller from the third balcony of the New Amsterdam Theatre and vowed to become a star. In 1927, on that stage, Claire portrayed Lenore Ulric to Paulette Goddard's Peaches Browning in a sketch that was part of that year's *Ziegfeld Follies.*

In the intervening years Claire Luce had danced in *Little Jesse James* (1923) and *The Music Box Revue* (1924). In 1925 she replaced Mistinguette, the reigning star of the French music hall, in the Casino de Paris in Paris.

Claire says that Spencer Tracy and Humphrey Bogart shared her dislike of filmmaking and that all three vowed not to repeat the experience after appearing together in *Up the River* (1930). She made a few more movies during the years she lived in England.

Two of her best-known English films were *Over She Goes* and *Mademoiselle Docteur,* both 1937 releases. In the latter she played opposite Erich von Stroheim.

She had made up her mind to accept dramatic roles when she met Cole Porter aboard the ocean liner *Normandie.* The actress was on her way to New York City to read for a play at the request of its author, George S. Kaufman. The composer invited her to his suite, where she heard "Night and Day" played for the first time. She immediately agreed to do his musical *The Gay Divorce* (1932).

When the late Clare Boothe married publisher Henry R. Luce in 1935, a confusion began in the minds of many that continues to this day. For a brief period the playwright was using the name Clare Luce, which created havoc at the bank that carried the accounts of both women.

"I knew Clare long before she married Luce and always liked her a lot," recalls

Claire Luce. "We'd call each other frequently because the mix-ups were endless and she always had some amusing remark about it. Then, when she converted to Catholicism, I phoned her and said, 'Now this too much!' You see, I'm a Catholic. But it was an awful nuisance and at the same time great fun."

The name Claire Luce means more in England than in her native country. She had made a great hit in the West End production of *Burlesque* in 1928. In 1933 she returned in *The Gay Divorce*. Fred Astaire and Claire scored an even greater success in that production than they had had in the original show on Broadway.

Six years later her English fans saw her recreate her dramatic performance in *Of Mice and Men*. She did several other plays in London that were never seen on Broadway. During World War II the actress spent more time on tour for ENSA than for the United States equivalent, USO.

In 1945 Ms. Luce played the leads in *Twelfth Night, Much Ado About Nothing, The Merry Wives of Windsor,* and *Anthony and Cleopatra* at the Shakespeare Memorial Theatre. As of 1988 she was the only American to act there for a full season. Her will specifies that her ashes be strewn around the theatre in Stratford-on-Avon.

Her one marriage was to Clifford Warren Smith, a society aviator, whose father was the president of Western Union. It ended after five years in a 1934 divorce.

It was Winston Churchill who interested Claire in painting during her brief engagement to his son, Randolph. She has since had three one-woman shows and has a painting in the permanent collections of the Rochester Museum and the Southhampton Museum, both in New York.

She designed the dust jackets of two of her more than two dozen record albums. Ms. Luce has set music to five of Tennessee Wil-

Michael Knowles

Claire Luce following an interview conducted by the author at WBAI-FM in New York City.

liams's poems when they were recorded and six albums of the works of George Jean Nathan.

Her other appearances on the New York stage include: Ziegfeld's *No Foolin'* (1926), *Society Girl* (1931), *Vintage Wine* (1934), *Love and Let Love* (1935), *Follow the Sun* (1935), three Shakespearean plays, *Vanity Fair* (1946), *With a Silk Thread* (1950), *These Are My Loves* (1960), her one-woman-show, and *The Milk Train Doesn't Stop Here Anymore* (1963).

She was never offered the screen version of *The Gay Divorce (The Gay Divorcée)* but was approached by the producers of the film version of *Of Mice and Men*. She declined even to test for the part she had originated on Broadway because: "I never saw myself as a film actress. Perhaps, even more importantly, I have never been a fan of movies. At a very early age I fell in love with the stage and I would be acting in some theatre today if my health would permit it."

Claire Luce is attended by a nurse part of the time. She lives alone in a Gramercy Park apartment. An insomniac, she reads and listens to talk radio. Her closest friend from her career is Julie Haydon. The two actresses talk via long-distance phone several times a week.

Picture-Play, *the most intelligently written fanzine of the period, had Dorothy Mackaill on the cover of its April 1926 issue. By then the English beauty had become a leading star of First National Pictures.*

Dorothy Mackaill

The star of silent and early talking pictures was born in Hull, England, on March 4, 1903.

In 1914, when her parents separated, Dorothy remained with Mr. Mackaill. She did not get along, however, with any of the housekeepers her father hired. When the ninth in a succession of these women married him, the teenager left for London.

Her mother had instilled in her a love of anything theatrical, and Dorothy decided to pursue a career on the stage. She and her father had a reconciliation, but only after he allowed her to remain in London and agreed to pay for her dancing lessons.

After her debut as a chorine at the Hippodrome, she went to Paris in an act that became part of a Maurice Chevalier revue. During the run she met Ned Wayburn, a well-known Broadway choreographer, who assured Dorothy she would appeal to Broadway audiences, adding, "You're perfect for a Ziegfeld show."

Dorothy had never heard of Ziegfeld, and her mother was named Flo; until she walked through the door of his private office, she assumed the impresario to be a woman. He was amused by her naîveté and taken by her looks. She was engaged for his *Midnight Frolic*. Despite her strong Yorkshire accent, Ziegfeld publicized her as "the typical American Girl."

Taken by her beauty, Marshall Neilan gave Dorothy an uncredited bit part in *Lotus Eater* (1921), a John Barrymore starrer that he directed. Then she became a leading lady to comedian Johnny Hines, who had a reputation for "discovering" talent. After playing with him in three of his popular "Torchy" two-reelers, she was an established name.

Throughout her screen career Dorothy Mackaill played a wide range of parts, something few stars of that era were permitted. She portrayed a blind musician, an heiress, a spinster, a Broadway star, and a murderess. Twice she played a drug addict.

The huge success of *The Man Who Came Back* (1924), seconded by the title role in *Chickie* (1925), established Dorothy Mackaill as a star. Her social status in Hollywood had been assured from her arrival by a close friendship with Marion Davies, a bond formed during their days under Ziegfeld's auspices.

Ms. Mackaill played opposite George O'Brien twice and Richard Barthelmess three times. But most moviegoers of the silent era would probably remember her for the pictures she made opposite Jack Mulhall. There were a dozen Mackaill-Mulhall features, nine of which were light comedies.

Some of the films that sustained her stardom throughout the decade were: *The Painted Lady* (1924), *Shore Leave* (1925), *Joanna* (1925), *The Dancer of Paris* (1926), *Lady Be Good* (1928), and *Children of the Ritz* (1929).

Dorothy made a successful, if unplanned, transition to talkies. Shortly after her scenes in *The Barker* (1928) were completed it became apparent that sound was "in." The A feature had been produced as a silent. Dorothy, Betty Compson, Douglas Fairbanks, Jr., and Milton Sills were reassembled under the direction of George Fitzmaurice for the reshooting of key scenes. The film was released as a part-talkie, did excellent business, and proved that all four screen veterans "could talk."

But studios were finding the conversion to talkies to be very costly. To offset these expenses many of the higher-priced stars were permitted to work out their contracts but were not offered new ones. In most cases the only producers willing to pay their established price were on "Poverty Row."

A year after Dorothy's commitment to First National Pictures ended, she made *Love Affair* (1932) with Humphrey Bogart at Columbia, a studio then considered a comedown for a star of her stature. The same year she made *No Man of Her Own* for Paramount, a major, but she had a supporting role. *The Chief* (1933) was an M-G-M picture but with Ed Wynn as its star; Dorothy was again leading lady to a comedian.

The next year Dorothy Mackaill made three quickies, the last of which, *The Cheat-*

Marty Jackson

Dorothy Mackaill has been a permanent resident of the Royal Hawaiian Hotel in Honolulu since the late fifties.

ers (1934), was her Hollywood swan song. The only film she did after that was *Bulldog Drummond at Bay* (1937), which was made during one of her trips to England.

Dorothy met her first husband, Lothar Mendes, on the set of *Prince of Tempters* (1926). They were divorced in 1928.

After leaving her profession Dorothy occupied herself with the care and comfort of her mother, who by then was almost a complete invalid. She told interviewer DeWitt Bodeen that everything she achieved professionally was for the approval of her mother. They lived together until the latter's death in 1956.

Dorothy Mackaill had wanted to live in Hawaii from her first visit, made when she filmed *His Captive Woman* (1929) in Honolulu. In 1931 she married a singer, Neil Albert Miller, whose specialty was Hawaiian melodies. Shortly after they were divorced in 1934 she married a man who was the largest orchid grower in the Hawaiian Islands. The marriage lasted until 1938.

The last time she was before a motion picture camera was at the urging of her friend Jack Lord, who persuaded her to play a part on a segment of his TV series, *Hawaii Five-O.*

In 1946 the **Harvard Lampoon** *proclaimed Catherine McLeod and Glenn Ford to be the "least talented newcomers" and her starring vehicle,* I've Always Loved You, *to be one of the worst films of that year.*

Catherine McLeod

The star of Republic Pictures was born in Santa Monica, California, on July 2, 1921. Mrs. McLeod was ill and confined to home for many years before she died of cancer in 1934. Catherine frequently acted out scenes from the recent movies she had seen to entertain her. Her mother strongly encouraged her to become an actress.

After his wife's death, Mr. McLeod, who was a lawyer, moved with Catherine and her younger sister to Texas. What was left of the family savings he invested in his brother's oil field. Shortly after the wells came up dry, Catherine McLeod's father died. He, too, believed his daughter should act and made her promise to pursue a career.

Returning to Hollywood, she supported herself in a variety of jobs while appearing in plays at little theatres. On the closing night of a play she did at the Bliss-Hayden Playhouse, Catherine intended to go to work the next morning in a defense plant. But when the curtain fell, Billy Grady, M-G-M's casting director, came backstage and signed her to a contract paying $150 a week.

At Metro she was tried out in very small parts and screen tests. Her first major role was on loan-out to Monogram Pictures for *They Shall Have Faith* (1945). She was fired when it was determined that she looked too much like the picture's star, Gale Storm.*

On her home lot Catherine played Elizabeth Taylor's older sister in *Courage of Lassie* (1946) and was then cast as one of the waitresses in *The Harvey Girls* (1946). During the filming of the latter, Catherine was chosen as spokesperson for all of the performers who were playing in the fight scene. Although their grievances were settled amicably, Catherine McLeod was immediately advised that her option would not be picked up.

Her next appearance was in an industrial film for Bell Jars, which was made at Republic Pictures. When the footage of Catherine McLeod canning tomatoes was run for studio chief Herbert J. Yates and director Frank Borzage, she was signed for the lead in *I've Always Loved You* (1946). She played a pianist, but Arthur Rubinstein did the actual playing heard in the picture.

Although Republic was not a major studio, it publicized Catherine and gave her leads in such features as *That's My Man* (1947) opposite Don Ameche, and *The Fabulous Texan* (1947) and *Old Los Angeles* (1948), both with John Carroll. But when the studio entered into a retrenchment program, she was asked to take a $40-a-week cut in salary. She refused and was dropped.

She spent much of the fifties in New York City, doing what she considers the best work of her career, on live TV dramas. When she returned to Hollywood it was for such pictures as *So Young So Bad* (1950), *My Wife's Best Friend* (1952), *A Blueprint for Murder* (1953), and *The Outcast* (1954) with Ben Cooper.[9]

Catherine worked at most of the studios during their heyday as a bit actress, featured player, star, and leading lady, but her only unpleasant recollections are of Twentieth Century-Fox: "Stars are treated like stars on any set, but at Fox everyone knew his or her place and were damned well kept in it at all times. Who got a table first in the commissary, where that table was located, who got a chair on the set, where you parked your car, who spoke to you and who didn't—*everything* was determined by one thing only—what salary bracket you were in. I could never wait to get off that lot."

She has been married to character actor Donald Keefer since 1950. Their oldest son is a press agent. The middle boy is an assistant director, and the youngest is a key grip on films.

Catherine found Charlton Heston, Dick Powell, MacDonald Carey, David Niven, Anthony Quinn, and Robert Ryan to be the most generous of all the actors she has worked with. She names Phil Carey and Richard Boone, in that order, as two of the three she would least like to encounter again. She singles out Richard Widmark as the "worst bastard of all time!"

Throughout the seventies Catherine was the West Coast editor of *Daytime TV* and Af-

Catherine McLeod in her Sherman Oaks home, which she and her husband, character actor Donald Keefer, purchased from the estate of the mother of Anne Jeffreys.

ternoon TV. Now she writes one-act plays.

Among her final acting jobs were roles in the films *Tammy Tell Me True* (1961) and *Ride the Wild Surf* (1964) and on stage in Los Angeles opposite Walter Pidgeon in *Take Her, She's Mine* in 1969.

She retired after playing a small role in *Lipstick* (1976), an experience she likens to "being back at Fox thanks to Mariel Hemingway."

The Keefers do not socialize within their profession. One exception is Piper Laurie, whom they have known since they lived in New York City. Another was the late Veda Ann Borg, who became Catherine's best friend after they met in the line for unemployment insurance.

Catherine McLeod is a heavy smoker, an active Democrat, and what she describes as "a deathbed Catholic." She is not related to the director Norman McLeod.

Most fans know her for *I've Always Loved You* and her westerns. For a few years in the early sixties, she was concerned that her wide exposure on an award-winning TV commercial for Anacin would eclipse her earlier celebrity. She played the exasperated housewife who exploded with "Mother, *please!* I'd rather do it myself!"

107

The 1959 Life *magazine cover story on Gardner McKay compared his looks and dash to those of Errol Flynn, Robert Taylor, and Tyrone Power: "This is the face that will—well, let's say probably will—launch a million sighs and burn its romantic image into the hearts of hordes of American females." Hedda Hopper pronounced his eyes "hazel-gray—restless and searching."*

Gardner McKay

The hearthrob of the years 1959 to 1962 was born George Cadogan Gardiner McKay in New York City. His birthdate is June 10, 1932. His father, an advertising executive, was credited with coining the Lux toilet soap slogan, "for that schoolgirl complexion."

The McKays moved about a great deal. For several years they lived in Paris. Altogether, Gardner attended more than a dozen schools before graduating.

After two years at Cornell, where he worked on the campus newspaper, Gardner

settled in Manhattan. He sculpted in his spare time, earning his living as a commercial model. On his return on the *Ile de France* from Paris, where he and Suzy Parker [10] posed for a Richard Avedon fashion layout, McKay's ship took on survivors of the *Andrea Doria*. The photographs Gardner took of the rescue were purchased by a national publication.

A photo of him in *Town and Country* magazine in the early fifties surrounded by his sculpture drew an agent, who promised a contract with a major movie studio. Years later Gardner described his feelings at the time: "It was all a stupid fluke. I'm an introvert and even in high school and college I was into writing. Acting had never appealed to me. It as as if I opened an invitation meant for someone else. But I *thought* I needed the money."

The zenith of his career as an actor was reached before he really got started. A *Life* magazine cover story by Shana Alexander proclaimed him the "new Apollo." His studio continued to hype him throughout his brief career. Gardner McKay was one of Hollywood's most oversold commodities.

Despite bad scripts and hostile notices, his series *Adventures in Paradise* ran on ABC-TV for three seasons, beginning in 1959. Many, including one much-quoted TV critic, believed the real viewer interest was not McKay but his boat, the *Tiki*. As the saying went, "no 'Tiki,' no watchee."

Fox executives knew differently. McKay received more fan mail than all the other actors at the studio put together. Most of the requests were for photos of Gardner stripped to the waist, as he frequently appeared on the shows.

When the series concluded in 1962, Gardner retreated for eighteen months into the deserts of Libya and Egypt. Next he went to Venezuela, where he spent long periods in the jungle. It was during this period that he began to write again.

Upon his return McKay told Hedda Hopper that the monkey she happened to notice perched on his shoulder was the son of the one he ate at one point during his adventures. He arrived for the interview in Tony Curtis's old Rolls Royce. Sitting in the back seat of the convertible was "Pussy Cat," the large shaggy dog the columnist described as "famous" to residents of Beverly Hills.

He made a few features, such as *The Pleasure Seekers* (1964) and *I Sailed Around the World with an All-Girl Crew* (1969), but he received very little media attention after *Adventures in Paradise* left the air.

His fame quickly faded nationally, but his profile within his immediate area remained strong due to the menagerie he kept on his property in Coldwater Canyon. Local papers reported the complaints of his neighbors when any of his three lions, two cheetahs, or five dogs caused disturbances or escaped. Eventually, he was forced to dispose of the lions.

When his play *Me* was produced in Los Angeles in 1973, its cast included Geraldine Fitzgerald and Richard Dreyfuss. McKay was quoted at the time as saying, "They're congratulating me not because I wrote the play, but because I directed it. This town always values the interpreter over the creator."

From 1979 through 1981 he was drama critic for the *Los Angeles Herald-Examiner.* Then he taught playwriting at a UCLA extension course.

His play *Sea Marks* won the Los Angeles Drama Critics' Award for Best Play of 1979 and was produced for television by the Public Broadcasting System. In 1981 it had a brief run off-Broadway.

McKay was linked romantically with the fashion model Dolores Hawkins and with Suzanne Pleshette, Diane McBain, and Ann-

Marty Jackson

Gardner McKay was seen frequently around Los Angeles, usually at play openings, until he and his wife went abroad to live.

Margret. His relationship with Greta Chi began when she was in her teens and continued for more than a few years. As he neared forty a newspaperman remarked on his perennial bachelorhood. "Yes," replied Gardner, "I just have affairs."

In 1984 McKay married a native of the Irish Free State, the mother of a teenage daughter by a previous union. Since then the couple have leased their New England–style farmhouse in Beverly Hills and traveled. They spent a year in the United Kingdom and have since spent periods in northern California and the Hawaiian Islands.

Adventures in Paradise is still seen in syndication in some parts of the world. In 1974 the former actor told journalist Bert Prelutsky about encountering fans: "It's like I used to be a hooker and I keep running into ex-clients. They'd either love and respect me or despise and resent me and it was for nothing."

He will be interviewed only as a writer, not on his acting career. Approached for inclusion in this book, he said, "Just say he was never heard from again."

Marion Mack was Buster Keaton's leading lady in **The General** *(1927), a silent picture which he also directed. Although it was not a financial success at the time of first release, the comedy is now generally thought to be among his best work.*

Marion Mack

The pioneer screen actress and film maker was born in Mammoth, Utah, on April 9, 1902. Her original name was Joey Marion McCreery. Her parents divorced when she was three years old.

An ardent movie fan, as a teenager she wrote to Mack Sennett asking if she could play a part in one of his productions. She enclosed a photo of herself in a bathing suit. In his reply the producer promised to consider her if she were ever in Los Angeles. He specified that he would see her personally, provided she was chaperoned.

Shortly thereafter Mr. McCreery, his daughter, and second wife came to Los Angeles on a business trip. Without his knowledge his daughter went almost immediately to the Sennett studios, accompanied by her stepmother. When the eighteen-year-old signed a contract paying $25 a week, her father, who thought Sennett's famous bathing beauties were vulgar, disowned her.

As Joey McCreery she made Sunshine comedies for Fox Films and Mermaid comedies for Educational Pictures. At Universal she was Art Acord's leading lady in several of his western starrers. But it was playing in the "Hallroom Boys" two-reelers that got her into features.

The popular "Hallroom Boys" shorts were produced by CBC, which evolved into Columbia Pictures. One of the first releases was *Mary of the Movies* (1923). Taking the name Marion Mack, she wrote the scenario and played the title role. By the time the picture was completed, she had married its producer, Louis Lewyn.

Her other starring vehicles were *One of the Bravest* (1925) and *Carnival Girl* (1926).

The part for which she is best known came to her through her hairdresser, Perc Westmore. He recommended Marion when he learned that Buster Keaton was looking for a girl with long curls to play a rather dumb southern belle. But by the time Westmore reached Ms. Mack she had just bobbed her hair. She tested for and played the leading-lady role in *The General* (1927) while wearing a wig made for her by Westmore.

Marion was in Oregon for five months shooting *The General*. Her husband and she agreed that they did not want to be separated again merely because she had to work on location. She retired from acting and became his production partner. Her final appearance before a movie camera was the lead in the two-reeler *Alice in Movieland* (1927), except for a few walk-ons she did in the shorts that she and her husband produced.

Louis Lewyn produced the *Voice of Hollywood* series of shorts (twenty-four in all) for Tiffany Productions. Marion worked with him as writer and coordinator of these two-reelers, which she has described as "magazines of the screen." She appeared in one, along with Anita Page, Paul Whiteman, Reginald Denny, and the female impersonator, Julian Eltinge.

The pair then went to Paramount to make a similar series of one-reelers, *Hollywood on Parade*. During the forties the Lewyns made musical shorts at Warner Brothers aimed primarily at servicemen.

Of their many short subjects, the one of most interest to film buffs is *Fiesta in Santa Barbara* (1935). Her old friend Buster Keaton played a brief role. Another part was played by a young singer named Frances Gumm, just before her name was changed to Judy Garland. It was instrumental in bringing her to the attention of M-G-M executives.

In 1960 the couple sold their seven-acre Beverly Hills estate and matching Rolls Royces and moved to Costa Mesa. Until her husband died in 1969 they had their own real estate brokerage firm in that small southern California town.

Marty Jackson

Marion Mack posed in her Costa Mesa, California, home fifty years after her last movie. She painted the portrait behind her from one of her old publicity stills.

Since being widowed, Marion has attended college courses in painting and sculpture. She has traveled to much of the world, appearing with showings of the "rediscovered" *The General*.

Her son, Lanny Lewyn, who did bit parts in the thirties, lives nearby in Laguna Beach. He is an electrical engineer and holds several patents in stereo compact-disc sound reproduction.

Marion Mack kept in touch with her friend, Clara Bow, until Bow's death. Rudy Vallee was the only other celebrity she remained close to after her retirement from Hollywood. She receives a Christmas card each year from Mary Philbin but has not seen her in more than fifty years.

In 1988 Marion Mack explained why she never received screen credit for her writing: "I got it finally when we moved to M-G-M to do the 'Sally and Mary in Hollywood' series. That was only because I insisted. The studios were always reluctant to acknowledge women who were behind the camera. They claimed a man's name on the screen is always more impressive to the public."

111

Jerry Maren made his screen debut as a "Lollipop Kid" (right) in The Wizard of Oz *(1939). On network radio he played "Buster Brown" (center) on* Smilin' Ed's Buster Brown Gang. *On TV he was on the* Andy Williams Show *as the little German general. In the movie* Little Cigars *(1973) Jerry and his longtime friend Billy Curtis were top-billed.*

Jerry Maren

The "little performer" of all entertainment media was born Gerard Marenghi in Boston, Massachusetts. His birthday is January 24, 1920. He is the youngest in a family of twelve children and the only one not of normal size.

From an early age Jerry took dancing lessons. During high school he formed an act with his teacher, another young man, and a girl, which they called "Three Steps and a Half." Booked into a hotel during the summer vacation, Jerry was noticed by an M-G-M executive. Three months later he was brought to Hollywood to be in *The Wizard of Oz* (1939).

At first he was to play a "winged monkey," but his agent held out for a role that would showcase his musical talents. Jerry portrayed the "Lollipop Kid" who presents a sucker to Judy Garland.

Fifty years after the filming Jerry commented: "I had no idea I was becoming a part of Hollywood history when I made the picture. It was my first, so everything was new to me. What really impressed me was all the other little people, young ones, old ones, lonely ones, pretty ones. I knew there were others my size, but I had never met one. You can just imagine what that's like for a guy about to turn twenty years old."

One of these "little people," Billy Curtis, who played the "Mayor of Munchkinland," became his friend and frequent partner over the years.

Maren and Curtis spent World War II in *Bits of Fun,* an act that toured as part of a USO unit.

From the mid-forties to 1952 Maren played "Buster Brown" on *Smilin' Ed's Buster Brown Gang.* The network radio show was broadcast first at 8:30 A.M. and was heard in the late morning in the eastern and central states. Three hours later he did a repeat broadcast for the remainder of the country. For both shows he wore the complete outfit of "Buster Brown," the trademark of the shoe manufacturer that sponsored the program.

In April 1988 he recalled the job: "Radio paid shit! And every week it cost me four cab rides because there was a two-hour gap between shows. I could hardly kill it by shopping or going to a restaurant. What do you do on a Saturday morning when you're dressed like 'Buster Brown'?"

The screen roles for which he is best known are the thieving "Light-fingered Lester" in the "Our Gang" short *Tiny Troubles* (1939), "Professor Anton" in the Marx Brothers starrer *At the Circus* (1939), the saloon owner in *The Great John L* (1945), and a cigar-smoking infant in *When My Baby Smiles at Me* (1948).

His most lucrative jobs were in commercials. For years Jerry wore a chef's hat and apron as "Little Oscar," the trademark of Oscar Mayer meat products on the West Coast.

Even more rewarding were the nationally televised commercials for McDonald's in which Maren played "Mayor MacCheese" to the "Big Mac" of Billy Curtis.

In the picture *Three Wise Fools* (1946) he and Billy Curtis played leprechauns. For three years the *Gong Show* ended with the pair throwing confetti at the camera and at studio audiences. Their best work together was on television, with Jerry playing "Truth" and Curtis playing "Consequences" on the game show of the same title.

Of his private life Jerry Maren said recently: "I dated many normal-sized women, except some were fatter than most. I took out the ones who were responsive. But I knew that I wanted to eventually get married to a lady like myself. I met Elizabeth through the newsletter put out by the Little People of America, the organization founded by my good friend Billy Barty. We corresponded. We met. We wrote back and forth some more. She too was from a family with eleven other normal-size children. We are both Roman Catholics, except she's the good one."

The Marens were married in May 1975. Although they consider themselves semiretired, Mrs. Maren occasionally accepts stunt work that child actors are not permitted to perform.

Jerry smokes a pipe, swims in his pool, and drives a standard station wagon with extension pedals. Mrs. Maren describes him as a "terrific golfer." He also pitches and plays shortstop on a baseball team called the Hollywood Shorties.

The Maren home has kitchen facilities, plumbing fixtures, and electrical switches considerably lower than in standard homes. Jerry has shortened the legs on some fur-

Elizabeth and Jerry Maren posed alongside their swimming pool with their neighbor, Stanton (center), *who is ten years old.*

niture but points out that most of theirs is as they bought it: "There are an awful lot of little people in the world. Maybe they're not as small as us, but they are much shorter than normal and things are manufactured for them."

Asked to name the most difficult aspect of being 4 feet 3 inches in height, he could not think of any that really bothered him. Neither could his wife, who is an inch taller.

The only time he ever wanted to be a larger man was when the home he and his wife designed was being built in the Hollywood foothills. After listening to the contractor's evasions and distortions for the umpteenth time, Jerry wanted "to slam him up against the wall and choke a straight answer out of him." He quickly added, however, that "a lot of men would be incapable of doing something like that because of health or age. It was a frustration, but a minor one because I get along very well with almost everyone."

113

To moviegoers of the late thirties and the forties, Marion Martin epitomized the flashy, gold-digging blonde. In three of the "Mexican Spitfire" features she played "Fifi" to Leon Errol's lecherous older man. In The Big Street *(1942) she was married to a gangster while having an affair with a younger man, played by William Orr.*

Marion Martin

"The World's Most Beautiful Showgirl" was born in Philadelphia, Pennsylvania, on June 7.

According to an RKO press release of the late thirties, her life began in the then-ritzy Germantown area in the year 1918. After graduating from Bayonne, a finishing school in Switzerland, she would have become a physician, had it not been for the Wall Street crash of 1929.

But Iris Adrian[8] remembers that when the Hollywood Restaurant nightclub opened on Broadway in 1928, Marion was featured in the show as the "leading nude." The same year she appeared along with Thelma White[9] in the *George White Scandals*. ("She *was* young," says Ms. White, "but ten years old???")

Although her widower insists that her real name was Marion Martin, Iris Adrian is adamant. "We called her mother and father 'Mr. and Mrs. Suplee.' They always came by to pick her up after the last show, cover up what everyone had been looking at all night, and take her home. . . . She wore pasties and had that platinum blonde hair. Marion really was a knock-out."

Although she had been around the Great White Way for five years, Marion always credited Flo Ziegfeld as her discoverer. She was in his *Follies* of 1931. Some of her other appearances on Broadway were in *Lombardi, Ltd.* (1927), *Shady Lady* (1933), and *New Faces of 1936*.

Marion made her movie debut in *Sinners in Paradise* (1938) with Madge Evans.[8] Among her forty-two other screen appearances were *The Man in the Iron Mask* (1939), *Tall, Dark and Handsome* (1941), *Tales of Manhattan* (1942), *Lady Scarface* (1941), *They Got Me Covered* (1943), *Lady of Burlesque* (1943), *It Happened Tomorrow* (1944), *Deadline for Murder* (1946), *Angel on My Shoulder* (1946), and *That Brennan Girl* (1946), with Mona

Freeman[8] and James Dunn.[8]

She supported Loretta Young[8] in *The Lady from Cheyenne* (1941) and *Come to the Stable* (1949), and Clark Gable in *Boom Town* (1940) and *Key to the City* (1950), her last film.

Iris Adrian, who worked with her in Hollywood as well as on Broadway, claims that "one of President Roosevelt's sons—I don't remember which—used to come to see her over and over. So did two of William Randolph Hearst's boys. I don't think they ever got anywhere with her. I doubt anyone did. She was a Catholic—the kind who reads the fine print."

In 1950 she married Jimmy Krzykowski, a Singer sewing machine repairman. They had been introduced by their parish priest. The couple lived in Santa Monica with their dogs, cats, turtles, and ducks. She lost touch completely with everyone from her career and seldom responded to fans. Marion was a volunteer worker at St. John's Hospital and St. Anne's Maternity Home until she died on August 13, 1985.

Marion retired from the screen, according to her widower, "because she didn't like the roles she was being offered and the changes that started taking place within the industry. She lived to see her instincts confirmed."

None of the mourners at her funeral had known her professionally. Complying with his wife's wishes, Mr. Krzykowski had her remains interred in the mausoleum at Holy Cross Cemetery in Culver City, "so she could be close to the altar where she so often heard Mass and near Metro-Goldwyn-Mayer Studios."

Shortly after her death there was a memorial service for her at the San Juan Capistrano Mission. It was conducted by the mission's pastor, who is Marion Martin's brother.

Marty Jackson

Marion Martin was a volunteer worker at St. John's Hospital and St. Anne's Maternity Home and a Santa Monica housewife. She died in 1985.

To Richard,
with all
good wishes
Peggy Moran
April 1988

Peggy Moran played opposite Johnny Downs in **I Can't Give You Anything But Love, Baby** *(1940). Of the fourteen movies she made that year all but* **Strike Up the Band** *were programmers.*

Peggy Moran

The pert leading lady of B pictures was born in Clinton, Iowa, on October 23, 1918. Her given name is Marie Jeanette. Her father was Earl Moran, a well-known illustrator who was one of the first artists to employ Marilyn Monroe as a model.

After Peggy's parents were divorced in 1924 her mother, who had been a member of the famed Denishawn Dance Company, brought her to Hollywood.

A chance remark about Peggy's attractiveness, made by a judge while Mrs. Moran was doing jury duty, led indirectly to a screen test, but not a contract. It did bring bit parts, such as a showgirl in *Gold Diggers in Paris* (1938) and the cigarette girl in *Ninotchka* (1939).

After casting her in small roles in *First Love* (1939) and *Spring Parade* (1940), Joe Pasternak, who produced the movies, and Henry Koster, who directed them, persuaded their studio, Universal Pictures, to sign Peggy.

When Ann Rutherford was unable to appear in *Seven Sweethearts* (1942) because of illness, Pasternak, who had moved to M-G-M, replaced her with Peggy.

Peggy made more than thirty features. Among them are: *Little Accident* (1939) with Baby Sandy; *Oh, Johnny, How You Can Love* (1940) with Tom Brown [10]*; *One Night in the Tropics* (1940) with Robert Cummings [9]; *Argentine Nights* (1940) with the Ritz Brothers [9]; *Horror Island* (1941) with Iris Adrian [8];

Johnny Downs is a retired realtor and the father of five daughters. He and his wife have lived in Coronado, California, for more than thirty years.

Peggy Moran and the late Robert Paige at the annual reunion of Universal Pictures players. She has been married to director Henry Koster for more than forty years. Paige died on December 21, 1987, four months after this photograph was taken.

Double Date (1941) with Rand Brooks[8]; *Flying Cadets* with Frankie Thomas[9]; *There's One Born Every Minute* (1942) with Elizabeth Taylor; and *Drums of the Congo* (1942) with Turhan Bey.[10]

Peggy Moran is known to horror-film enthusiasts for her appearances in *The Mummy's Hands* (1940) and *The Mummy's Tomb* (1942) with Turhan Bey.[10]. Western fans recognize her as leading lady to Roy Rogers in *The King of the Cowboys* (1943), her swan song.

On October 30, 1942, Peggy and director Henry Koster were married with the clear understanding that the bride would retire from the screen. She was promised, however, at least one appearance in every picture that he directed. He then had a bust sculpted by Yucca Salamunick which has been seen in all of his pictures.

Their older son, Nicholas, is a psychiatrist. The younger, Peter, is a probation officer.

In 1981 Peggy and her husband moved from their beach house to a complex in Camarillo, California. Among their neighbors are Adele Jergens and her husband Glenn Langan, Emile Sitka, Bill Quinn, who is best known for playing the blind man on *All in the Family,* and Ethelyne Clair, western heroine and a Wampas Baby Star of 1929.

Unbeknownst to Ms. Moran, the director Oscar Serlin wanted her to read for *Life with Father.* But her agent, probably because of the interest in her at Universal, never mentioned it. The part went to Teresa Wright, and the play became the longest-running non-musical in history.

Peggy Moran is an active member of the Science of Mind church in Camarillo, California.

Henry Koster died at the age of eighty-three on September 21, 1988.

In April, 1988, Mrs. Koster spoke of the four decades away from the public eye: "I knew I had become hopelessly typed as an actress in 'B's.' They are much harder work than 'A's' because of the fast pace at which they're shot. I never really missed the profession because my husband and I have had such a close marriage. Every picture he directed we thought of as 'ours,' because I was frequently on the set and frequently met him in the commissary for lunch. That in Henry is considered very peculiar. We've had very little contact with movie people since he retired over twenty-five years ago."

Patricia Morison became a star on Broadway and in London's West End in the title role of Cole Porter's Kiss Me, Kate. *Then she played the lead in Rodgers and Hammerstein's* The King and I *opposite Yul Brynner on Broadway. But when those musicals were filmed, Kathryn Grayson and Deborah Kerr, respectively, were cast in those parts.*

Patricia Morison

The international star of musicals was born in New York City to English parents. Her birthday is March 19, 1915.

In her early teens Patricia seemed inclined toward art. In high school she won a scholarship that would have taken her to Paris, but she chose instead to study acting at the Neighborhood Playhouse. Always supportive, her mother sent her to Martha Graham to study movement.

Her first Broadway role was to have been

the female lead in *Growing Pains* (1933) with Junior Durkin and Johnny Downs,[10]* but by the time it opened, Patricia's role was a very small one. She then understudied Helen Hayes in *Victoria Regina* but never got to go on. Playing opposite Alfred Drake in *The Two Bouquets* (1939) brought her to the attention of *New York Times* theatre critic Brooks Atkinson, who wrote that she could "sing with uncommon skill" and "act with willowy elegance." The musical also resulted in a contract with Paramount Pictures.

In the four years Patricia Morison spent on the Marathon Street lot, she made eleven films. One, *Romance of the Rio Grande* (1941), was a "Cisco Kid" feature made on loan-out. On her home lot she debuted as a gangster's moll in *Persons in Hiding* (1939), supported Bob Burns's "The Arkansas Traveler" in *I'm from Missouri* (1939), and played Akim Tamiroff's wife in *Untamed* (1940). She made two movies with Fred MacMurray, *Rangers of Fortune* (1940) and *One Night in Lisbon* (1941), and two with Ray Milland. The one time Paramount gave her co-starring billing was in *The Roundup* (1941), a western with Richard Dix. *The Glass Key* might have put her over, but at the last minute Veronica Lake[8] replaced her in the lead opposite Alan Ladd.

After leaving Paramount Patricia freelanced in *Silver Skates* (1943) with Belita[10] and *Where Are Your Children?* (1944) with Gale Storm,* both for Monogram. She played the Empress Eugenie in *The Song of Bernadette* (1943) and did small parts in *Without Love* (1945) and *Lady on a Train* (1946). Patricia also made one each of the "Sherlock Holmes," "Tarzan," and "Thin Man" series.

When she auditioned for Cole Porter, he promised her the lead in *Kiss Me Kate*, but was unable to offer her a contract because the Broadway musical had not yet found backers. By the time the show was financed, Patricia had signed for a TV detective series and had to negotiate her freedom.

Like most of the cast, she did not believe *Kiss Me Kate* would be a success when it was in rehearsals. Well-meaning friends and colleagues warned her that the song "I Hate Men" would permanently alienate her character from the audience. In fact, the number frequently drew the most applause of the evening.

On opening night, December 30, 1948, Patricia Morison became a hit in a hit. Three years later she and the musical became the rage of London.

In 1954 she returned to Broadway in *The King and I*, playing "Anna" to Yul Brynner's "King of Siam." She then took the Rodgers and Hammerstein musical on tour for almost two years.

Ms. Morison sang and acted frequently on television. In 1948 she was nominated as the media's Most Outstanding Personality. In 1950 she starred in televised versions of *Rio Rita, Trial by Jury,* and *Light Up the Sky.* Later she acted on *Screen Director's Playhouse, Schlitz Playhouse of Stars,* and *Hallmark Hall of Fame.*

The only time movie audiences have heard her sing was in *Sofia* (1948), the last picture she made before becoming a star on Broadway. And, despite all the successes Patricia Morison had as a singer and actress in other media during the last forty years, she has been in only one film: In *Song Without End* (1960) she appeared in a cameo as George Sand.

Originally, Alexander Korda was to produce *Kiss Me Kate* for the screen, using all of the original cast. But after M-G-M outbid him for the rights, Patricia was not considered for the film version. Even though Twentieth Century-Fox had to dub her songs, Deborah Kerr was cast in their production of

Patricia Morison lives in the Park La Brea Towers apartment, which she shared for many years with her late mother.

The King and I.

Follies was another major disappointment. At first Patricia was assured that she was "perfect" for the part that was eventually played by Alexis Smith. When the final casting was done, it was decided that what was needed in the role was an actress who did not sound like a singer.

Patricia Morison has remained active in the musical theatre. In 1973 she played opposite Dean Jones in a San Diego production of *Pal Joey.* In 1976 she portrayed the flamboyant feminist of the nineteenth century, Victoria Claflin Woodhull, in *Winner Take All,* but the musical did not make it to Broadway. In the early eighties she starred in a musical based on the history of Hawaii, where it was presented. In 1987 she reprised her part in *The King and I* for New Zealanders. In the spring of 1988 Patricia guested on the TV series *L.A. Law.*

The walls of her Los Angeles apartment are decorated with an ever-changing array of her oil paintings, which she sells. On the piano in her living room are signed photos of such luminaries as Cole Porter, Oscar Hammerstein II, and Bishop Fulton J. Sheen.

Patricia Morison has remained single.

119

Karen Morley is described in the book They Had Faces Then *thusly: "She wasn't conventionally pretty. She had high cheekbones, hooded eyes, a deep liquid voice. Not easy to cast. . ."*

Karen Morley

The blacklisted actress was born Mildred Linton in Ottumwa, Iowa. Her birthdate is December 12, 1910. She left the small farming community in 1924 when her family moved to Los Angeles.

She was class valedictorian at Hollywood High School and then attended UCLA briefly. At college she was coached and encouraged by Irving Pichel, who soon afterward left academe to become a screen actor and later a director.

In 1930 Karen supported Elsie Ferguson in *Fata Morgana* in a Los Angeles stage production. She was a member of the Pasadena Community Players when she got her "break." Ms. Morley was in the waiting room of M-G-M's casting department when Robert Montgomery was to do a makeup test. An actress was needed to read his cues. Both the actor and the director, Clarence Brown, were impressed with her, and she was given a small role in *Inspiration* (1931), a Greta Garbo starrer.

Karen Morley was signed to a contract from that feature and acquired a reputation while making it. Unlike so many actors, she was not intimidated by Garbo then or when she again supported her in *Mata Hari* (1932). The same was true for Lionel Barrymore, another actor in the cast of *Mata Hari* who was used to being deferred to. When they were reteamed in *Arsène Lupin* (1932), she held her own in the script's sophisticated verbal exchanges with Lionel and his brother, John Barrymore.

The word was out that the young actress "had something." Howard Hughes borrowed her for *Scarface, the Shame of a Nation* (1932). Paul Muni, who starred, playing a thinly disguised Al Capone, became one of her enthusiasts.

She stood out as the petulant leading lady to William Haines in *Are You Listening?* (1932) and in the mother-love weeper *Wednesday's Child* (1934).

The considerable attention she received from fanzines in the early thirties was most likely due to readers who had written to editors about her. Her studio seemed undecided as to how best to publicize her and to utilize her obvious talent.

Many fans and critics saw a potential in Karen Morley as an actress that was seldom realized on the screen. Becoming known throughout the film capital as an intellectual early in her career certainly did not work in her favor. She was one of the first to align herself with left-wing causes, which further alienated her from the Hollywood establishment.

In 1934 she had one of her best parts as a member of a Utopian commune in King Vidor's *Our Daily Bread*. The controversial drama did not fare well at the box office, however. The following year Karen again impressed audiences as Paul Muni's faithless lover in *Black Fury* (1935). It was her last role of any consequence.

Some of her other films are: *Politics* (1931), *The Sin of Madelon Claudet* (1931), *Washington Masquerade* (1932), *The Mask of Fu Manchu* (1932), *Gabriel over the White House* (1933), and *Dinner at Eight* (1933). She was in *Crime Doctor* (1934), which was not a part of the subsequent series, opposite Otto Kruger in the title role.

After supporting Shirley Temple in *The Littlest Rebel* (1935), Karen was leading lady to Richard Dix in *The Devil's Squadron* (1936) and to Warren William in *Outcast* (1937). There followed *The Last Train from Madrid* (1937), *Kentucky* (1938), *Pride and Prejudice* (1940), *The Unknown* (1946), *Framed* (1947), and *M* (1951).

She contributed most of her time during 1948 to support of the Progressive Party platform and candidates. Six years later she ran unsuccessfully for the office of lieutenant governor in the state of New York on the American Labor Party ticket.

When Karen Morley appeared before the H.U.A.C. in 1951, her legal counsel was the leftist congressman, Vito Marcantonio. She took the Fifth Amendment when asked if she was or had been a member of the Communist party. She was immediately blacklisted, but her screen career had all but ended in the early forties.

In subsequent hearings of the congressional committee, her fellow actors Marc Lawrence[9] and Sterling Hayden testified that

Marty Jackson

Karen Morley is seldom seen in public and usually refuses to sign autographs or pose for photos. The rare exception above was taken in early 1988.

Karen had been active in affairs of the Communist party in Hollywood. Hayden recalled that she had urged him to rejoin after his membership had lapsed and that some meetings were held in her home.

Karen kept her marriage of November 1932 to director Charles Vidor a secret at first, a violation of tradition in Hollywood. Neither her studio nor the press was informed for more than a month. Their son, Michael, was born the following year. The actress and director were divorced in 1943.

Her only other marriage was never announced. Karen and Lloyd Gough had appeared together in *The Banker's Daughter* (1952), her Broadway swan song. His obituary in 1984 listed her as his widow.

Lloyd Gough was a well-established Broadway actor who made such movies as *All My Sons* (1948), *Sunset Boulevard* (1950), *The Great White Hope* (1970), and *The Front* (1976). He had also written several plays and was working on a novel about the American Revolution at the time of his death. His name had appeared on the blacklist a few years after he was awarded the Bronze Star as an infantryman during the Normandy Invasion.

Karen Morley lives by herself in a house in Los Angeles. She does not respond to requests for interviews.

"Closer, hold me closer," said Esther Muir to Groucho Marx in A Day at the Races *(1937). "If I hold you any closer I'll be in back of you," he replied.*

Esther Muir

The featured player of stage and screen was born on March 11 in Andes, New York. She was one of ten children.

Esther won a scholarship to Vassar, but because it did not include expenses, she had to forgo college and seek work after her father died.

She moved in with her older sister, who had an apartment in Manhattan. Giving her high-school plays as professional credits, Esther auditioned for stage jobs.

Esther's debut was the two lines she had in *Greenwich Village Follies* (1922). During the days she earned even more money by modeling. She became a name on Broadway after playing the title role in *His Girl Friday*, a hit of 1929.

In *So This Is Africa* (1933) she was foil to the antics of the popular screen pair, Bert Wheeler and Robert Woolsey. She was in *Sweepings* (1933), a film based on the Marshall Field scandal, with Lionel Barrymore. She played with his brother, John, in *Here's to Romance* (1935).

In 1940 she and Ida Lupino's mother, Connie Emerald, supported Joan Blondell in the out-of-town tryout of *Good-Bye to Love,* a play that the star left before it opened on Broadway. In the film *Fury* (1936) she was the girlfriend of Spencer Tracy.

She went on to do dramatic as well as light roles, but was known mostly for the latter, both on stage and in pictures. Esther believes she learned her comedic skills from Charlie Ruggles, whom she supported on Broadway in *Mr. Battling Butler* (1923) and *Queen High* (1926).

Before *A Day at the Races* (1937) was filmed, she and the Marx Brothers tried out skits for possible use in the picture before live audiences in presentation houses. The friendship Esther formed with Groucho during that tour and the subsequent movie lasted until his death. She is still in touch with the widow of Harpo Marx.

The one role for which she was considered that might have changed her career was "Belle Watling" in *Gone with the Wind*.

Esther never worked with Busby Berkeley, but in 1931 she became the first of his five wives. "Living with him was enough of a strain," remarked the actress recently. "Buz was a lovely person in many ways, but a real momma's boy. I was more his keeper than his wife. He had great gifts but was very irresponsible."

In 1934, two years after divorcing Berkeley, Esther Muir married Sam Coslow. Eventually he produced for movies and TV, but he is best known as the lyricist of such standards as "Just One More Chance" and "Cocktails for Two." For the latter, his biggest hit, he wrote the words and collaborated on the music. The couple separated in 1947 and were divorced shortly thereafter.

Esther Muir still wears a miniature gold Oscar on her charm bracelet. It is a duplicate of the Academy Award won by Sam Coslow for *Heavenly Music,* the short he coproduced in 1943.

On her own, and completely without study or experience, she has financed and overseen the building of more than 400 tract homes, mostly in southern California.

The former actress has homes in Green Valley, Arizona, and San Dimas, California, as well as a villa in Kyparissi, Greece, which she maintains as a summer residence.

Esther's daughter Jacqueline, her only child, is by Coslow. She is married to actor-producer Ted Sorel and has a son and a daughter.

Esther is well aware that it is for her part in *A Day at the Races* that she is best remembered. Quite recently her grandson, Vassily, told her of his pride when in looking through the illustrated dictionary at his school he found, alongside the definition of the word *slapstick,* a still of the famous wallpapering scene. The third-grader immediately pointed to the picture and exclaimed to his classmates, "That's *my* grandmother!"

Marty Jackson

Esther Muir on a recent visit to Hollywood, awaiting her Cadillac in the portico of the Roosevelt Hotel after her interview with the author.

The Wild One was hailed in some quarters as a break-through film on its release in 1953. Its leather-clad hero, played by Marlon Brando, popularized an attire and an attitude that swept the Western world. Portraying a "nice girl" who falls for the biker-rebel established Mary Murphy immediately.

Mary Murphy

The Hollywood Cinderella was born in Washington, D.C., on January 26. Her family moved to Cleveland when Mary was six months old. Ten years later, after her father died, Mrs. Murphy and her daughter settled in Los Angeles.

When she graduated from high school in 1949, Mary Murphy had never met anyone connected with motion pictures and had never even fleetingly considered an acting career. She took a job wrapping packages at Saks Fifth Avenue in Beverly Hills with no thought of what she intended to do with her life.

One morning in April 1950 the teenager took the two buses necessary to get to work. Before punching in, Mary stopped for a cup of coffee at the Milton F. Kreis drugstore and luncheonette in the Beverly Wilshire Hotel. A paunchy man in his fifties introduced himself to her as Milton Lewis, head of the talent department at Paramount Pictures. She took his card and promised to phone his office for an appointment on her next day off. What she found so incredible about her "discovery" was that she had her hair up in curlers.

Paramount Pictures pacted Mary but, be-

cause the studio was going through a retrenchment program, immediately placed her on layoff. Technically, she was under contract to a major studio, but she was not being paid. So she continued working in the department store, a five-day-a-week job, for which she received (after deductions) just over $26.

Almost a year after she was signed, Paramount put her on salary. She made her screen test opposite William Reynolds, took lessons on the lot, and was assigned a studio publicist. She was proclaimed Miss Haystack of 1951, Miss Industrial Safety of 1952, Miss Eight Ball of 1953, and Miss Tomato Queen of 1954.

In *The Greatest Show on Earth* (1952) she was seen as a member of the audience. In the Bob Hope starrer *The Lemon Drop Kid* (1951) Mary spoke one line. In *Carrie* (1952) she had three lines. She played small parts in *When Worlds Collide* (1951) with Richard Derr,* *That's My Boy* (1951) with Eddie Mayehoff [9] and Ruth Hussey,* and *Off Limits* (1953), again with Bob Hope.

It was her prominent role in *Main Street to Broadway* (1953) that was expected to launch her career. But it was not a success at the box office and has little interest today, except for its exceptionally large cast of both stage and screen stars.

Her fame came from *The Wild One,* in which she played opposite Marlon Brando. It was considered one of 1953's most important films and immediately drew a cult following that has not diminished over the years.

Thirty-five years after working with Brando Mary laughed about the public's speculation over their off-screen relationship: "Marlon saw how green I was and couldn't have been sweeter about our scenes together—very supportive. But he and Movita were hot and heavy then. We didn't even flirt."

Dale Robertson and Mary became involved while they were making *Sitting Bull* (1954) together. Their 1956 marriage was annulled after six months.

Thirty-one years later the former Mrs. Robertson explained: "Dale is a lovely man. We're still good friends. There are a lot of men like that. They're great until they become your husband."

Her screen credits include: *The Outcast* (1954) with Joan Evans* and Ben Cooper[9]; *Beachhead* (1954) with Skip Homeier*; *The Mad Magician* (1954); *Hell's Island* (1955) opposite John Payne; *The Desperate Hours* (1955) with Arthur Kennedy; *Finger of Guilt* (1956) with Constance Cummings[9]; *Make Haste to Live* (1954); *A Man Alone* (1955); *The Maverick Queen* (1956); *Live Fast, Die Young* (1958); *Crime and Punishment U.S.A.* (1959); *The Electronic Monster* (1950); *Forty Pounds of Trouble* (1963); *Harlow* (1965); *Junior Bonner* (1972) and *Manhattan* (1979).

Her other long-running relationship was a stormy one with agent Kurt Frings. At one point in 1959, local newspapers reported Mary's accusation that he had kicked her. She

In recent years Mary Murphy has supported herself by working for Greenpeace and at a Los Angeles art gallery.

now denies the incident but admits that she found herself trapped in a triangle that was a Hollywood cliché. Frings was married at the time to the writer Ketti Frings, whose play *Look Homeward, Angel* was one of Broadway's most prestigious hits.

"Of course, he promised to marry me," says Mary today. "And, like a fool, I believed him—over and over. Not only did he control my private life, he represented me as well. I did not work one day during that whole period. And he was a 'big agent,' as they say."

In 1962 Mary Murphy became the wife of a Los Angeles retailer of lighting fixtures. They have a daughter who is studying acting. Her regret about the marriage is that she complied with her husband's request that she retire from acting.

In the early eighties, after she was divorced, Ms. Murphy made an effort to reactivate her career. As of 1988 the only work she had done was a one-day part on the soap opera *The Young and the Restless* in 1984. Not acting again would, she admits, disappoint her, but "not break my heart."

She was in touch with Milton Lewis until his death in 1986. During a recent interview she commented, "I shudder to think of what kind of a life I'd have had if that dear man hadn't 'found' me."

125

The brush cut and cigar became Ken Murray trademarks during his career of more than sixty years. After becoming a star in the mid-twenties as an emcee-comedian, he had success as a producer, author, and filmmaker.

Ken Murray

The man described by Anthony Slide in his book, *The Vaudevillians,* as a "show business phenomenon" was born Ken Doncourt in New York City on July 14, 1903. He was raised on a chicken farm in the Catskill Mountains.

His father, Jack Doncourt, well known then in vaudeville as a comedian, discouraged Ken's keen interest in a career as an entertainer. Doncourt saw no potential in a young man who could not sing, dance, or play an instrument.

Whenever his father appeared in the environs of New York City, Ken was backstage. He learned clog dancing as well as rope and whip tricks before making his debut in 1922 as one of the Pete Curly Trio. Within months he joined another trio, replacing a man whose name was Morey. So as not to change the sound of the act's name too drastically, he took the name Murray.

In September 1925 he married Charlotte La Rose, his partner in a duo. *Variety's* review of April 1926 called Ken "commendable" but found Charlotte nonessential to the act. Seven months later they had a separation, which eventually led to a divorce. Before the year was out Murray played New York's Palace Theatre, where he received fourth billing as a single.

During the final years of vaudeville's heyday Ken had his own unit, which headlined Radio-Keith-Orpheum Theatres throughout North America. His understudy then was Bob Hope.

His debut in motion pictures was with silent star Olive Borden in *Half Marriage* (1929), RKO's first all-talkie. He was also in *Leathernecking* (1930), which introduced Irene Dunne[8] to the screen.

Among his other screen appearances were roles in the films: *Crooner* (1932) with David Manners*; *Disgraced* (1933) with Helen Twelvetrees*; *You're a Sweetheart* (1937); *A Night at Earl Carroll's* (1940); *The Man Who Shot Liberty Valance* (1962); *Son of Flubber* (1963); and *Follow Me, Boys!* (1966).

Murray had his own radio show for a brief time and guested on many throughout the years, but television was much more his medium. He was on the first sponsored TV show that was done from the stage of Chicago's RKO Palace in 1930. *The Ken Murray Show,* which began on CBS-TV January 7, 1950, was one of the network's first hits.

On the evening of June 24, 1942, his comedy-variety show *Blackouts* opened in Hollywood to generally unfavorable reviews. A year later the smash hit was hailed as "fast, fleshy and funny" in *Life* magazine. Its run, which lasted for more than seven years and 3,844 performances, was the longest in the history of the legitimate theatre.

During the fifties Ken Murray frequently headlined in Las Vegas. In one twelve-month period his name was at the top of the bill for an unprecedented thirty-one weeks.

Ken Murray has written some songs, many articles, his autobiography *Life on a Pogo Stick,* and a biography of Earl Carroll. (He had been presented on Broadway for the first time by Carroll in the impresario's 1935 film, *Sketchbook.)* His book *The Golden Days of San Simeon,* which has a foreword by Ronald Reagan, has been in print for more than twenty years.

When Murray first came to Hollywood it was for a vaudeville engagement in 1927. He immediately purchased an 8mm movie camera, photographing most of the movie stars he met during his stay. He sent the films to his family in the east the way other tourists sent postcards. He has been filming screen and TV personalities ever since. Ken has shown his footage on network TV shows and in movie houses for years. Recently, three compilations of these films have been released on videocassette.

He met his wife, Betty Lou Walters, when they did a skit together in *Blackouts.* They were married in 1948 and had two daughters. Jane Murray, the oldest, is single and an actress living in New York City. Pamela is married and works in Hollywood as a theatrical

Marty Jackson

Ken Murray with the Oscar he won in 1947 as producer of Bill and Coo, *a short that featured trained birds. Thirty years after he received the plaque, the Academy of Motion Picture Arts and Sciences gave him a statuette with the same inscription. The cigar in his right hand was made of plastic.*

press agent. The Murrays spent much of their time with their three granddaughters.

Ken declined to name the big-time comic who hired him as a stooge early in his career. He soon lost the job when the man was fired for drunkenness. Subsequently, the comic took his own life. Murray credited his life-long abstinence to this experience. He gave up smoking his famous cigars years ago on his doctor's orders.

He concluded an interview in the spring of 1988 by saying: "The longer I live the more conscious I am of being a very lucky guy."

When he was admitted to Burbank's St. Joseph Medical Center in the fall it was the first time Murray had spent a night in a hospital. He was eighty-five years old when he died one month later on October 12, 1988.

Carmel Myers played opposite some of the major stars of the silent era: Douglas Fairbanks, Sr., Rudolph Valentino, John Gilbert, Rod La Rocque, Ramon Novarro, and John Barrymore.

Carmel Myers

The star of silent pictures was born in San Francisco on April 9, 1899, to Rabbi Isadore Myers and a mother she once described as a "very ambitious woman."

The facts about her beginnings in movies are nebulous, as is the actual year of her birth.

The generally accepted story is that when her father acted as consultant to D. W. Griffith during the filming of *Intolerance* (1916), Mrs. Myers persuaded the director to engage the teenage Carmel as an actress.

The actress maintained that she worked as Lillian Gish's stand-in and was given a contract for $12 a week. She always denied that she appeared in a bit part in *Intolerance.* In a 1965 interview she admitted that her daughter, actress Susan Adams, had recently seen the picture and claimed to recognize her in it. Ms. Myers insisted that she was mistaken.

In the same interview, which was recorded for radio, she stated that she debuted in pictures at the age of thirteen. When her contemporary Dagmar Godowsky heard the broadcast she commented, "Thirteen years old? Sounds too young, but then, was I not five and a half?"

By 1917 she had the first of her many vamp roles in *Sirens of the Sea* and played Elmo Lincoln's leading lady in *Haunted Pajamas.*

In 1918 Carmel Myers was cast opposite Rudolph Valentino in *All Night* and *A Society Sensation,* both for Universal Pictures, where she was under contract.

In 1919 she made her Broadway debut in *The Magic Melody,* a Sigmund Romberg musical that ran for 143 performances. Ten years later she returned in a vaudeville act at the Palace Theatre.

Her 1920 marriage to producer I. Kornblum lasted only three years.

Among the many films she made during the twenties were: *The Famous Mrs. Fair* (1923); *Beau Brummell* (1924) with John Barrymore; *Babbitt* (1924); *The Devil's Circus* (1925) with Norma Shearer; *The Demi-Bride* (1926) with Lew Cody; *Sorrell & Son* (1927); *Four Walls* (1928) with Joan Crawford; and *The Show of Shows* (1929).

Tell It to the Marines (1926), in which she played a Filipino vamp, was such a hit that it established William Haines as a star. But it was her portrayal as the wicked Egyptian "Iras" in *Ben-Hur* (1925) that was her greatest success.

Carmel continued to make pictures after Hollywood had converted to sound, but in 1930 she married an attorney, Ralph Blum, who eventually became the partner of super-agent Charles K. Feldman. After the Blums bought the vast Gloria Swanson mansion across from the Beverly Hills Hotel, she began to concentrate on her career as a Hollywood hostess.

Always very much a part of Hollywood's social life, Carmel was a frequent guest at San Simeon and at the parties given by Marion Davies at her Santa Monica beach house. Carmel stated repeatedly that it was she who introduced Mae Murray to David Mdivani and Pola Negri to his brother, Serge. The White Russian "princes" became known as "the Marrying Mdivanis."

Her early talkies include *Careers* (1929), *The Ship from Shanghai* (1930), *Nice Women* (1932), *The Countess of Monte Cristo* (1934), and the two she made in 1931 with John Barrymore, *The Genius* and *Svengali.*

After a twelve-year hiatus Carmel appeared in *Whistle Stop* (1946). *Won-Ton-Ton, the Dog Who Saved Hollywood* and *Gus,* both made in 1976, were her last films.

In 1932 the Blums' only child was born. Ralph Junior is the author of novels and nonfiction books. His latest, *The Book of Runes,* was published in 1987. Subsequently, the Blums adopted two daughters. Susan, an actress, is married to Adam Kennedy, the author of *The Domino Principle.* Mary is the wife of movie producer Pierre Cossette.

Shortly after being widowed in 1950, Ms. Myers moved to Manhattan. In 1951 she married A. W. Schwalberg, an executive with Paramount Pictures.

Carmel appeared for a time with Rudy Vallee on his early radio series. In June 1951 *The Carmel Myers Show* debuted on ABC-TV. The fifteen-minute program of celebrity interviews and the star's reminiscences lasted until February 1952.

She was really never completely out of the limelight she so dearly loved. In the mid-fifties, before scent was commonly worn by American males, Carmel acquired the franchise for a line of French fragrances made for men. She promoted her line with interviews and personal appearances, claiming that one

Two of the things Carmel Myers enjoyed most throughout her life were parties and publicity. When this photograph was taken, shortly before her death in 1980, she was on her way to a Hollywood reception.

of her line was the same cologne that Valentino had worn.

On November 8, 1980, the day before she died of a heart attack, the former star made a personal appearance at I. Magnin's Beverly Hills store to introduce "Carmel."

One of the relationships Carmel maintained over the years was with Mary Pickford. Long after "America's Sweetheart" became a virtual recluse in her Beverly Hills mansion, she continued to visit with her old friend by phone and in person. Along with many memories, the two stars shared a common birthday, April 9, and often celebrated together.

On her radio and television appearances she frequently played the ukelele and sang. After Carmel returned to Hollywood, following the death of her third husband, in 1974, she drove to Woodland Hills to do her act for the residents of the Motion Picture and Television Country Home and Hospital.

"It was agony for her," said Mary Cossette recently. "Illness, aging, and poverty were things that mother never had to contend with herself. But she *made* herself do what she could for people less fortunate. The luck she had all her life held to the end. She believed those who died suddenly like mother were truly blessed."

At her request, the ashes of Carmel Myers were strewn throughout the rose garden at Pickfair.

Alan Napier made more than sixty films, as well as many appearances on television, aside from Batman. *Yet it is his portrayal of "Alfred Pennyworth," butler to the "Dynamic Duo," that made his face familiar throughout much of the world.*

Alan Napier

The English actor who came to prominence as "Batman's" butler was born in Birmingham, England. His birthday was January 6, 1903.

When he decided to go on the stage he shortened his name from Alan William Napier-Clavering. He believed he was inspired to act by the stories read to him as a child by his mother. In his eighty-fifth year Napier expressed gratitude that both parents stressed good diction in their home. It gave him a "leg up" during his training at The Royal Academy of Dramatic Arts. Later he joined the Oxford Players.

Noel Coward chose him for a key role in the original West End production of *Bittersweet* in 1929. He considered himself a friend of George Bernard Shaw, who assisted in the direction of several of his own plays with Alan in the cast.

Napier believed the thing that held him back in his career was his height of 6 feet, 5 inches: "How many parts I lost by simply standing up! The damnable thing about it is that I could see their point. It's the same on stage as on a set. I throw everything off."

Alan had been in six other Broadway plays before Gladys George brought him from England again to be with her in *Lady in Waiting* (1940). He had lived in the United States ever since. He made three more appearances on the New York stage but lived and worked mainly in Hollywood.

Though he appeared in pictures since the early talkies, Napier was never typecast until he did the *Batman* series from 1966 to 1968. The one thing all of his characters had in common was their nationality. Frequently, he was what could be best described as "frightfully British."

Horror fans know him as the blackmailer in *The Invisible Man Returns* (1940), Ruth Hussey's beau in *The Uninvited* (1944), and the art critic murdered by Rondo Hatton in

House of Horrors (1946). Some of his other appearances in the genre were: *The House of the Seven Gables* (1940), *Cat People* (1942), *Hangover Square* (1945), *Isle of the Dead* (1945), and *The Premature Burial* (1962).

Among Alan's other screen credits were: *Loyalties* (1934), *The Revenge of General Ling* (1938), *A Yank at Eton* (1942), *Random Harvest* (1942), *The Song of Bernadette* (1944), *The Hairy Ape* (1944), *Ministry of Fear* (1945), *Unconquered* (1947), *Forever Amber* (1947), *Joan of Arc* (1948), *Criss-Cross* (1949), *Macbeth* (1950), *The Great Caruso* (1951), *Julius Caesar* (1953), *Desiree* (1954), *Journey to the Center of the Earth* (1959), *Marnie* (1964), and *The Loved One* (1965).

In April 1988 the octogenarian said: "My acting career, like my emotional life, is divided into two quite distinct parts—before and after *Batman*. Those shows were great fun to do, but I couldn't be cast for anything else when the series went on the air. Fans still write to me from around the world— always with questions for 'Alfred.' And yet, on balance I confess that I'm glad I did it.

"As to my heart: I discovered at a crucial point in my life that my first wife was a lesbian. That sort of thing has a very discouraging effect on a young man. But I then met a young woman whose love helped me put that experience behind me. I am still nourished by the many happy memories I bask in from our years together. She has been gone for over twenty years."

As late as 1979 *Batman* was a hit all over again in England. When newscasters on the commercial channel, ITN, went on strike, the network substituted reruns of the "Caped Crusaders."

Alan was not usually in touch with the other members of the *Batman* cast, but he was reunited with them in April 1988 on TV's *The Late Show*. Afterward he remarked:

Marty Jackson

Widower Alan Napier posed for this photo on January 6, 1988, the day he turned eighty-five. He died on August 8, 1988.

"Jolly good to see them all again and even the Batmobile! But I've never been able to work up much enthusiasm for the 'Boy Wonder.'"

Alan purchased his three-level home overlooking the Pacific Ocean in 1943 for $6,750. It was only a few hundred yards away from the Pacific Coast Highway and the structure that was once Thelma Todd's Sidewalk Café. It had an estimated value in 1988 of approximately $1 million.

He spent much of his time in a rose garden off his bedroom. At 4 P.M. daily Napier took tea, sometimes with fans, in his living room. The Lapsang Souchong was served by a young man who grew up in Rio de Janeiro watching *Batman* shows that had been dubbed into Portuguese.

131

Jane Nigh and Bill Williams were top-billed in Monogram's Blue Blood *(1951), her favorite of her films. Their other movies together were* Fighting Man of the Plains *(1949),* Operation Haylift *(1950), and* Blue Grass of Wyoming *(1950).*

Jane Nigh

The leading lady of the forties and fifties was born in Hollywood on February 25, 1925. Her birth certificate reads "Bonnie Lenora," but her parents and sister always called her "Jane."

Although she had been in plays during high school, an acting career had never occurred to her. A studio press agent noticed her working in the offices of McDonnell-Douglas Corporation and asked her to call him concerning work in movies. Jane took it as a joke, but after a month of his persistence she was tested and signed by Twentieth Century-Fox, where she remained for four years.

Jane Nigh made her screen debut in *Something for the Boys* (1944). She had a small part in *State Fair* (1945) and played Betty Hutton's roommate in *Red, Hot and Blue* (1949). In *Captain Carey, U.S.A.* (1950) she lost Alan Ladd to Wanda Hendrix. Her other credits include *Whistle Stop* (1946), *Dragonwyck* (1946), *Unconquered* (1947), *Give My Regards to Broadway* (1948), *Zamba* (1949), *Leather Gloves* (1948), *Cry of the City* (1948), and two in 1950 opposite Tim Holt: *Treasure Trail* and *Rio Grande Patrol.*

After Jane's reported engagements to com-

Bill Williams,9 husband of Barbara Hale and father of William Katt, attending the funeral of Horace Heidt8 in December 1986. The Williamses live in Heidt's apartment complex in Van Nuys.

In February 1988, when this photograph was taken, Jane Nigh was recuperating from a stroke and preparing to move to Bakersfield, California.

poser David Rose, architect John Lindsay (who subsequently married Diana Lynn), and Claude Cartier, of the jewelry dynasty, Louella O. Parsons scolded her in print and jokesters hung a sign on her dressing room door that read: "Miss Gadabout of 1949." But when Parsons met Jane she wrote that she was "taken off my feet by her beauty," declaring her to be "the nearest thing to Corinne Griffith of all the young actresses." (Griffith was a major star of the silent era, for whom the term *orchidacious* was coined.)

Her first husband was Victor Cutler, a Samuel Goldwyn contractee, who went on to a very successful modeling career. The couple had never even kissed when they eloped in 1946. Three months later they were divorced.

In 1952 Jane became the wife of a rancher, who is the father of her son and daughter. They were divorced in 1962.

Jane Nigh originated the role of "Lorelei Kilburn" on the TV version of *Big Town* in 1952 but left after the first season when she became pregnant.

The last time she was before a movie camera Jane did the pilot for a sitcom. Had it sold, she would have played the mother of the then boy actor Kurt Russell.

Her friends from her career are Elena Verdugo and Coleen Gray. The latter got the one part Jane wanted most, opposite Bing Crosby in *Riding High*.

Ms. Nigh married and divorced her third husband, a lumberman, twice. She lived in Costa Mesa, California, and ran her own business, "Jazzy Jewels," until 1985.

Her daughter by her third marriage was killed in an auto collision in 1985.

In April 1988 Jane Nigh spoke of her life: "My career was the most wonderful surprise because I never thought of myself as beautiful. I've had four divorces but never with any bitterness. My second husband and I are still dear friends. But I had watched my daughter poison herself with drugs and alcohol. She was twenty-one years old when she died. Then, after she was gone, I had the most terrible guilt because we'd been estranged. Within months, I had a stroke."

In May 1988 Jane Nigh sold her condominium in Costa Mesa and moved to Bakersfield, California, to be near her second husband and their daughter.

133

Marion Nixon was always in the shadow of Janet Gaynor throughout their years at Fox Films. Even Marion's favorite among her own pictures, Rebecca of Sunnybrook Farm *(1932), was one Gaynor had turned down.*

Marion Nixon

The leading lady of the twenties and thirties was born in Superior, Wisconsin. Her birthday was October 20, 1904.

Marion worked in a department store during high school to earn money for dancing lessons. She joined a troop of dancers touring vaudeville houses. When they disbanded in Los Angeles, she decided to try her luck in pictures.

She had bit parts in several comedy shorts before getting a small role in her first feature, *The Courtship of Miles Standish* (1923). The film proved disastrous financially and professionally for its star, Charles Ray. For the young actress it led to a walk-on in *Rosita* (1923), a Mary Pickford vehicle.

Her first real part came when Marion was chosen over Alice Day, who also tested, for leading lady to Buck Jones. *Big Dan* (1923) was the first of five features they made together that year. In 1924 she was leading lady to Tom Mix in *The Last of the Duanes* and *Riders of the Purple Sage,* both considered classic silent westerns.

Marion played opposite John Gilbert in the drama *Just Off Broadway* (1924) and Raymond Griffith in *Hands Up!* (1926), a comedy. *Spangles* (1926), a circus picture, was one of her early hits. She was in *The Chinese Parrot* (1927), the first time the character "Charlie Chan" was presented on the screen. Then she did *Red Lips* (1928) with "Buddy" Rogers, *The Fourflusher* (1928) with George Lewis, and *General Crack* (1929) with John Barrymore.

Among her personal favorites were *Out of the Ruins* (1928) and *Young Nowhere* (1929), both opposite Richard Barthelmess.

There has long been confusion over the proper spelling of Ms. Nixon's first name. This was caused when, on the advice of a numerologist, she insisted that she be billed as "Marian Nixon." She soon reverted to the original spelling.

Marion Nixon and Janet Gaynor entered movies at approximately the same time and were both under contract to Fox Films during the last years of silents and into the early thirties. They were much the same type, playing the sweetheart with unshakable faith, overcoming all adversity. Marion was every bit as good an actress as Gaynor, probably more versatile and definitely prettier. But Gaynor had such a huge following after *Sunrise* and *Seventh Heaven* that she was always able to command the best roles the studio could provide.

Marion Nixon made more than three dozen sound films. Her first all-talkie, *The Rainbow Man* (1929), in which she played opposite Broadway star Eddie Dowling, was well received. The same year she was in *Say It with Songs,* an Al Jolson starrer with Davey Lee.[10] Frank Borzage directed her with Charles Farrell in *After Tomorrow* (1932). She played opposite Spencer Tracy in *Face in the Sky* (1933) and opposite Joel McCrea in *Chance at Heaven* (1933). John Ford directed her in the Will Rogers vehicle *Doctor Bull* (1933) and *Pilgrimage* (1933).

When Marion met William Seiter he was married to Laura La Plante, the most important star on the Universal lot. He directed Marion and Reginald Denny in five features, all silents.

For a brief time Marion seemed about to marry a wealthy Chicagoan, Edward Hillman. But then she came under Seiter's direction again in *Chance at Heaven* (1933). By that time both were divorced. In 1934, the year they married, he directed her in *We're Rich Again* (1934). It was also the year she left Fox Films.

Marion made *The Reckless Way* (1935) opposite Kane Richmond and *Tango* (1936), in which she was top-billed over newcomer Chick Chandler. Her career ended in the mid-thirties in those and other Poverty Row releases.

Marion Nixon and Ben Lyon first met during the twenties. She had been widowed for

Marty Jackson

Ben Lyon and Marion Nixon had been married for almost seven years when he died during a cruise in 1979. She lived until 1983.

almost seven years when they began seeing each other again in 1971. His wife, Bebe Daniels, had died a few months before. They were married in 1972.

The Lyons traveled frequently. They were aboard the *Queen Elizabeth II* when Ben died suddenly in 1979.

Marion Nixon died of complications after open-heart surgery on February 13, 1983. She is survived by a daughter by Hillman, a son by Seiter, and five grandchildren.

135

Lucille Norman was brought to Hollywood by Metro-Goldwyn-Mayer because of her beautiful soprano voice, but she had few opportunities to sing in pictures. Western fans know her as Randolph Scott's leading lady in Carson City *(1952).*

Lucille Norman

The soprano of screen and radio was born in Lincoln, Nebraska, on June 15, 1926.

Her parents were singers on the Chautauqua circuit until her father became a Unity minister. Lucille sang as part of his religious services throughout her childhood.

The Normans settled in Cincinnati, where Lucille attended the Conservatory of Music. After winning a talent contest on a local radio program, she soloed at age fourteen with the Symphony Orchestra of Columbus, Ohio.

The first time Lucille Norman was scheduled to audition for the Metropolitan Opera Company, the tryouts and their live broadcast were canceled when Pearl Harbor was bombed on December 7, 1941.

When she did get to compete with the other aspirants, the contract she was offered was not from the famed opera house but with Metro-Goldwyn-Mayer.

She was at M-G-M only long enough to play a supporting role in *For Me and My Gal* (1942), though four years later one of her outtakes was included, along with some other musical numbers, in *The Great Morgan* (1946).

Among her other screen credits are: *Painting the Clouds with Sunshine* (1951), *Starlift* (1951), and *Sweethearts on Parade* (1953), a turn-of-the-century musical in which she costarred with the late Ray Middleton.

Lucille met her soon-to-be husband, Bruce Kellogg, when they did *Robert* together at Camp Roberts for the troops in 1944. Kellogg made a few films, such as *Barbary Coast Gent* (1944) and *They Were Expendable* (1945), but he concentrated mainly on his wife's career after their marriage.

If Hollywood had not made her a star, it had established her as a name. Kellogg booked her into light operas at the Hollywood Bowl and the Greek Theatre. Those shows, as well as her tours, had the benefit of her regular appearances on network radio programs, such as the *Carnation Contented Hour*. Her long-running weekly show over

Marty Jackson

Randolph Scott was a pallbearer at character actor Edgar Buchanan's funeral, where this photo was taken in April 1979. Scott died in March 1987 and is buried in his family's plot at the Elmwood Cemetery in Charlotte, North Carolina.

Marty Jackson

Lucille Norman is frequently seen in the company of the proprietor of a piano and organ store. It was he who coaxed her into posing for this photograph.

KNX was heard throughout the west coast during the early fifties. There was also a *Lucille Norman Sings* show on Los Angeles TV in the mid-fifties.

Lucille and Gordon McRae might have become a team if he had had his way. During the years he hosted radio's *Railroad Hour* she guested frequently. Together they recorded the songs from *The New Moon* and *The Vagabond King,* which were released as albums.

There was at least one announcement that Warner Brothers would present the pair in a technicolor remake of *Viennese Nights,* an early talkie musical.

The Kelloggs' investments in beach and Hollywood properties were very successful. For a while they had as many as 15,000 head of cattle on the ranch they owned in Cody, Wyoming. Their home on three acres was adjacent to the Beverly Hills estate of Arthur Rubinstein.

Through an intermediary, Lucille Norman expressed her willingness to be included in this book. For reasons she does not wish disclosed, she will not be interviewed. Since this friend did not know her during the years of her career, he was able to supply information only pertaining to the two decades she has been in complete retirement.

When Bruce Kellogg died in 1966, he and Lucille had been separated and were in the process of being divorced.

The only person she heard from on a regular basis after leaving her profession was Gordon McRae, who called until his death in 1986. She is a member of the Pacific Pioneer Broadcaster's Association and occasionally attends the luncheons held by the radio veterans.

She is a volunteer worker at Hollywood Presbyterian Church and has been a reader for the blind since the mid-seventies.

She plays golf occasionally and is one of the top-rated members in her age group at the Los Angeles Tennis Club.

Her only child, a daughter, is a business executive. Lucille Norman lives by herself in Hollywood.

Martha O'Driscoll made more than three dozen films during the thirties and forties, as a supporting player in A features and a leading lady in Bs. She was "Daisy Mae" in the first screen version of Li'l Abner (1940).

Martha O'Driscoll

The leading lady of the forties was born in Tulsa, Oklahoma, on March 4, 1922. An exceptionally pretty baby, she modeled children's clothes from the age of four.

In 1921 the O'Driscoll family moved to Arizona. Martha, who by then had had several years of dancing lessons, began appearing in local plays and pageants. When choreographer Hermes Pan noticed her in a production at the Phoenix Little Theatre, he suggested to Mrs. O'Driscoll that Martha might have a future in movies.

It was not long afterward, in 1935, that she and her daughter came to Hollywood. Upon learning that Pan was out of the city, the teenager answered an advertisement for dancers and made her screen debut in *Collegiate* (1936). Martha O'Driscoll also danced in *Here Comes the Band* (1935) with Ted Lewis, *Big Broadcast of 1936* (1935), and *Champagne Waltz* (1937) before she got her big break: a scout from Universal Pictures spotted her in *The Great Ziegfeld* (1936) and arranged for a screen test, which resulted in a contract.

Martha O'Driscoll was well known to all movie fans of the time. Even those who lived in areas where Universal pictures were not released were aware of her from magazines. Her studio contracted her endorsement and likeness to Woodbury Complete Beauty Cream, Charm-Kurl Supreme Cold Wave, Max Factor Hollywood Face Powder, Royal Crown Cola, and Frederic's Tru-Curl Permanent Waves. The advertisements always mentioned her most recently released film.

At M-G-M she appeared in *The Secret of Dr. Kildare* (1939) and *Judge Hardy and Son* (1940). Paramount cast her in *The Lady Eve*

(1941), *Henry Aldrich for President* (1941), *Reap the Wild Wind* (1942), and *Young and Willing* (1943). At Universal she made *Crazy House* (1943) with Olsen & Johnson; *Here Come the Co-eds* (1945) with Abbott & Costello; *The Daltons Ride Again* (1945); and *House of Dracula* (1945). Three times she made pictures on her home lot opposite Noah Beery, Jr. Among her last were *Blonde Alibi* (1946) with Tom Neal and *Carnegie Hall* (1947).

Fanzines covered her dates with William Lundigan, a romance that lasted for several years.

In 1943 Martha married a young Lieutenant Commander in the U.S. Navy, but she continued to accept screen assignments. When she filed for divorce ten months later, the actress explained to the press that her husband had no comprehension of the demands on her time made by the studio. She admitted at the same time that she had not fully understood her duties as the wife of a naval officer during wartime.

The court stayed her divorce for the duration and Martha continued to make pictures. In July 1947, less than forty-eight hours after her decree was final, she became the bride of another naval officer. This one, Arthur Appleton, was also the heir to an industrial empire. After returning to civilian life, he became the president of his family's electronics firm in Chicago.

At their wedding, which was held at El Rancho Vegas, Mrs. Appleton announced that she was "definitely through with pictures, stage and all of that."

Since then her time has been devoted to raising her three sons and one daughter. The latter was elected Dartmouth Winter Carnival Queen in 1971.

Now that her children no longer live in the family home in Wilmette, Illinois, and her husband is retired, the Appletons spend most

Marty Jackson

Martha O'Driscoll-Appleton leaving the annual reunion of Universal Pictures players in August 1987. It was her first public appearance in Hollywood since her retirement forty years ago.

of their time in their Miami Beach house and on their yacht. Martha is on the board of directors of Appleton Electronics, Appleton Oil Co., and The Gulf Stream Race Track. She shares her husband's interest in horse racing and golf.

Although the Appletons frequently visit her brother in Los Angeles, of her contemporaries Martha has kept in touch only with June Vincent and Marjorie Weaver.

Martha O'Driscoll is reluctant to discuss any aspect of her career or personal life with either fans or professionals. After agreeing to an interview in late 1987, her responses to all questions were either vague or noncommittal. She gave the impression of being very ill-at-ease throughout the brief exchange.

One of her contemporaries, who knew her in the forties and talked with her again at the annual reunion of Universal contractees in August 1987, said of her: "It was like being with her sister or double. She remembered everything but as though it happened to someone else. The Martha O'Driscoll I knew doesn't seem to exist anymore. There's only Mrs. Arthur Appleton."

Oliver's rendition of "Jean" was the number-two song in the United States in August 1969 and remained on Billboard magazine's "Hot 100 Chart" for fourteen weeks. His version of "Good Morning, Starshine" had made it to the number-three position three months earlier and was on the chart for thirteen weeks. "Sunday Mornin'" was among the nation's "top forty" records for nine weeks in late 1969.

Oliver

The singing sensation of 1969 was born William Oliver Swofford in North Wilkesboro, North Carolina, on February 22, 1945.

Shortly after he entered the University of North Carolina's Department of Television and Motion Pictures, Swofford became interested in music as a career. By 1964 he and two other students had formed "The Good Earth," a folk group that had an immediate success in and around the campus. It was still playing local engagements when the three young men signed a recording contract with Bob Crewe, a major influence then in all aspects of popular music and personalities.

Shortly thereafter, "The Good Earth" moved to New York City and became a duo. Then, after Swofford's partner left, Crewe decided to try him as a single.

He gives Bob Crewe full credit for his name and the huge success of his first record, "Good Morning, Starshine." "He thought that Donovan and Melanie had begun a vogue for one-named balladeers and chose my middle name. My rendition, which was from the Broadway show *Hair,* was released the same month as five or more other versions, and no one had ever heard of me. But Crewe had such clout then that all the top disc jockeys in Los Angeles were playing it even before it was in the stores."

The record, which had "broken big on the coast," appeared as the obvious hit version to stations across the nation. By May of 1969 Oliver's rendition of "Good Morning, Starshine" was the third most popular record in the United States.

His next single, "Jean," was an even bigger hit, reaching the number two position among the "top forty," this despite the fact the song's composer, Rod McKuen, had sung it during the credits of *The Prime of Miss Jean Brodie,* which was released months earlier.

Oliver attributes his success with "Jean" to

Crewe's promotion man, Tom Rogin: "After we made 'Oliver Again,' my second record album, Rogin sent dummies of the album to all the key disc jockeys along with a note asking them which song, in their opinion, had real potential. When the majority picked 'Jean' that single was sent out as the choice of all these heavyweight guys and went almost to the top."

"Jean" became the second most frequently played single in the nation. It was followed by "Sunday Mornin,'" which reached number thirty-five on *Billboard* magazine's "Hot 100 Chart." All three of Oliver's hits were released in 1969.

Swofford was never called "Oliver" by anyone except his fans. His three gold records, which hang on the walls of his office, have to be explained to potential clients. He is a salesman of Stancraft Homes, a builder-developer in and around Dallas, Texas.

When Oliver was "hot" he appeared on all the TV variety shows and played nightclubs in the Century Plaza Hotel in Los Angeles and San Francisco's Fairmont. When he was booked into New York's Copacabana, comedian George Carlin opened for him.

Oliver and Crewe came to a parting of the ways in 1970 over accompaniment. The singer insisted on extremely simple backing. Although he never again had the success or attention that came under Crewe's auspices, he does not view the split as a mistake. "I just wanted to stay with the things that first turned me on to becoming a musician," he said in 1987. "Bob really had the commercial touch, which I seem to lack. It was the music, itself, that I most cared about. I retired when I saw that I was at a point professionally where I'd soon be playing lounges of Holiday Inns. By then I was so weary of travel, it was not a hard decision. But those years were an enriching experience and I'm very grateful."

Oliver and his wife live in Dallas, Texas, where he sells real estate.

Oliver continued to perform into the early eighties. Most of his bookings in later years were on campuses or in coffeehouses. Probably because he does not play rock and roll, he is not approached for "golden oldies" shows.

He says that his hits and three LPs did not make him wealthy and that he receives no payments when his records are played on the air or sold.

The emotional highlight of his public life was the first of the three times he was presented on television by Ed Sullivan. His younger brother, John Swofford, had made three touchdown passes playing quarterback for the University of North Carolina the day before. When Sullivan learned he was in the studio audience, he asked him to stand up.

He has been married since 1974 to a talent agent-booker who specializes in industrial shows. She does not represent him. Swofford is stepfather to her son and daughter.

The major mistake of his career was, according to Oliver, not seizing the opportunity to be the first to record "If You Could Read My Mind." When Gordon Lightfoot played and sang his composition for him, he offered it to Oliver.

He recently explained: "I was so impressed by his delivery I told him to just perform it himself and, of course, he did."

Gigi Perreau marked her fifth birthday at Metro-Goldwyn-Mayer, where she was considered the "threat" to the star Margaret O'Brien. Both children were under contract to the studio at that time.

Gigi Perreau

The child actress of the screen was born in Los Angeles on February 6, 1941. Her original name is Ghislaine Elizabeth Marie-Therese Perreau-Saussine. Gigi, the diminutive of her first name, is pronounced with two hard gs.

Her father fled his native France when World War II broke out. Her mother was American-born.

While visiting a friend who was employed by Warner Brothers, Mrs. Perreau was approached by an agent who represented child actors exclusively. The woman assured her that M-G-M was looking for a boy like her pretty five-year-old son, Gerald, who was with her.

Gigi accompanied her mother and brother to the interview where she was noticed by producer-director Mervyn LeRoy. When he learned that the thirty-month-old child could speak French as well as English, she was cast as Greer Garson's daughter in *Madame Curie* (1943). Making her screen debut in the same feature was Margaret O'Brien, who became and has remained a close friend of Gigi's.

She was still a toddler when Metro-Goldwyn-Mayer signed her to a contract. After five years on the Culver City lot, she was pacted by Universal-International.

Gigi won an award from *Film Daily,* was chosen Top Juvenile Star by *Parents* magazine, and received the Golden Skillet, the highest accolade of the Screen Children's Guild.

Gigi's younger sister, Janine, and their brother made pictures also. All three were brought up to understand that acting was a profession and did not entitle them to any domestic privileges not enjoyed by their one sister who never turned professional. When they were not being tutored at a studio, the Perreaus attended Roman Catholic schools. When a screen role was offered to Gigi at the time she was studying for her confirmation, the Perreaus rejected the role.

Gigi was sixteen years old before she was

permitted to go out with a boy. Her first date was Sal Mineo.

Some of the pictures Gigi appeared in are: *Mr. Skeffington* (1944), *Green Dolphin Street* (1947), *Enchantment* (1948), *Roseanna McCoy* (1949), *My Foolish Heart* (1950), *Has Anybody Seen My Gal?* (1952), *There's Always Tomorrow* (1956), *Tammy, Tell Me True* (1961) and *Look in Any Window* (1961).

Gigi enjoyed making movies, but she believes she is one of the rare exceptions among those who had early careers. As a child she preferred adults but got along well with her contemporaries. Her only unpleasant recollection is of Natalie Wood, who was her classmate for a while. The late actress passed notes in class that Gigi did not really understand, but that disturbed her—messages worded as warnings, to the effect that she would never become a star but that Natalie would. (They were then in grammar school.)

Gigi was twenty when she married a man who was reputed to be an heir to the Gallo wineries fortune. He is the father of her older son and daughter. She had another boy and girl by her second marriage to a studio production manager.

"I am going to be an actress until I die," Gigi told an interviewer when still a moppet. She has continued to act over the years, although she is seldom seen on movie or TV screens. Until the Theatre Arts Program was canceled after Proposition Thirteen was passed, she was part of a troupe of actors who performed at Senior Citizen Centers, schools, and churches. In 1986 she was seen on a *Murder, She Wrote* episode.

Gigi Perreau teaches drama at parochial schools near her home in Sherman Oaks, California.

Her sister Janine was born on October 19, 1942. She had her first crush on Jimmy Hunt,[9] whom she played with in *Invaders from Mars* (1953). Van Heflin, whom she

Gigi Perreau teaches at a Roman Catholic school near her home in Sherman Oaks, California.

supported in *Weekend with Father* (1951), was the actor she liked the least. When he suspected she was stealing a scene, he threatened her with a knife.

Their brother Gerald was born on April 1, 1938. His billing was usually "Peter Miles." *Enchantment* (1948), *The Red Pony* (1949), *Roseanna McCoy* (1949), *The Good Humor Man* (1950), and *Quo Vadis* (1951) were his most memorable screen credits. He played Gigi's brother on *The Betty Hutton Show*, a sit-com that ran on CBS-TV during the 1959–60 season. The bachelor is an art appraiser and high school teacher in Los Angeles. His early novels were twice recipients of the Samuel Goldwyn Creative Writing Awards. Another of his books was filmed as *Cold Day in the Park* (1959). He lives under his original name and does not choose to be interviewed or photographed. Gigi describes him as resembling a "Young Ernest Hemingway." Janine thinks he looks more like a "young Santa Claus."

143

Mary Philbin was known for the innocence she projected in her silent films. Some called her "Universal's answer to Mary Pickford."

Mary Philbin

The silent star was born in Chicago, Illinois. Her birthdate is June 16, 1903.

Mary came to Hollywood as the result of a beauty contest. She and Gertrude Olmstead were chosen as winners by Erich von Stroheim, who was then a director at Universal Pictures. Both young women were placed under contract to the studio.

The moviegoing public first saw her in *Blazing Trail* (1921). Among her other films were: *False Kisses* (1921), *The Temple of Venus (1923), Human Hearts* (1922), *The Trooper* (1922), *The Rose of Paris* (1924), *Gaiety Girl* (1924), *Fifth Avenue Models* (1925), *Love Me and the World Is Mine* (1928), *Drums of Love* (1928), *Affairs of Hannerl* (1928), *The Shannons of Broadway* (1929), and *After the Fog* (1930).

She was publicized and usually cast as the child-woman, a concept of femininity popularized on the screen by superstar Mary Pickford. One of her pictures, *Stella Maris* (1926), was a remake of a film that had been a successful vehicle for "America's Sweetheart" eight years before.

Mary made pictures, such as *Merry-Go-Round* (1923), which were important in their time. She played opposite the Russian star Mosjukine in *Surrender* (1927) and costarred with Conrad Veidt in both *The Man Who Laughed* (1928) and *The Last Performance* (1929). D.W. Griffith borrowed her from Universal for *Drums of Love* (1928), which he directed. She is best remembered, however, for *The Phantom of the Opera* (1925), which is considered one of the all-time great films of the silent era.

When *The Phantom of the Opera* was released with sound added in 1930, Norman Kerry dubbed the dialogue for its male star Lon Chaney, Sr., and Ms. Philbin was heard speaking her own lines.

During her years at Universal, Mary was thought by many to be the personal favorite of studio head Carl Laemmle, Sr. Her fiancé for much of that time was Paul Kohner, who was at first casting director and then headed the studio's production of foreign-language versions.

The Philbin-Kohner romance had the enthusiastic encouragement of Louella O. Parsons, then the unchallenged queen of Hollywood columnists. Fans have long been curious why the long and highly publicized engagement never led to marriage. When the breakup was announced in the spring of 1927, no explanation was given.

In late 1987, a few months before his death, Paul Kohner talked about the relationship: "Mary was the lovely demure girl people saw on the screen, but she was almost completely dominated by her parents. Her father, a dour man, was adamantly opposed to our getting married. The chief obstacle was that they were Roman Catholics and I am not. But I was young and determined. Then, one night, she told me she could not go out with me. I became suspicious and my jealous nature was aroused. I drove to her house and parked across the street. Soon after I arrived, Guinn 'Big Boy' Williams came by to pick her up. It was obvious that she was dating him. The next day she received my wire asking for the return of the engagement ring I had given her."

Both Paul Kohner and Dorothy Gulliver, who was under contract at Universal during some of the same years, used the exact same words to describe the actress they once knew: "very sweet and very shy."

Mary Philbin made a few talkies, but her career ended in 1930. Since then she has turned down countless invitations to film festivals, tributes, and Hollywood gatherings. She has been known to sign autographs but answers all queries with the remark: "Interviews, parties, personal appearances—they are all part of a life I no longer live."

Mary still resides in the same house she shared with her parents during her heyday in movies. Whether or not she ever married is unknown. Because she did not wish to displease them, she never married.

Marty Jackson

Mary Philbin made her first public appearance in over fifty years at the annual memorial service for Rudolph Valentino, held at the Hollywood Memorial Park Cemetery on August 23, 1988.

145

Marc Platt was teamed with Janet Blair in Tonight and Every Night *(1945), the Technicolor musical that starred Rita Hayworth.*

Marc Platt

The actor-dancer of Broadway and the movies was born in Pasadena, California. His birthdate is December 2, 1913. His original name was Marcel Emile Gaston Leplat.

His father, a classical violinist, and his mother, a soprano, settled in Seattle when their son was nine years old. They strongly encouraged him when, two years later, he asked to be enrolled in the Mary Ann Wells Dancing School. Unbeknownst to them, however, his interest was not in dance but in one of the little girl students.

As a teenager he danced in the chorus of *Peer Gynt* at the Seattle Repertory Play-

house. Later he played the lead in a production for the same company and had prominent roles in several of the Henry Duffy Players productions.

By 1935, when he became a member of Colonel de Basil's Ballet Russe de Monte Carlo, his name was changed to Marc Platoff. Within three years he was a soloist. When Leonide Massine broke away from the Ballet Russe, Marc became a member of the dancer-choreographer's new company. During the three years he spent under Massine, Platoff toured Europe and North and South America and choreographed the *Ghost Town* ballet to the music of Richard Rodgers.

He left the ballet for an opportunity to dance in the Broadway show *The Lady Comes Across* (1942) under the direction of George Balanchine and under the name Marc Platt. His next show was *Beat the Band* (1942). The third of what he refers to as "my three flops in a row" was *My Dear Public* (1943), which starred Joe E. Lewis and Mischa Auer.

In *Oklahoma!* (1943) he danced as "Curley" in the dream ballet sequence. Agnes de Mille's choreography was thought to revolutionize dancing in Broadway shows. The attention it brought Marc landed him a contract with Columbia Pictures.

Marc had married a dancer in 1942. When they divorced in 1947, their son remained with his mother. In 1951 he married a member of the road company of *Kiss Me Kate* in which he played the lead during a two-year tour.

He made his movie debut in *Tonight and Every Night* (1945), a Technicolor musical that starred Rita Hayworth. It was a major hit of World War II and brought about *Down to Earth* (1947), also a musical vehicle for the "Love Goddess" with a featured role for Marc.

His other pictures were *Tars and Spars*

Marty Jackson

Janet Blair in August 1987 at the American Cinema Awards.

Jean Platt

Marc Platt photographed by his wife in early 1988 at their Fort Myers, Florida, home.

(1946) with Janet Blair; *The Swordsman* (1948) with Larry Parks and Ellen Drew;* and *Her Wonderful Lie* (1950) with Marta Eggerth,* Gil Lamb, and Janis Carter. He was one of the brothers in *Seven Brides for Seven Brothers* (1954).

His movie career, which came about as a result of *Oklahoma!* on stage, ended with the movie version of the Rodgers and Hammerstein musical. In that film, which was released in 1955, Marc played a character that did not appear in the original.

In 1987 Platt explained his early retirement from performing: "With a few notable exceptions, a dancer's career is a relatively brief one. Mine was shortened considerably by what Jack Cole put me through in three pictures. He loved people sliding all over them on their knees, and mine were bothering me a lot when I quit."

The one part that would have kept him before the cameras was the TV series *Mr. Ed.* Marc tested for the lead and was very disappointed when it went to Alan Young.[8]

The Platts moved to the East Coast where he earned his living as a choreographer of industrial shows and TV commercials. In

1962 he took over as producer and director of the ballet company of Radio City Music Hall, a post he held until 1970.

For a brief time he and his wife operated an ice-skating rink and school in Naples, Florida. Since 1971 they have been the proprietors of the Ballet Arts Studio in Fort Myers, Florida. For a while he appeared regularly as the theatre critic on a local television station.

His son by his first marriage is the aspiring actor Ted Leplat. Neither Donna nor Michael, his children by his present wife, are in the profession.

Recently, Marc Platt spoke of his career: "I've never known bitterness over what didn't happen. I did the work I loved most and got paid for it. For a guy who was never a star, I certainly had some terrific highlights: a featured spot in *Oklahoma!,* the musical that changed musicals and modern dancing forever, being chosen by Balanchine, and receiving high praise from the great Fokine. Dancing with Rita Hayworth wasn't so bad, either. I don't frequently think about those years, but when I do the memories are very pleasant ones."

For ten consecutive weeks in 1955—April to early July—the Perez Prado rendition of "Cherry Pink and Apple Blossom White" was the number-one record in the nation according to Billboard's "Top 100 Chart."

Perez Prado

The King of the Mambo was born on December 11, in Matangas, Cuba.

Because Perez Prado insists he neither speaks nor understands English, little is known of his background. Questions addressed to him in Spanish are responded to with vagueness.

He says his first musical group was made up of friends during his youth in Cuba. His sound, which swept North America and western Europe in the fifties, first caught on in Mexico City during the late forties.

Anglos in Southern California were made aware of Perez Prado by disc jocky Gene Norman. By 1950 Norman's late-night radio show was one of the most listened to programs in the Los Angeles area and was considered the hippest. Latinos could hear Prado records on the Spanish-language station, but exposure on the Norman program made him a crossover artist.

It was under the auspices of Gene Norman that the Prado aggregation made its debut in the United States. Their first concert, on August 20, 1951, was held at Pasadena's Civic Auditorium, and according to Norman, it set the tone for the musician's career in this country.

The Perez Prado concert was a success financially and critically. It heralded the mambo craze of the fifties. But it was also the first of a number of times that he was to claim his manager had run off with his share of the proceeds.

In spring 1954 Perez Prado's recording of "Patrica" was a smash hit. By June it was number one on *Billboard*'s "Top 100 Chart." He had a verbal commitment to play the Crescendo, a Sunset Strip nitery that was then owned by Gene Norman. At the last minute, a rival club, Mocombo, offered better terms, which Prado accepted.

One veteran of Hollywood's music scene recently recalled what happened after the maestro acquired the services of Billy Regis, an exceptional trumpet player: "After Billy began to draw applause for his solos, Prado used to stand directly in front of him *pretending* to play a trumpet . . ."

He had a reputation among musicians for paying the lowest possible wages and for being a demanding conductor. Anyone who played with Prado was well disciplined and thoroughly rehearsed.

His mastery of the salsa beat, seconded by his showmanship, kept the name Perez Prado before the public for more than a decade. Two more of his records, "Guaglione" and "Paris," were on hit charts in 1958 and in 1962, respectively. A new rendition of his earlier success, "Patricia Twist," was on *Billboard*'s "Hot 100 Chart" for five weeks in 1962.

The maestro readily admits to having proclaimed himself the "King of the Mambo." When his brother, Pantaleon, began using the title, Perez sued him in a French court and won his case. But when Pantaleon died in 1983, a widely syndicated obituary was headed, "Mambo King dies in Milan."

That story, and the fact that Perez Prado had absented himself from the United States after the IRS had questioned his returns, led many to believe he was deceased.

In the fall of 1987 the name Perez Prado was on the marquee of the Hollywood Palladium, promoting his first local appearance in many years. That same day the theatre's house manager assured one journalist that the attraction was "his son or cousin, maybe."

The promoter of the event, reached a day before, said he had never met Prado and could not guarantee it was the original "Mambo King."

An hour before the show, the Palladium's longtime stage doorman confirmed the generally held belief that "the real guy has been dead for years."

When these remarks were repeated to

Marty Jackson

"The King of the Mambo" headed the bill at the Hollywood Palladium on September 12, 1987.

Prado in his dressing room, he laughed heartily and then walked onstage to a packed house. Anyone who remembered his pear-shaped body and trademark high collar recognized him immediately. To those who knew him only from recordings, his beat was unmistakable.

The King of the Mambo tours Mexico and Latin America and has recently begun making appearances in Japan, where his sound has gained wide popularity. He is the father of a son and a daughter. Perez and his wife, a nonprofessional, live in Mexico City.

149

Wayde Preston starred on Colt .45 *as "Christopher Colt," a government undercover agent who posed as a gun salesman. The half-hour western series ran on ABC-TV from October 1957 to September 1960.*

Wayde Preston

The TV hunk of the late fifties was born in Steamboat Springs, Colorado. His birthday was September 10, 1930. His original name was William Erskine Strange.

After attending high school in Laramie, he studied pharmacy at the University of Wyoming from 1947 to 1950. He then served as a First Lieutenant in the U.S. Army Artillery during the Korean War. After his discharge from service, he spent some time as a park ranger in Wyoming.

He was a licensed pilot and an employee of McDonnell Douglas Aircraft when, during a flight to San Francisco, he met a talent representative.

The agent introduced him to Carol Ohmart, an actress under contract to Paramount Pictures, who agreed with his professional assessment of the 6-foot 4-inch young man. After her coaching, he was signed to a term contract at Twentieth Century-Fox. In late 1956 the two were married.

Preston was not long at Fox and did nothing during that period but take various lessons. He went from that studio to Warner Brothers, where he was cast in *Colt .45,* the television show for which he is remembered.

In 1988 Preston spoke of his three seasons as "Christopher Colt," the undercover government agent in the Old West: "My contract paid $250 a week the first season. That sounds like good money for 1957, but they had me shooting six segments a month, which worked out to 80 to 85 hours a work week. The most I ever made, and that was after four years, was $750 a week."

Very much the man about town when *Colt .45* was on the air, Preston made front pages in 1959 when he challenged attorney Arthur Crowley to a judo match at a party given by Lance Reventlow.

Wayde walked off the set of *Colt. 45* in a well-publicized dispute with Warner Brothers. He did return to the series but found the working conditions and hours very much the same. When he staged a protest on the set, the show's producer suggested he quit. He did and virtually vanished from theatre and TV screens in the United States.

In 1958 Preston had established Commanche Aero Service, a flying firm that operated out of the Van Nuys Airport. After selling the company in the early sixties, he moved to Rome.

Preston had wider exposure in Europe than in the United States. He made more than three dozen features during the decade he lived in Italy. Most of these were of the genre known as "spaghetti westerns." He believes none were ever released in the United States and admits that he was only able to sit through "two or three of the things."

Wayde owns property in Reno, Nevada, and spends part of his time there but keeps an apartment off Wilshire Boulevard in Los Angeles.

Preston says he was married to Carol Ohmart for "something like five or six years." He has not been in touch with her since their divorce, but he has remained friendly with Rory Calhoun, Lee Van Cleef, and Clint Walker.

Wayde does not regret breaking his Warner Brothers contract, which had three years to run. He holds no grudges but has not had an acting job since his return to Hollywood. While Charlton Heston was a regular on *The Colbys,* Preston worked as his stand-in.

Marty Jackson

Wayde Preston lives in an area of Los Angeles known as the "Miracle Mile."

In 1960, when Jon Provost turned ten years old, he was given one of the original Lassie's puppies as a birthday present.

Jon Provost

The second boy to play Lassie's master on television was born in Los Angeles. His birthdate is March 12, 1950.

The Provost Family were members of an Episcopalian church near their home in Pasadena. Their older son and daughter attended the Sunday school classes while three-year-old Jon was placed in the church nursery school.

The woman who supervised the younger children thought him to be an exceptionally obedient child. When she read in Hedda Hopper's column that Warner Brothers was looking for a very young boy to play in the film *So Big* (1953), she brought it to the attention of Jon's mother.

Thirty-five years later Mrs. Provost recalled her attitude at the time: "My husband thought it was just a publicity stunt. I would never have given it another thought if the piece hadn't mentioned that the picture was to star Jane Wyman. She was one of my favorites, and I was so green I expected to see her in person at the audition. Anyway, I'd always wanted to see the inside of a movie studio."

Jon was chosen from more than two hundred little boys to play the star's son in the early part of the film. Later in the picture the character is played by Tommy Rettig.

Next Jon played the son of Bing Crosby and Grace Kelly in *The Country Girl* (1954).

The "Lassie" series was then owned by the late Jack Wrather. His wife, the former movie actress Bonita Granville, was the show's producer. When it was decided to replace Tommy Rettig, the first boy to play Lassie's master on TV, she chose Jon Provost. The casting was done on the strength of his work in *So Big*. He was never tested for the role.

The press were offered a wide choice of flavors of ice cream, and ice cream only, at the parties the Wrathers hosted for the preschooler at the Beverly Hills Hotel and New York's Plaza. It was generally agreed that he lacked the precociousness expected of child stars as well as the shyness found in most younger children. He appeared to like everyone every bit as much as they liked him.

The public, too, took to the "new" *Lassie*

Jon Provost and his family live in Santa Rosa, California. He is partnered in a real estate business with offices in nearby Sebastapol.

show and kept it among the highest rated every season that Jon Provost was on.

Along with his salary from *Lassie,* Jon received considerable fees for guest appearances on other shows with such stars as Jack Benny, Bob Hope, Danny Thomas, and Tennessee Ernie Ford. There were additional earnings from the line of boys' wear—shirts, pants, sneakers, and socks—marketed under the label "Jon Provost, Timmy of the *Lassie* series."

Mr. Provost, who was an aeronautical engineer, saved and invested everything his son made and placed it in trust for him. His mother was paid a salary and expenses for being with him on the set.

Jon Provost says he left the lead role after seven years because "I just got so sick of being called 'Timmy.' They called you that even when you're not shooting. After *Lassie* the only part I wanted to play was a cold-blooded killer. But there were no such offers, so I did *The Computer Wore Tennis Shoes* for Disney in 1970 and then I split."

His other feature films were: *Back from Eternity* (1956), *Escapade in Japan* (1957), *This Property Is Condemned* (1966), and *The Secret of the Sacred Forest* (1970).

For Provost the late sixties and seventies consisted of "university courses, traveling, protesting, having hair all the way down my back, wearing an earring—doing what everyone I knew was doing."

In 1980 Jon backed his car into one owned by a young woman who thought his name "sounded familiar." Three years later they were married. They live in Santa Rosa with their son, daughter, and two dogs of mixed breed. Provost is partnered in a real estate firm in nearby Sebastapol, California.

His older brother Bill, who appeared frequently on *Lassie* in small roles, is a telephone company executive in Los Angeles.

Because *Lassie,* like most TV shows, was never filmed in sequence, Jon used to watch it at home on Sunday evenings with the same interest as millions of other viewers. Now he runs videotapes of the programs for his own children.

"It was the fans who have made me understand why *Lassie* was so popular," he said recently. "The plots and dialogue might seem corny today, but the values don't. The only acting that would interest me in the least would be a *Lassie* reunion on TV. I'm very proud to have been part of the series."

153

William Reynolds is best remembered as "special agent Tom Colby," the role he played from 1967 to 1973 on The FBI, *but he was the star of three other TV series. On* Pete Kelly's Blues, *during the 1959–60 season, he had the title role. On* The Islanders, *which ran from October 1960 to March 1961, he played a commercial pilot. He also played a U.S. Army officer on* The Gallant Men, *a show that began a one-year run in the fall of 1962.*

William Reynolds

The film actor and star of several TV series was born William DeClercq Reynolds in Los Angeles on December 9, 1931. He was a pre-schooler when his mother, an aviatrix, died in a plane crash. His aunt brought him up in northern California.

"The highlights of my childhood," he says today, "were listening to serials on the radio after school and going to the movies on Saturday afternoons. Actors got to wear neat clothes, carry guns, and do things ordinary people would never experience. I knew that was the life for me. After I got to appear in some plays done on a San Mateo radio station, I couldn't wait to crash the movies."

Meyer Mishkin, the agent who still represents him, picked the teenager out of the cast of a little theatre production in Los Angeles. But the contract he got him with Paramount Pictures was terminated after six months. "I hadn't yet learned discipline," he explains. "I behaved very immaturely right from the start, but after I eloped and they couldn't even publicize me as the eligible bachelor, I was dropped."

He was not quite twenty years old when he married actress-model Molly Sinclair, who had recently been chosen "Miss Irish Linen." Before retiring from the profession, she appeared as an on-camera assistant to Johnny Carson when he hosted the quiz show *Earn Your Vacation* in 1954.

Reynolds made his debut as Mona Freeman's[8] boyfriend in *Dear Brat,* followed by *No Questions Asked* with Mari Blanchard and *The Desert Fox,* in which he played James Mason's son, all in 1951. After William Wyler chose him to portray the son of Lawrence Olivier in *Sister Carrie* (1952), William was signed to a contract with Universal.

Most of the pictures his studio made appealed to a youthful audience. Bill was in the Universal training program along with Rock Hudson, whom he supported in *Has Anyone*

Seen My Gal? (1952). His appearance in that movie, as well as several others that year—*Francis Goes to West Point, The Cimarron Kid,* and *Son of Ali Baba*—drew favorable remarks when they were previewed. When he was cast in the Tyrone Power starrer *Mississippi Gambler* (1953), he thought his career was about to ascend, but instead he was drafted into the army.

He worked in features until Jack Webb picked him for the lead in his TV show *Pete Kelly's Blues* in 1959. Among them were: *Cult of the Cobra* (1955) with Faith Domergue; *There's Always Tomorrow* (1956); *All That Heaven Allows* (1956); *Away All Boats* (1956); *Mr. Cory* (1957); *The Big Beat* (1958) with Gogi Grant;[8] and *The Thing That Could Not Die* (1958).

After heading the cast of the series *The Islanders* in 1960 and *The Gallant Men* in 1962, he made the pictures *A Distant Trumpet* (1964) and *Follow Me, Boys!* (1966). It was his part in the movie *FBI Code 98* (1964) with Jack Kelly[10] that brought him to the attention of the producers of *The FBI.* He joined the cast of the TV show in 1967 at the beginning of its third season on the ABC network.

As "special agent Tom Colby," Reynolds was featured, but Efrem Zimbalist, Jr., was the star of *The FBI.* In 1968, during his second season in the role, William gave a lengthy interview to *TV Guide* in which he was quoted as saying: "I want to be a movie star. I'd hate to be a second banana ten years from now, a forty-seven-year-old who never made it." The article was entitled "Unwrinkled, Unscarred, Unnoticed."

From 1970 to 1979 William Reynolds served on the board of the Screen Actors Guild, but he has no close friends within his profession. The last acting job he did was in 1985, when he substituted for Ed Nelson on the TV soap opera *Capitol* for two days.

William Reynolds is now an executive of an insurance agency that issues medical malpractice polices. The firm is owned by a group of physicians.

The Reynolds and their teenage son live in Van Nuys, California. Their daughter is away at college.

Recently, William Reynolds explained why he is now in the insurance business: "I was top billed in three series, but none ran longer than one season. Then I was on the hit show *The FBI* for six years, but I wasn't the lead, so I didn't emerge a star—even by TV standards. And by then I was overexposed in the medium. Actors in my category seldom get into features."

Bill was advised early in his career to be seen around town more in Hollywood, but neither he nor his wife cared for social life, and they have always lived quietly.

"Often actors are cast in roles just because they ran into the right person at the right time. You have to keep reminding people that you exist," he said in 1986. "Am I sorry? I don't know. I'm still thinking about it."

Elizabeth Russell **(standing and encircled)** *made more than twenty feature films but is best known for her brief appearance in* Cat People *(1942), in which she spoke only two words: "Moia sestra." Greeting Simon Simone* **(right, center)** *in Serbian as "my sister" indicated that she recognized the film's star as being, like herself, a person who at times became a cat. After the scene was filmed the director, Val Lewton, had the line dubbed by Ms. Simone since, unlike Elizabeth, she had a European accent.*

Elizabeth Russell

The actress known for her appearances in cult films was born on August 2, 1916, in Philadelphia. She is the oldest of the nine children of the Convery family.

Elizabeth became a close friend of Rosalind Russell when they were students at Rosemont College. After graduation, had Roz had her way, Elizabeth, too, would have enrolled at the American Academy of Dramatic Arts. Instead, Ms. Russell's older sister brought her to the attention of John Robert Powers, who headed one of the two top modeling agencies in the country. Her hauteur and high cheekbones immediately established her as a "cover girl" and drew interest from the movie studios.

By 1936, when she accepted a contract from Paramount Pictures, she had become the wife of Rosalind Russell's brother and the mother of a son. "None of my career makes any sense," she said in 1986, "except I know now that everything in life is for a purpose. I came to Hollywood with no real ambition because I rather looked down on pictures. I only came out because Roz insisted I give it a chance. Actually, I had made more money modeling, so Paramount was doing me no favor. When I was all but ordered to attend a party for Adolph Zukor, I complained bitterly. I had an early call the next morning and considered it an imposition. They didn't care for my attitude. Nor did I much like theirs. The name for me around the lot was 'Mrs. Rich Bitch.'"

Elizabeth had the lead in *Girl of the Ozarks* (1936) opposite Leif Erickson,[10] but it is for supporting roles in horror movies that she is well known to buffs. Randy Vest wrote in his *Films in Review* article on the actress: "It was producer Val Lewton who brought out her sultry, slightly sinister quality, which, with her sculptured facial beauty, were perfectly suited to his films."

For Lewton she played the "cat woman" in *Cat People* (1942) and the pathetic alcoholic in its quasi-sequel *Curse of the Cat People* (1944). In *The Seventh Victim* (1943), also under Lewton's auspices, she was a beautifully coiffed and gowned tubercular. *The Corpse Vanishes* (1942) has a following because of its star, Bela Lugosi. The same is true of *Bedlam* (1946), in which Elizabeth supported Boris Karloff. *Weird Woman* (1944) and *The Uninvited* (1944), two of her other credits, are of interest to fans of the genre.

Among her other movies are: *A Date with the Falcon* (1941), *Hitler's Madman* (1943), *Adventure* (1945), *So Big* (1953), and *From the Terrace* (1960).

Billie Burke was one of several actresses who refused to have Elizabeth in scenes with them because of her beauty. The two important might-have-beens in her career were when Elizabeth was tested by Cecil de Mille for the roles that eventually went to Jean Arthur[10] in *The Plainsman* and *The Prisoner of Zenda*. She tested for the latter opposite David Niven, but the two lost out to Madeleine Carroll and Ronald Colman.

After returning to the East Coast, Elizabeth acted on radio and toured in the play *Ramshackle Inn* with her friend Zasu Pitts. Eventually she settled into a maisonette in Washington, D.C.

Amaryllis Beime-Keyt

Elizabeth Russell in the lobby of the Beverly Hilton on her first visit to California in more than twenty years.

She recently completed writing the life story of her longtime friend, Maria Montez.

Elizabeth Russell is a Roman Catholic and a passionate anti-Communist.

In 1986 the former actress spoke of her experience in Hollywood: "Professionally, I found it very frustrating, and it was the ruin of my marriage. I considered myself a failure in pictures, but my husband felt sufficiently threatened by seeing me on the screen to take up serious drinking. George Sanders asked me to marry him repeatedly, but I *was* married. By the time we decided to get a divorce, he had stopped asking.

"Billy Grady, the casting director, certainly knew I was married when he arranged for my RKO contract. But, as soon as I was signed, he asked me out. I explained that I took marriage seriously and was dropped at the first option period."

Elizabeth Russell is amused by the many letters she receives from around the world inquiring about her role as the "cat woman" and commenting on how feline she appeared. "I'd always been told I was beautiful," she once said. "But I guess if cats are beautiful, people who are like cats can be beautiful. I just don't much fancy cats. I don't dislike them, but I am by no means what is called a 'cat person.'"

John Smith was very much a part of Hollywood's younger set during the fifties. Fanzines ran photos of him with the girls he took out in his red convertible: Terry Moore, Venetia Stevenson,[9] Lori Nelson,[9] and the daughter of Darryl F. Zanuck. Although it was not reported at the time, he also dated Phyllis Gates, his agent's secretary and the future Mrs. Rock Hudson.

John Smith

The leading man of movies and television was born in Los Angeles on March 6, 1931, and named Robert Van Orden.

While still in grammar school he attracted attention singing in St. Agatha's, his parish church. He became a member of the Bob Mitchell Boys Choir, appearing with them in the Bing Crosby starrers *Going My Way*

(1944) and *The Bells of St. Mary's* (1946) and on tour. Another member of the group at that time was Joseph Paparella, who became a comedian under the name of Steve Rossi.

Van Orden was a football hero at Susan Miller Dorsey Senior High School. After graduation he became a messenger at M-G-M. The casting director suggested the teenager to play James Stewart's younger brother in *Carbine Williams* (1952). It was a small part, and when his scenes were completed he went back into the mail room. During the filming he had become friendly with several of the young players under contract at the studio. When he began sitting in on their acting lessons, he was fired off the lot.

Dismissing his screen debut as a fluke, Van Orden then took a job selling silverware and china. On his day off he dropped by M-G-M, "just to say 'hello' to my friend in casting." During that brief visit he caught the attention of Henry Willson, an agent with a well-deserved reputation for discovering young talent.

"That's with two *l*s," Willson said as they shook hands.

"That was always Henry's opening line," said the actor thirty years after that introduction. "Little did I know, but the entire course of my life had just dramatically shifted."

Willson had turned complete unknowns into stars, giving them new names, such as Rock Hudson, Troy Donahue, and Tab Hunter. When he named his new "find" John Smith, the agent stated publicly that he was doing so to disprove the rumor that his clients got so much attention in the press because of their odd names.

When the young actor appeared in court to have his name changed to John Smith, the media was alerted and were informed that the Van Ordens were direct descendants of Peter Stuyvesant. One of his witnesses, the wife of Tommy Noonan, was named Pocahontas. The proceedings were pure Hollywood hype of the period.

His career as John Smith began in *The High and the Mighty* (1954). He and Karen Sharpe played newlyweds on a troubled airliner. The star and coproducer of that box-office hit, John Wayne, put him under personal contract.

John Smith headed the cast of some low-budget pictures and was featured in A productions. He had three TV series but never quite became a star in either medium.

His movies include: *We're No Angels* (1955); *Ghost Town* (1955) with Kent Taylor;* *Desert Sands* (1955) with Ralph Meeker* and Marla English;* *Friendly Persuasion* (1956); *Quincannon, Frontier Scout* (1956) with John Bromfield;* *Hot Rod Girl* (1956); *Women of Pitcairn Island* (1956) with Lynn Bari[8] and Arlene Whelan;* *The Kettles on Old MacDonald's Farm* (1957); *The Crooked Circle* (1958); and *Island of Lost Women* (1959) with Jeff Richards* and Venetia Stevenson.[9]

In 1964 Smith headed the cast of a stage production of *The World of Suzie Wong*. The following year he made his last feature, *Waco* (1966), which starred Jane Russell and Howard Keel.

John Smith was a running character on *That's My Boy*, a sit-com that ran from 1954 to 1959 and later in syndication. Its stars were Eddie Mayehoff[10] and Gil Stratton, Jr.* On *Laramie* he shared top billing with Robert Fuller. The television western was seen from 1959 to 1963 and featured Bobby Crawford, Jr. in the role of John's younger brother.

His second series, also a western, was *Cimarron City*, which starred George Montgomery* and Audrey Totter.[10] After Luana Patten guested on one of the segments, the young actress and John Smith began dating.

Clint Brown

Ruth Conte, John Smith's companion in recent years, author's associate Marty Jackson, and John Smith (right) posed for this photograph in mid-April 1987. Less than a week later Ms. Conte, a former Miss Ohio and the ex-wife of Edward G. Robinson, Jr., died in her sleep.

In 1960 John and Luana were married in a well-publicized Roman Catholic ceremony. They settled into a hilltop home, very near the estates of Dan Duryea and Errol Flynn.

In 1964, a year after *Laramie* left the air, the couple were divorced. The marriage was childless and ended without hard feelings. John and Luana still talk frequently over the telephone.

John Smith's only child, a daughter now in her twenties, was born out of wedlock.

He recently lamented to a fan about residual payments from his extensive work on television: "If in my day actors had the agreements regarding reruns that they have today, I'd be calling myself 'retired' instead of merely 'out of work.'"

In 1987 he could not remember the last time he had appeared in front of a camera. His only work as an actor in recent years has been doing voice-overs.

He lives by himself in the Crenshaw area of Los Angeles. Memorabilia from his career and Roman Catholic religious articles are scattered throughout the bungalow, the same house in which he grew up.

His stock response to anyone remarking on the commonness of his name is to ask, "So, how many John Smiths do you know?"

159

K. T. Stevens was directed by her father, Sam Wood, in the screen test she made for Columbia Pictures. K. T. spent a year under contract to that studio but made only one film, **Address Unknown** *(1944), opposite Peter Van Eyck. The German actor died in 1969.*

K. T. Stevens

The leading lady of stage and screen was born in Los Angeles on July 20, 1919. Her father, Sam Wood, who had directed some of the early films of Gloria Swanson, named his second daughter for the star.

Her screen debut was in *Peck's Bad Boy* (1921), the Jackie Coogan starrer which her father directed.

Her mother had performed on stage before her marriage and discouraged her daughter's interest in acting When she graduated from high school at age sixteen, Mrs. Wood insisted she go to college. A family squabble resulted in Gloria moving out of the family home and in with her older sister, Jeana Wood, who had a brief career in movies.

With money she had earned as an extra on her father's picture *Navy Blue and Gold* (1937) she took drama lessons and then went into summer stock in the east.

The first week she was in New York City she got a part in the road company of *You Can't Take It with You.* Next she played the title role in the Chicago company of *My Sister Eileen.*

Her first appearance in a New York play was in a walk-on part in *Summer Light* (1939), which starred Louis Calhern and was directed by Lee Strasberg.

Some of K. T.'s other Broadway appearances were in *The Man Who Came to Dinner* (1940), *Yankee Point* (1942), and *Nine Girls* (1943). She went on for Margaret Sullavan during one 1944 performance of *The Voice of the Turtle.*

She liked Gloria Swanson but did not identify with her. And she was determined not to be known as Sam Wood's daughter. When she signed with David O. Selznick, his press agent Russell Birdwell suggested she be billed as K. T. Until then she had gone by Katharine (for her favorite actress, Katharine Hepburn) Stevens.

The only experience she had before a camera under Selznick was in Gene Kelly's screen test. He never cast her in a film and did not loan her to another studio. She was permitted to act in plays and on radio's *Junior Miss.* The only real disappointment of her career came when the title role in *Rebecca,* which K. T. read for, went to Joan Fontaine.

She and Alfred Gwynne Vanderbilt were an "item" to the press during the early forties and at one point were reported to be engaged.

She had known Hugh Marlowe when they had appeared together in the play she considered her Broadway debut, *The Land Is Bright* (1941). After they were paired in the Chicago company of *The Voice of the Turtle* they began going together. The actors celebrated the end of a twenty-two-month run by getting married in 1946.

Although K. T. Stevens and Hugh Marlowe never made a feature together, they costarred in more than twenty summer stock productions. In the Broadway production of *Laura* (1947), which was produced after the film's release, she played "Laura" and he had the Dana Andrews part. They were frequently teamed on television dramatizations during the fifties.

On her own K. T. Stevens appeared on such television shows as *Alfred Hitchcock Presents, The Real McCoys, Wagon Train, Line-Up, Hawaiian Eye,* and *The Big Valley.*

In the mid-fifties K. T. and Russell Nype shared billing in the Chicago run of *The Tender Trap,* which they brought to Los Angeles's Carthay Circle Theatre in 1955.

Her father directed her in a small, but very showy role in *Kitty Foyle* (1941).

Her next film, *The Great Man's Lady* (1942), starred Barbara Stanwyck. K. T. said of her recently: "She is so beautiful on the screen because she is a very genuine person."

She found Joan Crawford very agreeable throughout the filming of *Harriet Craig* (1950), but she still cringes when she recalls the star's verbal abuse of their director: "Joan and Vincent Sherman were having an affair at the time, and she would light into him right in front of all of us. He'd just get red in the face. I don't think he ever responded."

Her other movies were *Port of New York* (1950), which was Yul Brynner's screen debut; *Vice Squad* (1953) with Paulette Goddard; *Tumbleweed* (1953) with Audie Murphy; *Missile to the Moon* (1959) with Tommy

In January 1988 K. T. Stevens began her third term as President of the Los Angeles local of the American Federation of Radio and Television Artists.

Marty Jackson

Cook* and the late Richard Travis; *Bob & Carol & Ted & Alice* (1969); *Pets* (1974); and *They're Playing with Fire* (1984).

After her 1967 divorce from Marlowe, Ms. Stevens withdrew from acting to get a degree in nursery school education. But in less than three years she felt "burned out" and resigned.

The Marlowe's son Jeffrey, born in 1948, is a physical therapist's aide. Christian, born in 1951, acted until 1984, when the volleyball team he captained won the Olympic Gold Medal. He has since become well known as a TV sportscaster under the name Chris Marlowe. Both sons are single.

Her self-imposed retirement ended when she joined the cast of *The Young and the Restless.* The role continued on the TV soap opera for more than five years, ending in 1982.

K. T. Stevens's best friend is Julie Warren, wife of John Forsythe. Her next-door neighbor in the Brentwood area of West Los Angeles is Evelyn Venable, leading lady of the early talkies and widow of Oscar-winning cameraman Hal Mohr.

161

The Freddie Stewart B musicals were made for the teenage market. Others in which he costarred with the late June Preisser were: Junior Prom *(1946),* High School Hero *(1947),* Sarge Goes to College *(1947), and* Vacation Days *(1947).*

Freddie Stewart

The singing star of Monogram Pictures was born Morris Joseph Lazor on March 25, 1925, on Manhattan's Lower East Side. His mother and father, a cantor in a Sephardic synagogue, spoke little English.

He left school during the Depression to contribute to his family income, working most of the year as a stock clerk. During the summers he had a job at the Kiamesha Lodge in the Catskills. For room and board, plus $2.50 a week, he sang, acted, and worked backstage as well.

The name Freddie Stewart was a composite of the names James Stewart, his favorite movie actor, and Freddie Bartholomew. A friend thought the fourteen-year-old Lazor resembled the young star.

By the late spring of 1939, Freddie Stewart

was part of the Cappy Barra Harmonica Band and came at that time under the management of Maurice Duke, then a top agent. By the beginning of 1940 he had been hired away from the group to be a vocalist with Clyde McCoy's orchestra. His salary went from $35 to $60 a week.

Although he toured with McCoy's aggregation for about a year, Freddie never adjusted his singing to their fast dance tempos. He left McCoy for a Monday-through-Friday, fifteen-minute radio show, *Freddie Stewart Sings,* which was broadcast from WJZ in New York City over NBC's Blue Network.

His screen debut was in *She's a Sweetheart* (1944), singing a song in support of Larry Parks and Jane Frazee. In October of the same year he joined Tommy Dorsey's orchestra as a vocalist. His starting salary was $500 a week. Stewart was heard with the Dorsey orchestra on radio's *Fitch Bandwagon,* at military installations, and in their recording of "I Dream of You" and "I'll Walk Alone."

Eventually Dorsey paid Freddie $650 a week, but the group's up-tempo arrangements and his sweet-soft tenor were never really a perfect blend. Nor was the singer comfortable working for Dorsey, because of the latter's drinking. Freddie does not remember ever having seen his employer when he was completely sober.

His manager sold his services to Monogram Pictures, a low-budget studio that was to produce eight musicals tailored to the teenage market and starring Freddie Stewart.

His leading lady in seven of those features was the late June Preisser, who had begun her career at the prestigious M-G-M. Although they always played sweethearts, Stewart remembers her thusly: "On her very good days she was extremely condescending. Like it was my fault she was now working in B pictures. Once, when she was supposed to slap my face, she hit me so hard I saw stars. Totally unnecessary and very unprofessional."

June Preisser once walked off the set of one of their pictures and obtained her release from Monogram Pictures. The studio immediately announced that Jean Porter* would be Freddie's next costar. After her agent convinced Preisser that no other studio was interested in her services, a new agreement was negotiated, but at a lower salary.

Freddie Stewart went from $2,500 per film to $3,000 at Monogram Pictures. Most of his movies were shot in eight to ten days. Along with starring in the teenager series, he was featured in another cheapie musical, *Louisiana* (1947).

Freddie sang in his pictures to the music of such bands as Russ Morgan, Gene Krupa, Charlie Barnet,[10] and Jimmy Dorsey. Some of the songs were his own, such as "Baby, You Can Count on Me," which was introduced in *Campus Sleuth* (1948) and was subsequently recorded by Peggy Lee.

After leaving Monogram in 1948, he played engagements throughout Europe and the

Freddie Stewart attended the annual reunion of Universal Pictures players, which was held in August 1987 in Glendale. He lives in Woodland Hills, California.

United States. For a while he had his own club, Freddie Stewart's Matchbox, in Miami Beach. He continued to make his living mainly in nightclubs until the early seventies.

In 1988 he toured Florida's condo circuit. His name was on the marquee of the Sportsman's Lodge in Studio City, California, several weeks of the year until its change of policy in 1987. But his chief source of income is as a fundraiser for charities, something he has done from his Woodland Hills home for more than fifteen years.

He has a teenage daughter, April Stewart, by the second of his two marriages, both of which ended in divorce. He is now single.

The man who turned down the subsequent hit "Now Is the Hour" says he has no regrets or complaints: "I still work from time to time, always in nice rooms and with good people. I do all the old stuff, which I sprinkle with Michel LeGrand and the Bergmans."

Freddie and Warren Mills, who played his sidekick in Monogram musicals, formed a friendship during the filmings that lasted until Mills committed suicide. Phil Brito,* Stewart's costar in *Music Man* (1948), his last picture, is the only person from his movie-making days with whom he is still in touch.

163

Joe De Rita (right) made personal appearances and movies with Moe Howard (left) and Larry Fine until 1969 when the last "Three Stooges" picture was produced. The above photo was taken backstage in 1960 at one of their nightclub appearances.

Joe Besser (top) became one of the "Three Stooges" after Shemp died suddenly in 1955. He made sixteen comedies with them before the association ended in 1958. Moe Howard (center) died on May 4, 1975. Larry Fine died on January 24, 1975.

"The Three Stooges"

Joe De Rita

When "The Three Stooges" films proved to be even more popular on TV than they had ever been in the theatres in their original release, a comeback was conceived. The late Norman Maurer, son-in-law of Moe Howard, proposed that the trio play to live audiences. Joe Besser, however, was unavailable.

The second and last of the Shemp replacements was Joe De Rita, a native of Philadelphia. His birthdate is July 12, 1909.

De Rita spent his childhood traveling with his parents, a stage technician and a dancer. He was a "banana" (comic) on the burlesque wheels for more than a decade before making a series of two-reeler comedies for Columbia Pictures in 1943.

De Rita has been married to a vocational nurse since 1966. He was married previously but has no children. Because of poor eyesight, he leaves his home only when he goes to his physician. He did not attend the ceremony in 1983 when "The Three Stooges" were honored with a star on Hollywood's Walk of Fame at 1560 N. Vine Street. Joe Besser unveiled the star. Most of De Rita's time is spent listening to classical music in the company of his cocker spaniel, "Missy."

Joe De Rita remained in touch with Moe until his death but had seldom heard from Larry. De Rita and Joe Besser lived within a few blocks of each other for many years but never met.

The last time De Rita performed was in *Kook's Tour*, a feature made in 1969, but never released theatrically or shown on television. It was also the swan song of the comedy team with the longest active career in motion-picture history.

Joe De Rita waving to a fan from the front porch of his North Hollywood home.

Marty Jackson

Joe Besser

Movie audiences first saw "The Three Stooges"[8] in *Soup to Nuts* (1930), a Rube Goldberg feature. By 1965, when *The Outlaws Is Coming!*, their last film, was released, only Moe Howard and Larry Fine remained of the original trio. Shemp Howard died in 1955, Curly Howard in 1952.

Moe and Larry considered continuing as a duo until their studio, Columbia Pictures, suggested Joe Besser. The comic became a Stooge in their short, *Hoofs & Goofs* (1957).

Joe Besser was born in St. Louis, Missouri, on August 12, 1907.

He ran away from home at a very young age by stowing away in one of the trunks of Howard Thurston, a famed magician of the day.

For five years in the early twenties he was part of the comedy act of Alexander & Olsen. Olsen was the brother of Ole Olsen of the team of Olsen & Johnson. Twenty years later Besser spent another five years with Olsen & Johnson's *Sons O' Fun*, a sequel to *Hellzapoppin'*, which played Broadway's Winter Garden in 1941 and toured nationally.

Besser was well established in his profession when he joined two of the original Stooges. His was a familiar voice over network radio to listeners of Jack Benny, Milton Berle, and Fred Allen. His character "Stinky,"

Joe Besser in 1987 in the doorway of his home in North Hollywood. He died on March 1, 1988.

Marty Jackson

which he did with Abbott & Costello, had brought him a following. Most of the mail he received, however, came from fans who knew him for his appearances in "Three Stooges" pictures.

Besser most likely would have continued with the Stooges had he not been committed when their hiatus ended. He worked steadily on TV and in features until the early seventies, when his wife's health began to fail.

In 1987 *Once a Stooge, Always a Stooge* was published. It is a book of Joe Besser's recollections, written with the assistance of Greg and Jeff Lenburg.

Joe Besser died suddenly on March 1, 1988. His biographers, Emile Sitka and Iris Adrian,[8] were the only professionals at his burial service.

165

Columnist Hedda Hopper once wrote of Grady Sutton: "With a moon face, pained expression, and sad grin, he's a master at stepping up in the middle of the most horrendous situation and delivering a tag line that rolls 'em in the aisles."

Grady Sutton

The quintessential screen boob was born in Chattanooga, Tennessee, on April 5, 1908.

He came to Hollywood during a summer vacation from his school in St. Petersburg, Florida, with his roommate, the younger brother of director William Seiter. Grady stayed with the director and his family and was invited onto the set of Seiter's current film, *The Mad Whirl* (1924). Before the May McAvoy starrer was completed, Seiter had given Grady a job as an extra. He has lived in the film capital ever since.

Laura LaPlante,[8] whom he supported in *Midnight Sun* (1926), showed him how to apply his makeup effectively. Thelma Todd, a fellow Hal Roach contractee, taught him camera angles.

Grady Sutton worked steadily in pictures throughout the twenties but did not receive screen credit until 1932. He once told Leonard Maltin in an interview that he never took his acting seriously enough to insist on billing.

He played a student in Harold Lloyd's *The Freshman* (1925), thereby getting himself typecast into the thirties as a collegiate. Universal used him in their *The Collegians* series, Hal Roach featured him in his *Boy Friends* shorts, and he supported Bing Crosby in *College Humor* (1933). As late as *Pigskin Parade* (1936) he was appearing in a beanie and raccoon coat on the screen.

His rolling eyes and blank look were as effective in talkies as they had been in silents. His slow southern drawl was a great plus for the characters he played.

Of all the many stars he supported in the approximately two hundred features he made, Katharine Hepburn is his favorite among the women. In *Alice Adams* (1935) he is the pudgy dunce who asks her to dance and then steps on her feet. The man he liked the best was W. C. Fields, who was a great enthusiast of Grady's. They met when he did *The Pharmacist* (1931), the two-reeler Fields made for Hal Roach. In *The Man on the Flying Trapeze* (1935), Fields had him as a live-in brother-in-law, so lazy he took after-breakfast naps. In *You Can't Cheat an Honest Man* (1939), another Fields starrer, Grady played a hapless carnival trainee.

Fields saw to it that parts were written for Sutton and insisted that only he could play them. When he agreed to make *The Bank Dick* (1949) for Universal, he stipulated that Grady was to play "Og Oggilby," the lardy fi-

166

ancée of Una Merkel,[8] who played his daughter. The studio strongly objected, but Fields held firm and got him as a screen son-in-law.

Kevin Thomas of the *Los Angeles Times* has written of him: "What Margaret Dumont was to Groucho, Grady Sutton was to W. C. Fields."

Some of his other movie roles were as the butcher's assistant in *Stage Door* (1937); the nasty hotel clerk in *Having a Wonderful Time* (1938); a stagehand in *It's a Wonderful World* (1939); an office worker in *Torrid Zone* (1940); a short-order cook in *The More the Merrier* (1943); Jean Arthur's suitor in *The Lady Takes a Chance* (1943); a victim of laughing gas in *The Great Moment* (1944); Lynn Bari's jilted date in *Captain Eddie* (1945); a telegraph operator in *A Bell for Adano* (1945); Kathryn Grayson's boyfriend in *Anchors Away* (1945); a counterman in a diner in *Nobody Lives Forever* (1946); a sissified secretary in *Philo Vance's Gamble* (1947); a bowler in *Madison Avenue* (1962); a spectator at the Ascot races in *My Fair Lady* (1964); an undertaker in *I Love You, Alice B. Toklas* (1968); and John Huston's poker cronie in *Myra Breckenridge* (1970).

One of his biggest laughs came in *Valiant Is the Word for Carrie* (1936). After Grady elopes with Arlene Judge, the couple return to her home, arriving in the middle of a knock-down, drag-out family quarrel. As the threats and shouts subside, Grady has one line: "Well, I sure am glad to meet you all." Another classic line was in *Three Smart Girls Grow Up* (1939), when he approaches Helen Parrish at a dance, asking, "Would you mind terribly if we had this dance?"

On television he played the bank manager on the *Batman* segment that featured Tallulah Bankhead as "The Black Widow." Grady was "Sturgis," butler to Phyllis Diller on *The Pruitts of South Hampton* during the 1966–67 season and was a regular on *The Odd Cou-*

Grady Sutton lives by himself in an apartment in the heart of Hollywood.

ple from 1970 to 1975.

Grady remained on good terms with Mae West until her death. He was in attendance at her funeral and memorial service. George Cukor was thought to be another close friend of long standing. For years Sutton was a regular at Sunday brunches hosted by the director. But, for reasons Cukor never understood, the actor refused all of his many invitations during the last years of his life.

At about the same time, Sutton was dropping other acquaintances of many years. He was also withdrawing professionally. He turned down the offer of a featured role in a revival of *A Funny Thing Happened on the Way to the Forum*.

Failing health and reluctance to drive after dark may account for his semi-seclusion. Grady was very close to his brother, who died in 1987.

The work he did in motion pictures is being seen and appreciated more today than when the films were originally released. He has more fans today than at any time in his career. When one approached him in 1988, he reluctantly signed an autograph. After being thanked, Sutton asked, "Haven't you anything better to do with your life than this?"

Gloria Talbott

Gloria Talbott's screen career was recently summed up by Tom Weaver and John Brunas in an article that ran in the magazine Fangoria: "She was the girl-friend of a rampaging one-eyed giant in The Cyclops (1957), legal ward of a werewolf in Daughter of Dr. Jekyll (1957), bride of an alien invader (played by Tom Tryon—above) in I Married a Monster from Outer Space (1958), and romantic rival of an ageless murderess in The Leech Woman (1960)."

The scream queen of the fifties was born in Glendale, California, on February 7, 1931. Her father owned a dry-cleaning establishment. Mrs. Talbott was a Christian Science practitioner.

Before she was three years old, Gloria could sing and dance. During high school she won a trophy for acting. By graduation she had done bit parts in *Maytime* (1937), *Sweet and Lowdown* (1944), and *A Tree Grows in Brooklyn* (1945).

While learning her craft performing in plays at the Eagle Rock Theatre, she fell in love with an aspiring young actor. They were married just before she turned eighteen.

In 1947 she was voted "Miss Glendale." The following year she played in *One Fine Day,* a stage vehicle for the screen duo Mary Boland and Charlie Ruggles. They played in San Francisco and Los Angeles, where Gloria came to the attention of professionals in the movie industry.

Northern Patrol (1953) was her first movie, but *We're No Angels* (1955) was hailed as her debut. In it she supported Humphrey Bogart and Joan Bennett[10]. The same year she appeared in two other successful, big-budget films, *Lucy Gallant* and *All That Heaven Allows.* Among her others were: *The Young Guns* (1956), *The Oklahoman* (1957), *The Kettles on Old MacDonald's Farm* (1957), *Cattle Empire* (1958), *Alias Jesse James* (1959), *Oklahoma Territory* (1960), and *Arizona Raiders* (1965).

Gloria tested for *Rio Bravo,* in which she would have played opposite John Wayne. She believes she lost the part to Angie Dickinson because "I just wasn't sexy enough." She was thought "too pretty" to play Debbie Reynolds' best friend in *A Catered Affair,* a role she wanted. She was signed for a running part on the *Mr. Novak* TV series but injured herself just prior to shooting and had to be replaced.

The only part she remembers refusing was on *Sea Hunt*—a part that required her to wear diving gear. She has a phobia about being in any small, enclosed space, stemming, she believes, from having been buried alive in another lifetime.

Gloria also appeared on many dramatic television programs from both the East and West Coasts throughout her career. However, she is remembered chiefly for her horror films: *The Cyclops* (1957), *Daughter of Dr. Jekyll* (1957), *I Married a Monster from Outer Space* (1958), and *The Leech Woman* (1960).

To film historian David Del Valle, Gloria always seemed cast against type in her horror films: "She had the face and figure of a hot heavy, but always played the sympathetic role."

Her first marriage ended in divorce after five years. She was then the wife of a physician for six years. They were divorced shortly after she gave birth to a baby girl. Her daughter, Mea Mullally, is now a wife, an aspiring actress, and has won three gold medals in local ice-skating competitions.

The last the public saw of Gloria Talbott was in the feature *An Eye for an Eye* (1966). When her daughter was born in 1967, she resolved to be with her as much as possible. The former actress still feels guilty that her son was virtually raised by her mother.

When she was thirteen years old she frequently flirted with a fifteen-year-old filling-station attendant. They met as adults and were married in 1970. Gloria's third husband is a Roman Catholic dentist. She is a student of metaphysics.

Gloria recently spoke of her life since her retirement from acting: "I'm a total contradiction to the feminist argument. My career

Richard Schaeffer

Gloria Talbott is the fourth generation of her family to live in Glendale, California.

was something I, alone, made happen. I worked constantly, but not through the casting couch, although Darryl F. Zanuck once chased me around his desk. Finally I burst out laughing. I don't know why women don't do that. It works every time. I should add that it was eight years before I worked again at Fox.

"The decision to quit was completely mine. My husband would give anything for me to be in movies or on TV, so he could brag to his patients and Irish relatives. I have a son-in-law who calls me 'Mom,' and three dogs and a cat. My life is corny as hell and I just love it!"

George Tobias had the ability to inject humor instantly, with a look or quick remark, into his portrayals of heavies. Many considered it his trademark. It was certainly his specialty. The subheading of his obituary in the New York Times was "Often Portrayed Genial Tough Guy."

George Tobias

The character actor was born on New York's Lower East Side to parents who acted in the Yiddish Theatre. His birthdate was July 14, 1901.

By 1920 George was appearing in a Neighborhood Playhouse production of Galsworthy's *The Mob.* Later he became a member of the Provincetown Players, acting there in O'Neill's *The Hairy Ape* (1922).

On Broadway he was seen in *What Price Glory?* (1924), *S.S. Glencairn* (1929), *Red Dust* (1929), *Black Pit* (1935), *Paths of Glory* (1935), *The Emperor Jones* (1936) with Paul Robeson, and *You Can't Take It with You* (1937).

His screen debut was in *Maisie* (1939), the first in the series. His earliest important film was *The Hunchback of Notre Dame* (1940).

Because of his impressive Broadway credits, the pact he signed with Warner Brothers in 1940 began at $2,000 a week and provided regular raises during the many years in which it was in effect. Eventually he bought up his contract after his loan-out fee rose to $85,000 per picture. He came, however, to regret leaving the Burbank lot. Although he worked steadily as a free-lance actor, Tobias missed the perks and security that came as a contractee to a major studio.

For many years the actor lived on a twenty-one-acre ranch in California's Lucerne Valley. Descriptions of those with whom he shared his home vary. Some of his friends refer to his guests as "old pals from back East." Others considered them "hangers-ons, spongers." All agree that Tobias enjoyed their company and that he never gave a thought to his financial future.

When he was not cast as a heavy, he was playing the "best friend" of the male lead. Tobias supported James Cagney in *Torrid Zone* (1940), *City for Conquest* (1940), *The Bride Came C.O.D.* (1941), *The Strawberry Blonde* (1941), *Captains of the Clouds* (1942), and *Yankee Doodle Dandy* (1942). He was in *Out of the Fog* (1941), *Air Force* (1943), *Between Two Worlds* (1944), and *Nobody Lives Forever* (1946) with John Garfield. He appeared with Ronald Reagan in *Juke Girl* (1942) as well as the all-star *Thank Your Lucky Stars* (1943) and *This Is the Army* (1943). In *Mis-*

sion to Moscow (1943) he played the chauffeur of the U.S. ambassador.

Some of his other movies were: *East of the River* (1940) with Brenda Marshall;* *Saturday's Children* (1940) with Anne Shirley; *They Drive by Night* (1940); *My Sister Eileen* (1942); *Passage to Marseilles* (1944); *My Wild Irish Rose* (1947); *The Set-Up* (1949); *Southside 1–1000* (1950); *Rawhide* (1951); *Ten Tall Men* (1952); *The Glenn Miller Story* (1954); *Marjorie Morningstar* (1958); *The Glass Bottom Boat* (1966); and *The Phynx* (1970).

He returned to Broadway in 1952, taking over the role of "Stosh" in *Stalag 17*. Tobias then joined the national touring company, which had John Ericson[8] in the leading role.

Tobias listed *Sergeant York* (1941), *Object Burma* (1945), *The Seven Little Foys* (1955), and a *A New Kind of Love* (1963) as his favorite films. He was especially proud that he was allowed to play the same role in the screen version of Cole Porter's *Silk Stockings* (1957) that he had created in the original Broadway company in 1955.

Of the many stars he worked with, James Cagney was the one he most admired. Two he did not care for were Ricardo Montalban and Ronald Reagan. George always insisted that when the future president broke his leg during a studio baseball game, it was because he had tripped him.

George Tobias never married. He courted actress Millicent Patrick off and on for almost forty years, proposing twice in attempts to keep her from marrying other men.

"I knew he didn't really want to marry," reasons Patrick, "so I went ahead. It resulted in two divorces. George and I dated until he died."

Sandra Gould knew George Tobias as a family friend and sometime babysitter since she was in grade school. Despite their age difference, she played his wife on *Bewitched*

Marty Jackson

Bachelor George Tobias shortly before his death in February 1980.

from 1966 to 1972, after the original "Gladys Kravitz," Alice Pearce, died. Like Patrick, Ms. Gould believes the actor was a man who "just didn't have the need for a wife."

He had a wardrobe that included everything from handmade western outfits from Nudie (a well-known Hollywood custom clothier) to Saville Row business suits and formal wear. But Tobias seldom wore anything other than casual attire. He is remembered by friends as a man who loved to eat, drink, and laugh. Sandra Gould and Millicent Patrick agree that George would have thoroughly enjoyed what happened to his corpse.

George Tobias died on February 27, 1980. Hours later his body was being driven from the hospital to a mortuary when there was a minor collision with another vehicle. While the two drivers stood on the curb exchanging information, two young men drove off in the undertaker's station wagon.

Within minutes it was found a few blocks away, where it had been left in the middle of a busy street, with both doors open and the motor running. Witnesses to the abandonment told police the thieves "ran like hell" into the traffic.

Playing opposite James Mason in The Seventh Veil *(1946) established Ann Todd as an international star. It resulted in David O. Selznick bringing her to Hollywood for* The Paradine Case *(1948). In France her coiffure became the rage. The French referred to the British actress as "La Petite Garbo."*

Ann Todd

The British star was born in Hartford, Cheshire, England, to Scottish parents. Her birthdate is January 24, 1909.

Her socially ambitious mother permitted Ann to act in school plays in the hope that she would acquire poise and self-confidence.

The shyness she felt as a teenager held her back scholastically and made relationships with her peers almost impossible. She trained for several years at Albert Hall.

Ann was still a student in 1928 when she replaced an ailing actress in the play *The Land of Heart's Desire*. Ian Hay, a well-known writer and a friend of her family, saw her performance and gave her a very small role in his next play, *A Damsel in Distress* (1929).

She appeared on the stage in London and New York and in British films throughout the thirties. One of her pictures, *South Riding* (1937) with Ralph Richardson, she ranks among the best of her career, but she remained virtually unknown until she appeared in *The Man in the Half Moon Street* (1939). That West End play starred Leslie Banks.

Three years later London saw her play "Peter Pan" to Alastair Sim's "Captain Hook." Her portrayal of the title role in *Lottie Dundass* (1943) was very well received by London critics and theatregoers who braved the Blitz.

It was *Lottie Dundass* that convinced producer Sidney Box to cast her as the young pianist in his film *The Seventh Veil* (1946). Because her name meant almost nothing on a movie marquee, there was a frantic search for a male star to play opposite her. After several weeks of shooting, James Mason accepted the role, just when it looked as though the production would have to be abandoned. *The Seventh Veil* won the Oscar for the Best Original Screenplay and Ann was immediately pacted by J. Arthur Rank.

Todd had received a contract offer from a Hollywood studio after she was seen in *Vacation from Marriage* (1945). She declined, because no specific project was promised. But she leapt at the chance to play under Hitchcock's direction in *The Paradine Case* (1948). Despite the prestige of the Selznick picture, it meant little to her career. It was not a box-office hit, and most of the publicity went to the newcomers Louis Jourdan and Valli. She lingered in the United States long enough to appear in full-page, color magazine advertisements for Chesterfields and costar with Cary Grant on radio's *Suspense*.

Ann Todd's first marriage, to the grandson of Lillie Langtry, the famed "Jersey Lily" of the Belle Epoque, was brief. Her next was to Nigel Tangye, a writer and aviator. In 1949 he filed for divorce, naming David Lean as respondent. At the same time, Lean's wife, Kay Walsh, named Ann in her petition for divorce. She became the director's wife as soon as their decrees were final.

During the five years the Leans were together, he directed her in *One Woman's Story* (1949), *Madeleine* (1950), and *Breaking the Sound Barrier* (1952). Ann had done the latter on the London stage in 1944 under the title *The Rest Is Silence*. The playwright Terrance Rattigan had written the female lead with her in mind. When they divorced in 1957, the couple had been separated for several years.

Her successes in the United States were on television. The premier of *The Alcoa Theatre* in 1955 costarred Ann and Wendell Corey.

Her other West End appearance of note was in *Duel of Angels* (1958). She took over when Claire Bloom left the cast, playing opposite Vivien Leigh under the direction of Jean-Louis Barrault.

Most of her energies during the last twenty-five years have been channeled into the writing of two novels and her autobiography, and the producing and directing of documentaries. The half-hour films were well received when they played in cinemas in the United Kingdom.

Her filmmaking career began in 1964, when she woke from a sound sleep with the word *Katmandu* before her eyes. Within

Roger Karnbad

Cornel Wilde[10] escorted his old friend Ann Todd to the American Cinema Awards in 1987. It was the first time the British star had been in Hollywood in almost forty years.

three weeks Ann had assembled a crew and flown to that city, the capital of Nepal. She made brief on-camera appearances in the pictures. Others in the series are on Iran, Jordan, Greece, Egypt, and Australia. They were well received in the United Kingdom, where they played in cinemas as the second feature.

Ann Todd has written in her memoir, *The Eighth Veil,* and stated in interviews, that she never felt she had the true nature of an actress: "The only times I've been able to really bring a part to life is when I've found things very much like myself in the character. I was that desperately insecure girl in *The Seventh Veil,* and I found much in 'Lady Macbeth,' which I did at the Old Vic, to identify with. Probably most revealing of all is that I loathe to be photographed and cringe inwardly when I hear applause."

Among her interests are UFOs, out-of-body experiences, and human auras. She is a firm believer in most forms of parapsychology.

173

Playing a handsome young Scot who is doomed by a fatal disease in The Hasty Heart (1950) *established Richard Todd as an international star. The understated machismo he projected brought him many roles as a British military officer.*

Richard Todd

The movie star of the fifties was born in Dublin, Ireland, on June 11, 1919. His original name is Richard Andrew Palethorpe-Todd. As a toddler he was taken to live in India where his father, a physician in the British army, was stationed.

After schooling at Shrewsbury and then Sandhurst, Richard became one of the founding members of the Dundee Repertory Company. At the outbreak of World War II in Europe, he enlisted in the British army's Sixth Airbourne Division. On D-day he was one of those who parachuted into Normandy.

Todd returned to the repertory company after the war but was soon chosen to play a dour young Scot with a fatal disease in *The Hasty Heart.* He did the part in the West End for eighteen months and was then cast in the movie version, which was shot in England.

Richard Todd remembers Ronald Reagan, who supported him in *The Hasty Heart* (1950), as disliking the weather, food, and working conditions during the filming. He recalls, also, that the future president was very helpful to him in learning to act before a camera. He described Reagan to one journalist as "as generous and professional an actor as I've ever worked with."

The Hasty Heart did very well at the box office, with most of the notices singling out Richard as a handsome new star. In England he was awarded *Picturegoer* magazine's Gold Medal.

His next motion picture, Hitchcock's *Stage Struck* (1950), was less successful, probably due to the basic dishonesty of the script. But Todd was well cast as the intense younger man in love with and betrayed by Marlene Dietrich.

Walt Disney put the actor's dashing quality to good use in *The Story of Robin Hood* (1952), *The Sword and the Rose* (1953), and *Rob Roy* (1954).

After the Disney productions, he was pacted by Twentieth Century-Fox, where he was starred in *A Man Called Peter* (1955).

The feature costarred Jean Peters[9] and was based on the life of a Scotsman who became chaplain of the United States Senate. He was then cast in *The Virgin Queen* (1955), playing Sir Walter Raleigh to Bette Davis's Elizabeth I. In *D-day, the Sixth of June* (1956), he had one of his many roles as a British military man. Another of the kind, in the same year, was in The *Dam Busters,* which was made in England and became one of that nation's box-office champions.

Among his other screen credits are: *Interrupted Journey* (1951) with Valerie Hobson[10]* *Venetian Blind* (1952) with George Coulouris; *Portrait of Clare* (1951) with Jeremy Spenser;* *Lightning Strikes Twice* (1951) with Ruth Roman; *Flesh and Blood* (1951), playing a dual role opposite the late Joan Greenwood; *The Assassin* (1953) with Eva Bartok;* *24 Hours of a Woman's Life* (1952) with Merle Oberon; *Marie Antoinette* (1956) with Michelle Morgan; Otto Preminger's *St. Joan* (1957); *The Naked Earth* (1958) with Juliette Greco; *Intent to Kill* (1959) with Betsy Drake; *Yangze Incident* (1957) with Keye Luke; *Breakout* (1961) with Lee Patterson; *Crime Does Not Pay* (1962) with Danielle Darrieux;[10] *Never Let Go* (1963) with Peter Sellers; *The Battle of the Villa Fiorita* (1965) with Maureen O'Hara* and Rossano Brazzi;* *Operation Crossbow* (1965); *The Love-Ins* (1967); *Subterfuge* (1969) with Gene Barry; *Dorian Gray* (1970) with Helmut Berger; *Asylum* (1972); *The Big Sleep* (1978); and *Home Before Midnight* (1979).

In 1967 Todd and his wife of many years were divorced. He was then named corespondent in the divorce of a former model, who was more than twenty years his junior. In 1970 she became the second Mrs. Todd.

He produced one of his starring movies. *Why Bother to Knock* (1965). He has since become involved in play production both in

Laurie Butcher

Richard Todd recently at the stage door of London's Mayfair Theatre prior to a performance of The Business of Murder. *The thriller, which the actor also produced, entered the eighth year of its run in 1988, with Todd in the leading role.*

the West End and on tours of the United Kingdom.

When not acting or producing, Richard lives with his wife and son on the large dairy farm he owns and operates in Sussex, England.

In the late sixties Todd returned to the stage as "Lord Goring" in *An Ideal Husband.* He took the Oscar Wilde play on tour throughout the Republic of South Africa. In the early seventies England saw him in revivals of *The Constant Husband* and *The Winslow Boy* on stage.

On television he was seen opposite Dyan Cannon in *Jenny's War,* a made-for-TV movie that ran in 1985 in the United States.

Richard Todd survived a heart attack in 1975 but continues to smoke approximately one pack of cigarettes a day.

Richard Todd and Ann Todd share the same shield and tartan but are not related.

The first volume of his memoirs, *Caught in the Act,* was published in England in 1987.

Raquel Torres made her debut in White Shadows of the South Seas *(1928), a silent feature that had synchronized sound effects and music added. It was a box-office hit and resulted in the actress being signed to a contract with Metro-Goldwyn-Mayer.*

Raquel Torres

The screen beauty was born Paula Marie Osterman in Hermosillo, Mexico. Most sources give November 11, 1908, as her birthday. After her French-Spanish mother died, she and her younger sister Renee were placed in a boarding school run by nuns.

The teenager was movie-struck at a very early age, but her father, a prosperous German-born businessman, refused to take her yearnings for an acting career seriously. But, when a man he knew, an officer of the Mexican consulate, offered to bring his older daughter to the attention of Metro-Goldwyn-Mayer, he relented.

The diplomat had learned from his friend, director W. S. Van Dyke, that the studio was looking for a complete unknown to be featured opposite Monte Blue in a big-budget film. An "exotic, virginal type" was being sought to play a beautiful South Seas native girl.

Paula was introduced to the public as Raquel Torres in *White Shadows of the South Seas* (1928), which was filmed mostly in the Marquesas Islands. She was chaperoned on location by her sister. Her father died during the making of the movie.

Her next major film was *The Bride of San Luis Rey* (1929), the screen adaptation of Thornton Wilder's Pulitzer Prize-winning novel, which starred Lily Damita* and Duncan Renaldo. There followed: *The Desert Raid* (1929) in support of Tim McCoy; *The Sea Bat* (1930) with Charles Bickford and Nils Asther; *Under a Texas Moon* (1930) with Myrna Loy and Frank Fay; *Aloha* (1931) with Ben Lyon[8] and Thelma Todd; *So This Is Africa!* (1933) supporting the comedy team of Wheeler & Woolsey; and *The Woman I Stole* (1933).

She is probably best known for her appearance in one of her last films, the Marx Brothers vehicle *Duck Soup* (1933).

She had the lead in *Adam Had Two Sons,* a play that had a brief Broadway run in 1932.

From the beginning of her career Raquel and her sister had enjoyed the Hollywood party circuit. Renee was seen frequently with John Gilbert, and it was expected that Raquel would marry superagent Charles K. Feldman. But in 1934 she became the wife of Stephen Ames, a multimillionaire and an intimate of movie moguls Harry Cohn and Louis B. Mayer. He had recently been divorced from another screen personality of the period, the beautiful Adrienne Ames. He eventually produced more than a dozen features including *Sinbad, The Sailor* (1947), *The Boy with Green Hair* (1949), and *Ride, Vaquero!* (1953).

Ames was less than enthusiastic about Raquel acting in movies. As Renee recalls: "My sister began asking herself why she was getting up every morning at 5 A.M. and turning down invitations when she was on a picture. So she quit." Her last time on the screen was with Greta Nissen in *Red Wagon,* which was released in the United States in 1935 but had been made two years earlier in England.

After retiring from the screen Raquel Torres lived for more than fifty years in a style few movie stars ever achieve.

The Ameses commissioned architect Joseph Reith to design a mansion to be built in Bel-Air in a style that has been described as Hawaiian-modern. They liked it so much they had an exact duplicate constructed in the Malibu colony. Raquel maintained both homes for the rest of her life.

In 1959, five years after the death of Stephen Ames, she became the wife of former actor Jon Hall. Throughout their brief marriage, which ended in a divorce, Raquel financed a number of Hall's inventions and business schemes. He remained a friend and a frequent guest in her homes until his death in 1980.

Former Hearst columnist May Mann said of her close friend: "Raquel was always used to grande luxe, but she never became jaded about it. She thoroughly enjoyed her wealth and was very generous with it. I once expressed absolute awe over a huge ring she was wearing, one of many. She slipped it off right there and insisted I take it. I was embarrassed and astonished. Several days later when I tried to return it she said, 'I've always wanted to give you something I *knew* you liked. It's yours. Thank you for allowing me to make you happy.'"

Jon Hall

This, the last photograph of Raquel Torres, was taken by her former husband, Jon Hall,[8] shortly before he committed suicide in December 1980.

Her sister Renee, the wife of actor Edward Ashley, said recently: "My beautiful sister married a very handsome and enormously rich man. They remained deeply in love until the day he died. Raquel had it all—everything!"

Just before guests were to arrive for one of their frequent parties Raquel sprayed each of the many rooms with Joy, her favorite perfume.

After suffering a stroke in June 1987, the former actress was attended by round-the-clock nurses. From her oversized bed Raquel had a view of her tiered gardens, which led to the shores of the Pacific Ocean. The two steps leading to her raised bed were upholstered in ermine, which matched the bed throw.

Raquel Torres is buried in an alcove above her husband in the Hall of Celestial Peace at Forest Lawn Cemetary in Glendale, California.

Teddy Getty, one of the wives of billionaire J. Paul Getty and one of her closest friends, was one of the mourners at her Roman Catholic funeral. Another was her only child, an adopted daughter, who inherited two million dollars, a fraction of the estate of Raquel Torres.

Beverly Tyler considers her scenes with Tom Drake in The Green Years *(1946) to be the best work of her career. When they made the screen version of A. J. Cronin's best-selling novel, Beverly and Tom were two of M-G-M's most promising young contract players. They appeared together again in* The Beginning Or the End *(1947).*

Beverly Tyler

The screen ingenue was born in Scranton, Pennsylvania, on July 5. Her name was originally Beverly Jean Saul.

Her mother, a secretary, saw that her daughter had music lessons from a very early age. Beverly was in her early teens when, after a summer with one of the best vocal coaches in the country, she debuted on radio.

Her first professional job was singing on *Aunt Jenny's Real Life Stories.*

After a radio actress remarked that Beverly should be heard by "someone at M-G-M," Mrs. Saul took her daughter to the Manhattan offices of that studio, then best known for screen musicals. Although they arrived without an appointment or a contract, when they left she had been pacted.

For two years she took various lessons and attended the lot's "Little Red Schoolhouse." Her first time on screen was a bit part in *The Youngest Profession* (1943) in support of Virginia Weidler, who by then had become Beverly's best friend.

M-G-M initiated and publicized her dates with Tom Drake. On her own Beverly saw a lot of Rory Calhoun for a while. She broke off her relationship with Johnny Stompanato after a studio executive advised her of his unsavory reputation. He then began dating Lana Turner.

Her path again crossed that of Lana Turner when she was cast in *My Brother Talks to Horses* (1947) opposite Peter Lawford. Her leading man informed her that Ms. Turner, whom he was then dating, had "more appeal in her little finger than you could muster in a year."

At the urging of Kitty Carlisle, the still teenage Beverly auditioned and signed for the lead in *Firebrand of Florence* (1945), but the Kurt Weill musical ran for only four months on Broadway.

Beverly spent the evening of her twenty-first birthday as guest soloist with the San Francisco Symphony Orchestra under the baton of Miklos Rozsa.

Despite excellent notices in the title role of the musical *Miss Liberty* at the Greek Theatre in Los Angeles in 1950, Beverly never emerged as a singer on the screen.

She was tested for *That Midnight Kiss* and *The Romance of Rosy Ridge,* roles that boosted the careers of Kathryn Grayson and Janet Leigh, respectively.

Beverly was the first girl Audie Murphy dated in Hollywood and his leading lady in *The Cimarron Kid* (1951).

Her other screen credits include: *Chicago Confidential* (1947); *The Fireball* (1950) with Mickey Rooney and Marilyn Monroe; *The Palamino* (1950) with Jerome Courtland; and *The Toughest Gun in Tombstone* (1958) with George Montgomery.

On television she sang on *Cavalcade of Stars* and *Shower of Stars.* On *Climax* she was seen in a dramatic role. When Jane Nigh left the role of "Lorelei Kilbourne" on *Big Town,* Beverly took her place on the series in 1953.

In 1962 Beverly married comedy writer-director Jim Jordan, Jr., the divorced husband of Peggy Knudsen, and then retired.

Marty Jackson

Beverly Tyler and her husband, Jim Jordan, Jr., the son of the famed show business couple known professionally as "Fibber McGee and Molly."

In 1972 the Jordans moved to Nevada where they were already involved in land development. Their son, a student, lives with them in a ranch home on the outskirts of Reno.

After appearing in several plays in recent years at Reno's Little Theatre, Beverly has come to realize that she misses performing. Now that her husband has retired, he has no objection to her working.

Beverly Tyler has said: "My mother showed such promise as a young girl she was asked to join a dance company, but her mother would not permit it. What happened to me was none of my doing and yet I enjoyed it very much."

When they were in Hollywood for the funeral of his father, Jim "Fibber McGee" Jordan, in April 1988, Jim Jordan, Jr., commented on his wife's career: "As a very young child she showed such promise as a pianist, her teacher begged her mother not to concentrate on her voice. But she developed into a lovely singer. That's why she was brought to Hollywood, but about the only time they let her sing was in *Best Foot Forward.* Such a waste!"

Beverly Tyler still plays the piano but never sings.

179

When Virginia Valli married Charles Farrell on Valentine's Day, 1931, her screen career was virtually over. But within a very short time she would have another career as the "First Lady of Palm Springs."

Virginia Valli

The star of silents, once billed as "the outdoor girl of films," was born in Chicago, Illinois. Her birthdate was June 12, 1898. Her family name was McSweeney.

Virginia began as a dancer and got her acting experience in a Milwaukee stock com-

pany. She did some film work at the Essanay Studios in Chicago before going to New York City, where she played ingenues on stage.

The moviegoing public first saw Virginia in the motion pictures she made at Chicago's Essanay Studios. *Efficiency Edgar's Courtship* (1917) with Taylor Holmes and Rod La-Rocque was one.

She was brought to Hollywood as leading lady to the Broadway star Bert Lytell in three films. Among her screen credits are: *Plunger* (1920), *The Silver Lining* (1921), *The Village Blacksmith* (1922), *A Lady of Quality* (1923), *Wild Oranges* (1924), and *Siege* (1925).

By the mid-twenties Ms. Valli was Universal Pictures' most prominent female star and remained so until Laura LaPlante somewhat overshadowed her in about 1928.

Virginia Valli costarred with Thomas Meighan in *The Confidence Man* (1924) and *The Man Who Found Himself* (1925) and with George O'Brien in *East Side, West Side* (1927) and *Paid to Love* (1927). She and Adolphe Menjou were supported by Louise Brooks in *Evening Clothes* (1927). Virginia was the star of *Ladies Must Dress* (1927), which introduced Nancy Carroll[8] to the screen, and of *The Storm* (1927), with House Peters.

Virginia Valli was a perfect example of a star whose established salary was considered too high at a time when studios were incurring large expenses in converting to sound films.

Her voice was fine, but after making *Isle of Lost Ships* (1929) for First National, a "major," she did *Guilty* (1930) at Columbia, which was a definite step down professionally. Tiffany, where she filmed *The Last Zeppelin* (1930) was on "Poverty Row." Two others who starred in prestigious silents, Conway Tearle and Ricardo Cortez, were in it with her. Those were her last films.

Virginia was known among her set for her

intelligence and flair for clothes. When she married Charles Farrell in 1931, he was considered one of Hollywood's most eligible and best-looking bachelors. He was also almost a decade younger than Virginia. His name had been linked with Janet Gaynor and Lois Moran,[10] among others. Unlike fans, Hollywood insiders were not surprised by the match, since the couple had been seeing each other quietly for several years.

Although Virginia had left the screen, she was still very much in the Hollywood social scene. The Farrells lived in a house across from Gloria Swanson's. Without a tennis court or swimming pool, it was considered modest by Beverly Hills standards. But the newlyweds had open invitations to play tennis on Lawrence Tibbett's court and swim at the Richard Barthelmess estate.

On Christmas Day, 1934, the Racquet Club opened in Palm Springs. The Farrells and Ralph Bellamy had bought several buildings on fifty-three acres of land for $35,000 and turned it into a private club. When their partner found the enterprise too time-consuming, they bought him out. Within only a few years it became *the* place in the desert, especially among what was considered the elite in filmdom.

During World War II, while Charles served in the United States Navy, Virginia ran the Racquet Club by herself. She remained active in its management until 1966, when she suffered a stroke. From 1948 until 1954 Charles Farrell served as the mayor of Palm Springs. Unofficially, the couple had long been considered "Mr. and Mrs. Palm Springs." Virginia retained the title until she died on September 24, 1968.

Her funeral mass was said by her nephew, a Roman Catholic priest.

Virginia Valli Farrell is buried in the Home of Peace Cemetery in Palm Springs, California.

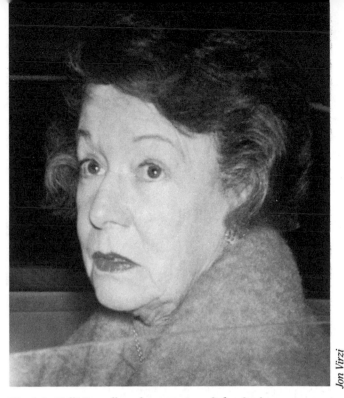

Jon Virzi

Virginia Valli-Farrell on her way to a Palm Springs party shortly before her death in 1968.

Marty Jackson

Charles Farrell recently in his Palm Springs home.

181

Norma Varden even tittered with hauteur. Her laughter gave the impression that she had just smelled something foul.

Norma Varden

The character actress-comedienne was born in London on January 20, 1898. Her father was a retired sea captain who was married late in life to a much younger woman.

Norma, at a very early age, showed promise at the piano. The Vardens, who were financially secure, took her to Paris for advanced study. Considered a prodigy, she concertized in England while still in her early teens.

But by the time she had reached eighteen, Norma had become aware of the difficulties of establishing a career as a concert artist. After her father died, she became a professional actress. At the Guildhall School of Music she had been taught by Kate Rorke, a well-known actress on the London stage. Rorke and her schoolmate, Edna Best, encouraged her to go on the stage.

When Norma Varden debuted as "Mrs. Darling" in *Peter Pan,* she was younger than the actors playing her children. She toured with a Shakespearian repertory company before making her West End bow in *The Wandering Jew* (1920). She supported the play's star, Matheson Lang, again in *Carnival* (1923) and was the "Player Queen" to his "Hamlet" in the first modern-dress production of the classic in 1925.

Norma was well established as a serious actress in England when she made her first trip to the United States in 1929. Producer John Golden cast her in *When in Rome,* but the play never made it to Broadway. Upon her return to London, she joined the group of actors who performed at the Aldwych Theatre. The comedic aspects of Norma's height (5 feet, seven and a half) and her imperiousness were used to maximum effect, especially when she played opposite the short, wimpish Robertson Hare.

Two of the Aldwych Farces, as they were known, were made into motion pictures—*A Night Like This* (1932) and *Turkey Time* (1933)—with Ms. Varden and Mr. Hare in their original roles.

By the early thirties Norma Varden was not only a star in Great Britain, but one who had proven her skills at both the classics and comedy.

Among her other English pictures were: *The Iron Duke* (1935) and *East Meets West* (1936), both with George Arliss; *The Amazing Quest of Ernest Bliss* (1936), Cary Grant's first English film; *Fire over England* (1937) with Raymond Massey;[8] *Rhythm Racketeer* (1937) with Judith Wood;[9] *You're the Doctor* (1938) with Googie Withers;[10] and *Shipyard Sally* (1939) with Gracie Fields.

When the actress and her widowed mother came to Hollywood, it was only supposed to be for a visit. But the outbreak of World War II made it seem practical to remain there, at least for the duration. Norma was kept busy with screen work, and she was happy to accommodate Mrs. Varden, who had quite fallen in love with the climate. Norma now regards the move, which proved permanent, as a great professional compromise.

The longest running of Norma's many radio roles was as Basil Rathbone's housekeeper on *Sherlock Holmes*. On television she played Jack Benny's mother. She was a regular on *The Betty Hutton Show* as the star's aunt and as the next-door neighbor on *Hazel*. Her proudest accomplishment on TV was as a pioneer woman on *Bonanza,* a role she played without a trace of her very English accent.

The most notable of the parts she played in sixty-five American movies are: Robert Benchley's wife in *The Major and the Minor* (1942); the woman whose husband's pocket gets picked in *Casablanca* (1942); a phony countess in *Fancy Pants* (1950); George Sander's bitchy mother in *Jupiter's Darling* (1955); the wealthy woman whom Tyrone Power is accused of murdering in *Witness for the Prosecution* (1958); the von Trapp's housekeeper in *The Sound of Music* (1965); Rock Hudson's mother-in-law in *A Very Special Favor* (1965); and the hypochondriac patient of *Doctor Doolittle* (1967). She is the woman Robert Walker almost strangles in

Author's associates Michael Knowles and Lester Glassner during a visit with the eighty-nine-year-old actress in her Carpenteria, California, home.

Strangers on a Train (1951), and in *Gentlemen Prefer Blondes* (1953), her husband, Charles Coburn, gives her diamond tiara to Marilyn Monroe.

Norma had a close, long-running relationship with a well-known criminal attorney, who is deceased. She has never married.

The Vardens had been living in Santa Barbara for several years when Norma's mother died in 1969. She has been virtually retired since then.

In 1987 she spoke of what might have been: "Because my darling mother was kept happy and healthy by the lovely weather, and that is what was most important to me, we stayed. But I never got used to the way one is cast here. It's based on one's salary. If your agent can get you so much per week, then you are considered only for parts that are budgeted at that amount. In 1934 I was a star when I made my third English film, *Evergreen*. Yet I played a small role as a barmaid. But it was a *good part*. You can't do that here. I don't mean to sound ungrateful for the success I've had in American films, but this system is so limiting for serious actors."

Yvette Vickers began her career as TV's "White Rain girl." Film historian David Del Valle once said of her: "Honey-eyed and blonde, she always appeared to be right out of a Tennessee Williams play. Whether confronting a giant leech or a 50-foot woman, Yvette managed to be sexy."

Yvette Vickers

The quintessential floozie of fifties films was born Yvette Vedder in Kansas City, Missouri.

Her parents, who were musicians, brought their family to California when Yvette was in grammar school.

Although the Vedders were not Catholic, Yvette was taught in high school by nuns. For a time she considered converting and entering the convent, but ballet classes made her interested in a more public life.

She was sixteen years old when she entered UCLA, where her majors were motion pictures and theatre arts. She graduated with a Bachelor of Arts degree.

Her screen debut was in *Sunset Boulevard*

(1950) as a giggly girl who monopolizes a telephone during a New Year's Eve party. She was still in high school when director Billy Wilder spotted her at a party and gave her the bit. At that point Yvette was interested in writing and made no attempt to pursue acting.

After college she became involved in little theatre and appeared in eight plays before James Cagney chose her for *Short Cut to Hell* (1957), which he directed. The same year she was seen in *The Sad Sack* and *Reform School Girls.*

Yvette Vickers has appeared in fifteen features, a dozen television programs, and was seen on Broadway in *The Gang's All Here* (1959). She is best known, however, for her roles in two science-fiction films that are revered by cultists.

Jim McPherson of the *Toronto Sun* remembers her in *The Attack of the 50 Ft. Woman* (1958) playing "the little roadhouse tramp found fooling around with the outsized heroine's husband. In one of the great scenes of the genre, the 'Woman'—looking about the size of a five-story building—lifts the roof off the joint where 'Honey Parker'— that's Yvette's name in this—is carrying on with her man. Unforgettable!"

Ted Okuda, in his 1987 article for *Filmfax* magazine, described her role of 'Liz' in *Attack of the Giant Leeches* (1959) as "little more than a cheap tart, and Yvette plays the part for all it's worth. 'Liz' wiles away her time primping herself in front of her dresser mirror and lounging seductively in a Japanese houserobe as she rubs skin lotion on her shapely legs. For Yvette Vickers fans, this is nirvana."

Although they were highly profitable pictures, both were "B"'s, which was not in her favor according to Hollywood's casting code of the time. Neither added to the momentum of her career.

Juvenile Jungle (1958), *I, Mobster* (1958), *Pressure Point* (1963), *Beach Party* (1963), *What's the Matter with Helen?* (1971), and *Vigilante Force* (1978) were some of her other motion pictures.

Directors and fans were impressed with the dimension she managed to bring to the women she played, no matter how preposterous the situation or dialogue. Yvette's characters were always understandable to the audience.

Despite the fact that she was identified with widely distributed B pictures, by the early sixties there was serious interest in Yvette Vickers as star material. The actress believes there were two reasons she never fulfilled her potential: *"Hud* was a part that really could have put me over. Instead it held me back. Had I read the final script before arriving on location, I would have refused. I should have, even then, but I was chicken. It had been cut down to almost nothing. It was precisely the wrong time to be doing a bit part."

There was a role in *This Earth Is Mine* that Henry King, the film's director, thought Yvette perfect for. The producer agreed, but Rock Hudson, who had the starring role, vetoed their choice in favor of a friend of his.

She admits that she would have liked to have become a star, but "probably not enough. My personal life always seemed to come first. That could only have been my decision. I'm not blaming the men in my life, because I always did about what I wanted."

Early in her career she was married to and divorced from bass player Don Prell. Her second husband, a writer, gave her an order the morning after their wedding night. Yvette walked out on him and filed immediately for divorce. She admits, also, that he had just learned that his bride was appearing in the current (July 1959) issue of *Playboy* as the Playmate of the Month. Her marriage to ac-

Marty Jackson

This photo was taken in December 1987, when Yvette appeared at Osco's discotheque in West Hollywood, where she sang the song "Those Leeches Are Crawling All Over Me," accompanied by the group "Nyck Varoom's Tomb." The door behind her leads to the club's men's room.

tor Tom Holland was annulled after a few months. There was also, she says, a brief affair with Cary Grant and a lengthy one with Mort Sahl.

Her greatest professional liability may have been her tumultuous relationship with Jim Hutton, whom she has described as "a classic Irish-Catholic—a hard drinker and a male chauvinist." Whenever they were together publicly, she recalls, Hutton introduced her not as actress, Yvette Vickers, but as "my date, Yvette." At times during the affair Hutton, who was married and a father, lived with her. The affair with the man she refers to as "the love of my life" lasted off and on, from 1964 until his death in 1979.

Afterwards Yvette leased her Beverly Hills house and moved to the Palm Springs area, where she had a real estate business. In 1987 she returned to the home she owns in Beverly Hills. Friends who asked her why she had not stayed in touch were told: "I was in love again for a few years. Now that's over."

Yvette Vickers has begun to resume her acting career and is preparing to do a one-woman show as Zelda Fitzgerald.

Before Bea Wain and Andre Baruch became radio's first husband-wife disc-jockey team in late 1946, she was nationally famous as the vocalist with Larry Clinton's band and for her many appearances on Your Hit Parade. *Baruch had one of the best-known voices in the country as an announcer for the CBS Radio Network.*

Bea Wain and Andre Baruch

The big-band singer was born in New York City on April 30. Her name was originally spelled Bea Wayne.

From the age of six she sang regularly on radio after her debut on *The Horn and Hardart Children's Hour.* She was heard as a teenager on the Frank Sinatra and Dinah Shore shows.

After high school she became part of "Bea and the Bachelors." Ken Lane, who has for years been Dean Martin's accompanist, was one of the "Bachelors." Another was former "Rhythm Boy" Al Rinker.

Next she sang with seven males in "The V-8," a group Fred Waring presented weekly

on the network shows he did for the Ford Motor Company.

Bea and three of "The V-8s" merged with the group Kay Thompson * formed for the Andre Kostelanetz broadcasts.

Bea was singing in the chorus, along with Dorothy Kirsten, on Kate Smith's radio show when she got an offer to go with the newly formed Larry Clinton band. She had been dating Smith's announcer, Andre Baruch, and took the job hoping they would remain in touch while she was on tour. Bea was on the bandstand with Clinton at the Glen Island Casino seven nights a week when she and Andre were married on May 1, 1938. NBC announcer Ralph Edwards was one of their ushers.

Bea was hired away from Clinton in 1939 by Lucky Strike cigarettes, the sponsor of *Your Hit Parade,* a radio show that had one of the largest listening audiences in North America. Through sheer coincidence her husband was the program's announcer. For eighteen months during the four years she sang on *Your Hit Parade,* she also appeared on the *All-Time Hit Parade.* On that show, which was broadcast live from Carnegie Hall, she sang only standards.

After four years Bea left *Your Hit Parade*

and began a tour of presentation houses and nightclubs.

In his book *The Big Bands,* musicologist George Simon refers to her as "one of the most outstanding stylists of her day."

Two of her recordings, "Deep Purple" and "My Reverie," were hits at the time she made them with Larry Clinton and are still marketed. Her fee for those sessions was $30 each.

Both Bea and Andre are charter members of the broadcasting union, AFTRA. They are also among the founders of The Society of Singers, an organization that aims to establish a retirement home for singers, much like the one that Giuseppi Verdi brought about in Italy.

Andre Baruch was born in Paris, France, on August 20. When he was thirteen years old his father, a Dutch-born diamond cutter, brought his French wife and son to New York City.

Andre was an art student at Columbia University when he was literally pulled in off the street into a small Coney Island radio station when a scheduled performer failed to appear. He worked there briefly as a piano player. Answering an advertisement for musicians, he came to audition at CBS Radio, where he somehow got into the wrong line. Because of his rich voice he was tested as an announcer and hired. Throughout the thirties and into the early forties, his voice and name were familiar to millions. He was the announcer on the network broadcasts of Irish tenor Morton Downey, *The American Album of Familiar Music, Just Plain Bill, Second Husband, Myrt and Marge,* and *The Shadow.*

Baruch spent much of World War II in North Africa, assisting in creating what became Armed Forces Radio. When he left the army it was with a Purple Heart and the rank of major.

When Red Barber, who had announced the

Bea Wain and Andre Baruch at a meeting of the Pacific Pioneer Broadcasters a few months before they celebrated their golden wedding anniversary in April 1988.

Brooklyn Dodgers baseball games, left to do the same for the Yankees, Baruch stepped in. He did the play-by-play during the 1954–55 seasons, but declined to go along when the franchise moved to Los Angeles.

Andre Baruch is the first cousin of the late Miranda Marais.[10]

The couple debuted as "Mr. & Mrs. Music," disc jockeys over WMCA in New York City, in December 1946. By the fifties they had dropped the title and were doing essentially the same show over WABC. By the time the Baruchs moved to the NBC affiliate, they had evolved into a talk show. Then, in 1971, they moved to WPBR in Florida, where they interviewed celebrities and chatted with listeners who called in. They were on the air live four hours a day, five days a week. The job, which required much socializing, lasted for eight years.

Since they moved to Beverly Hills in 1980, Baruch has continued to do voice-overs in commercials and narration. Bea appears occasionally at a big-band revival or on a cruise. Together they host *Your Hit Parade,* a syndicated radio show.

The Baruchs have done more than 5,000 radio broadcasts together, with Bea always billed first.

Those Whiting Girls ran on CBS-TV as a summer replacement for I Love Lucy for three seasons beginning in 1955. It was a sit-com in which Barbara (left) and Margaret Whiting appeared as themselves with the late Mabel Albertson playing their mother.

Barbara Whiting

The younger of the Whiting sisters was born in Los Angeles on May 19, 1931. Her father was Richard Whiting, the composer of such standards as "Ain't We Got Fun?," "On the Good Ship Lollipop," "Too Marvelous," "Japanese Sandman," and "Louise." He died in February 1938, when Barbara was seven and her sister, Margaret, was fourteen.

The Whitings were never competitive, Barbara reasons, because of the differences in their ages and natures: "Margaret started so young that she was established professionally while I was still a little kid. She always helped and encouraged me. She's like our mother, who always insisted we make the most of every opportunity in our lives. Mom was the force behind dad. If she hadn't made him move to Hollywood, he would have been content to stay in Detroit, playing other people's songs. I'm more like him, except for the talent, which went to Margaret."

Barbara's only acting before her professional debut was as "Becky Thatcher" in a grammar-school production of *Tom Sawyer*. But her next-door neighbor, Valentine Davies, thought she would be right for a part in the film version of *Junior Miss* (1945). Davies had written the scenario and suggested her to the film's director, George Seaton. She was, she says, a "fat, funny little thirteen-year-old" when she made the picture.

Her performance in *Junior Miss* brought her a contract with Twentieth Century-Fox. She went to school on the lot along with Roddy McDowell, Barbara Lawrence, and Connie Marshall.

Another of her classmates was Peggy Ann Garner, the star of *Junior Miss*. The teenagers made another picture together *Home, Sweet Homicide* (1946), and became best friends. When Mrs. Garner was sentenced to prison for passing bad checks, Peggy Ann went to live with the Whitings.

Her other movies were *Centennial Summer* (1946) with Cornel Wilde [10] and *Carnival in Costa Rica* (1947), which starred Dick Haymes and Vera-Ellen. She supported Susan Hayward and Dan Dailey in *I Can Get It for You Wholesale* (1951), and Ida Lupino [10] in *Beware, My Lovely* (1952). In *City Across the River* (1949) she is raped. Her last feature was *Dangerous When Wet* (1953) with Esther Williams and Denise Darcel. [9]

She sang a few times on the screen but never presented herself as a singer, so that she would not be compared to her sister. They sang together on the *Ed Sullivan Show* and were paired in the film *Fresh from Paris* (1955), a feature.

Three years after *Junior Miss* became a hit movie, she headed the cast of the radio series. On the air she had the title role with Beverly Wills,* daughter of Joan Davis, playing "Fluffy Adams," the part Barbara had in the picture. Gale Gordon [9] was cast as her father in this series, which ran from 1952 to 1954.

In 1959 Barbara became the wife of Gail Smith, the director of advertising and promotion for General Motors. Until a few months before they met, Smith had been engaged to Jane Wyman. Their son, who is now a nuclear engineer, was born in 1960.

At one point the Smiths got a divorce, but they are now remarried. Shortly after their second wedding, they had a third one in the Roman Catholic Church.

Barbara and her husband live in Birmingham, Michigan. Although she works on voice-overs for industrial films and occasionally in commercials made in Detroit, there has not been a single offer from Hollywood since she left thirty years ago.

In 1986 she was seen in Grandparent's Day advertisements for Florist Telegraph Delivery. In 1987 she appeared in F.T.D.'s Mother's Day campaign.

Jack Wrangler

The Whiting sisters spent the 1987 Christmas holidays together at Barbara's (left) home in Birmingham, Michigan. Margaret was accompanied by her longtime companion, actor Jack Wrangler.

She much prefers auditioning for such jobs to seeing someone about a part in Hollywood: "Nothing that serious hangs on what I now do professionally. I'm old enough so I don't have to shop for a new dress for every audition or hold my stomach in. They want you looking just this side of frumpy."

About being the sister of a star, she says: "I much prefer it to the other way around. The queen is always on. It's much easier to be Princess Margaret, believe me."

Barbara is still in touch with Joel Grey and the daughter of Ed Sullivan. She hears from Lon McCallister at least once a month. She has not heard from Gary Crosby for more than twenty years, but she read his book, *Going My Own Way,* and found it "completely believable."

"Secretary to star" was the theme of Dorothy Wilson's publicity when she debuted in Age of Consent *(1932). RKO Radio press releases claimed there was a clause in her contract guaranteeing that if her option was dropped, she could return to her job in the studio's secretarial pool.*

Dorothy Wilson

The studio secretary who became a movie star was born in Minneapolis, Minnesota, on November 14, 1909. Dorothy's mother took

her to plays and movies throughout her childhood. She became a fan but never entertained the thought of becoming an actress.

After graduation Dorothy and her best friend took secretarial jobs in Chicago. After a year away from home, her friend decided to return to Minneapolis and get married. Intent on some more travel and experience before settling down, Ms. Wilson moved to Los Angeles in 1930.

Several days after registering with an employment agency, she was sent to what was then Radio Pictures studios. Hired as a secretary, she worked in that capacity for almost two years. None of the young men she dated during that period was connected with movies.

Dorothy was sent one morning to the office of Gregory LaCava. The director was then preparing his next production, *Age of Consent*. One of the two female leads was to be played by Arlene Judge, a contractee and a "name." Richard Cromwell, at the height of his appeal and on the verge of stardom, was set to head the cast. Dorothy Wilson was to take LaCava's dictation. One letter concerned his search for a complete unknown to play opposite Cromwell. To her surprise, LaCava began asking her questions about herself. Would she like to act? Did she think she could act? Before the day was over, Dorothy had been introduced to studio head David O. Selznick, who approved LaCava's suggestion of a screen test. She got the part, was signed to a contract, and became one of the legends of Hollywood.

Dorothy Wilson was the female interest of William Boyd, Bruce Cabot, and William Gargan in *Lucky Devils* (1933). She played opposite Stuart Erwin in *Before Dawn* (1933) and Tom Keene in *Scarlet River* (1933). She was leading lady to Richard Dix in *His Greatest Gamble* (1934) and supported Loretta Young[8] and John Boles in *The White Parade*

(1934). She and the late George O'Brien headed the cast of *When a Man's a Man* (1935). Her studio, which had by then become RKO-Radio Pictures, cast her in *The Last Days of Pompeii* (1935), one of its most ambitious productions. Dorothy was borrowed by Fox Films for the Will Rogers starrer *In Old Kentucky* (1935). She was teamed with James Dunn in *Bad Boy* (1935), also by Fox. One of her last was *The Milky Way* (1936), the Harold Lloyd comeback film at Paramount.

Ms. Wilson's favorite role was in *Eight Girls in a Boat* (1934). During its filming she began dating Lewis R. Foster, who worked on the script. They were married in 1936.

Lewis R. Foster wrote for the screen and directed throughout most of his career. He won the Academy Award as the original author of the screenplay for *Mr. Smith Goes to Washington* (1939). He shared an Oscar nomination with three other scenarists for the script of *The More the Merrier* (1943). The screenplay of *It Happened Tomorrow* (1944), which was much admired, was also his.

He directed Ronald Reagan in *Hong Kong* (1952), Mickey Rooney in *The Bold and the Brave* (1956), and more than a dozen other features.

Dorothy Wilson made pictures on her home lot and was loaned out to other studios and then free-lanced until 1937. After marrying Foster she made *Craig's Wife* (1936) and *Speed to Spare* (1937), both for Columbia, and tested for the role of "Melanie" in *Gone with the Wind*. The latter, she maintains, is the only role that could have induced her to return to the screen.

The couple bought a ranch in Canoga Park from one of the founders of the Pierce Brothers Mortuaries. It was there they raised their two sons and lived until Foster's death in 1974.

Marty Jackson

Dorothy Wilson-Foster (left) *with her close friend, an interior decorator whom she calls "the King who became a Queen." (After being widowed by Louis King, she married a businessman whose last name was Queen.)*

Her only friends directly or indirectly associated with Hollywood are the widow of Louis King, the widow of singer Kenny Baker, and Ruth Hall. The latter was, like Dorothy, one of the Wampus Baby Stars of 1932. Both Ms. Baker and Ms. Hall, the widow of cinematographer Lee Garmes, are Christian Scientists. Dorothy Wilson, too, is a student of Christian Science.

Retirement was Dorothy's idea, but her husband heartily concurred in the decision. Fifty years later she explained: "I wasn't cut out to be an actress and I never meant to continue. It seemed to me very much like hard work and long hours with very good pay. People ask me about some of the stars I worked with, and I have to tell them that I barely knew any of them. Most of the people we ran around with during our courtship drank an awful lot. So did we, and when we stopped, we were no longer a part of their crowd. My husband and I were very glad to get away from Hollywood."

Dorothy Wilson Foster keeps her late husband's Oscar and his nomination certificate on display in her luxury mobile home in Buellton, California.

In 1976 Estelle Winwood posed beside a blow-up of her photo on the cover of a 1917 fanzine. The actress had become a star on Broadway in 1916. She is generally credited with being the first stage personality to wear lipstick off the stage, thereby causing something of a sensation in the United States.

Estelle Winwood

The high comedienne of stage and screen was born on January 24, 1883, in Lee, England. Her family name was Goodwin.

At a very early age Estelle was taken to a circus, where she saw a girl on a white horse. She decided then to become an actress, an idea frowned upon by her father, a civil engineer. Her mother, however, encouraged her daughter and helped her get expert training when she was in her early teens.

Estelle Winwood had many starring roles both in the West End and on Broadway, where she debuted in 1916. She played opposite John Drew, William Gillette, and William Farnun, three of the major male stars in the world at the time. She also shared the stage and billing with such female stars as Ethel Barrymore, Sybil Thorndike, Flora Robson, Pauline Lord, Fay Bainter, and Tallulah Bankhead.

Throughout the twenties and early thirties Estelle went back and forth between the United States and England. Broadway audiences knew her for such hits as Maugham's *The Circle* (1921), *Trelawny of the Wells* (1927), *Ladies in Retirement* (1940), and *Ten Little Indians* (1944). She appeared in New York in three plays in 1926, four in 1927, and three in 1935.

In England she had played in *Arms and the Man* under the direction of its author, George Bernard Shaw.

She long maintained that she preferred supporting roles, such as the one she played in *The Pirate,* a Broadway production of 1942 that starred The Lunts, or as Leslie Caron's fairy godmother in the movie *The Glass Slipper* (1955).

Her United States film debut was in *Quality Street* (1937), which was followed by a hiatus of almost twenty years of only stage work.

Among her other motion pictures are: the English-made *The House of Trent* (1933), *The Swan* (1956), *Darby O'Gill and the Little People* (1959), *The Misfits* (1961), *Dead Ringer* (1964), *Games* (1967), and *Camelot* (1967). In *The Producers* (1968), at the age of eighty-four, Estelle Winwood played a woman almost violently enamored of Zero Mostel.

In 1938 she was the star and producer of a

When this photograph was taken in late 1983, Estelle Winwood was one hundred years old. With her are silent stars (from left) the late Billie Rhodes, the late Mary MacLaren, and Wampus Baby Star of 1924 Ruth Hiatt.*

Marty Jackson

Broadway production of *The Merry Wives of Windsor.* The following year, again on Broadway, Estelle Winwood was the star of *The Importance of Being Earnest,* which she also directed.

When the actress played in the London production *Gigi* in 1956, it was her first appearance in the West End in more than twenty-two years.

The highlight of her stage career was "Madame Constance, Madwoman of Passy" in the original Broadway production of *The Madwoman of Chaillot* in 1949.

In early 1960, when Lucille Ball's initial offers to appear with her in *Wildcat* were declined, the star went to Estelle Winwood's West Hollywood home to "flatter, plead or bribe." But the aged actress did not choose to appear in the eventual Broadway musical.

Even as a young woman her features were not what would generally be considered beautiful. Yet for many years she was totally believable in parts that called for great attractiveness. The actress with the mannered speech and cow eyes once advised young actresses: "Don't worry about your looks. The very thing that makes you unhappy in your appearance may be the very one to make you a star."

Estelle Winwood was first married to Arthur Chesney, the brother of Edmund Gwenn, whom she once described as "an actor and a drunk." She was then married to and divorced from Guthrie McClintic. She was widowed by her third husband, a New Zealand rancher. Her last marriage was to Robert Barton Henderson, an actor who ran an acting school in London. They separated in 1948 but never divorced.

It was Tallulah Bankhead, her best friend, who once commented on the tiny actress's seeming fragility: "A snowflake would give Estelle a concussion."

Estelle Winwood lived to be more than one hundred years old and enjoyed good health until the last few months of her life. She celebrated her one hundredth birthday with a bridge game, during which she smoked cigarettes and drank champagne. Dozens of cards, wires, and calls were received from such admirers as the Queen of England, Doris Day, and George Cukor, who died hours later.

When a friend asked her how it felt to have lived for more than a century, she replied, "How rude of you to remind me!"

She had stated upon turning ninety-nine: "I wouldn't mind being dead. It would be something new."

On June 20, 1984, the oldest member of SAG died at the Motion Picture And Television House And Hospital in Woodland Hills, California.

Ian Wolfe

Ian Wolfe played on stage with Lionel Barrymore, Katherine Cornell, and Helen Hayes. Among his more than two hundred screen roles were the stool pigeon in Mutiny on the Bounty *(1935), the psychotic lawyer in* Bedlam *(1946), the doctor in* A Place in the Sun *(1951), and the astronomer in* Rebel Without a Cause *(1955). The above still is the actor in character from* Witness for the Prosecution *(1958).*

The character actor of exceptional versatility was born in Canton, Illinois, on November 4, 1896. His ancestors can be traced back in the United States to 1730 on his father's side and 1640 on his mother's.

After studying with Ruth St. Denis and Ted Shawn, Ian began acting on the stage in 1919. In 1921 he debuted on Broadway in *The Claw.* He first worked with Katherine Cornell during her tour with *The Age of Innocence* in the late twenties and joined her cast of *The Barretts of Wimpole Street* shortly after it opened on Broadway in 1930. His characterization of a fop in that play caught the attention of Irving Thalberg, M-G-M's production chief. He was engaged to re-create his performance in the screen version in 1934.

Wolfe played on Broadway in the original productions of *Lysistrata* (1930), *Winesburg, Ohio* (1958), *The Deputy* (1964), in which he portrayed the head of the Jesuits, and *Murderous Angels* (1970). The remainder of his career was taken up almost entirely by movies and television.

The actor was never under contract to a studio and was never typecast.

The size of his parts, like the quality of his pictures, varied greatly. The precision of his work, however, was a constant.

He was seen in such prestigious productions as: *You Can't Take It with You* (1938), *On Borrowed Time* (1939), *Hudson's Bay* (1941), *The Brighton Strangler* (1945), *The Bandit of Sherwood Forest* (1946), *Mr. Blandings Builds His Dream House* (1948), *They Live by Night* (1949), *The Magnificent Yankee* (1951), *The Great Caruso* (1951), *Julius Caesar* (1953), *Seven Brides for Seven Brothers* (1954), *The Court-Martial of Billy*

Mitchell (1955), *Gaby* (1956), *The Wonderful World of the Brothers Grimm* (1962), *Pollyanna* (1960), *Diary of a Madman* (1963), *The Terminal Man* (1964), *The Fortune* (1975), and *Seniors* (1978).

His last TV credit was a guest appearance in 1986 on *Scarecrow and Mrs. King.* His most recent feature is *Checking Out* (1988), in which he plays an undertaker.

He is well known to fans of the horror genre for his parts in *The Invisible Man's Revenge* (1944), *The Raven* (1935), *Zombies on Broadway* (1945), *The Lost World* (1960), and *Games* (1967). The favorite role of many is his portrayal of Colin Clive's hateful stepfather in *Mad Love* (1935).

He was considered for many parts that went to other actors, but the only one that deeply disappointed Wolfe was the role of the High Lama in *Lost Horizon* (1937). Although raised as a Baptist, he gravitated to metaphysics as an adult and has been a longtime student of Eastern thought. To have played the High Lama would have capped his career, but Sam Jaffe was cast instead.

One of the Wolfe's two daughters was married for a time but had no children. Neither is in her father's profession. Ian and his wife, a native of Australia, have been married for more than fifty years. They have a shared interest in the study of comparative religions and philosophies. The actor said in his ninetieth year: "We will continue to search—even among the seemingly increasing number of crank groups. As the Orientals say, 'There are many paths up the same mountain.'"

Mountains, in the earthly sense, are also one of the actor's enthusiasms. He has climbed some of the nation's highest peaks by himself, some by moonlight. In 1954 he was alone at the top of Mt. Whitney for thirty-six hours because of a storm. Wolfe spent most of that time singing "The Lord's Prayer," "The Star-Spangled Banner," and

Marty Jackson

Ian Wolfe climbed down a ladder from the roof of his Sherman Oaks home, where he had been sweeping leaves, to pose for this photograph. The actor had just celebrated his ninety-first birthday.

chanting mantras toward global unity. He also stood on his head on the 14,496-foot summit.

Recently he explained why he never rose to the high salary brackets, as did many of his contemporaries: "I took any part, regardless of the size or billing, that I thought I could do something with. I tried never to repeat a characterization or to play myself. I didn't become an actor to play myself, a trap so many character people fall into. I got along well with everyone I ever worked with, but never kissed any asses. Now you know precisely how *not* to become a 'name,' as they call it, in Hollywood."

195

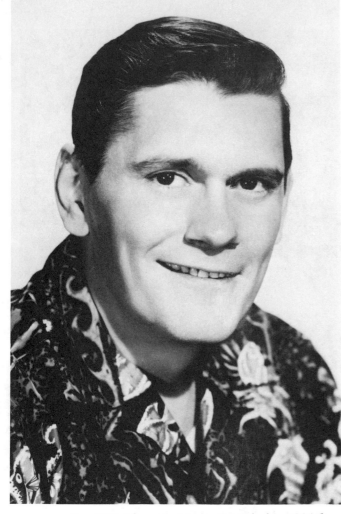

In a TV Guide cover story on Bewitched *in 1965 there was concern expressed that Dick York might become, "the first actor in television history to play the leading role in a number-one hit show—and remain practically invisible in the full glare of success." In 1987, eighteen years after he vacated the role, there was a musical group calling themselves "The Real Darrin."*

Dick York

The actor best known for his role on TV's *Bewitched* series was born in Fort Wayne, Indiana. His birthdate is September 4, 1928.

Because the Yorks were usually behind in

the rent, one member of the family had to remain at home at all times to ensure that the landlord could not padlock their apartment. Dick spent much of his time while doing this listening to radio soap operas and juvenile adventure serials.

Nuns, who taught him in a Roman Catholic grammar school, encouraged his interest in acting and suggested he join the local Jack and Jill Players. He also worked for this little theatre and was given speech and acting lessons as payment.

Dick York began acting on radio in Chicago in the late thirties. That city was then second only to New York City as the nation's most active radio hub. He appeared on many network and local shows, and wrote for as well as acted on *Junior Junction,* a children's program heard in the Midwest.

When the actor who originated the title role on *That Brewster Boy* went into military service, Dick replaced him. He was on *Jack Armstrong, the All-American Boy* for six years and was the last actor to portray "Jack Armstrong's" best friend, "Billy Fairfield."

In September 1950 York was retained in that same part when the series underwent a change in title and format. He portrayed "Billy Fairfield" as a young man until *Armstrong of the Scientific Bureau of Investigation* went off the air in June 1951.

The actor then moved to New York City where he worked steadily on such radio shows as *Young Dr. Malone, Rosemary,* and *The Romance of Helen Trent.* One of his fellow actors on *Michael Shayne, Private Eye* raved so about York that he was asked to read for Elia Kazan. The director cast him in *Tea and Sympathy* (1953) as the central character's best friend. The part brought him a nomination for the Best Supporting Actor award from the New York Drama Critics and a contract with Columbia Pictures for two films a year.

Dick took over the male lead in the Broadway production of *Bus Stop* from Albert Salmi, who originated the role. He considers the experience to be one of the four things in his career to give him "complete artistic satisfaction." The others are the part he played in the film *Inherit the Wind* (1960), an appearance on *Playhouse 90* with Paul Muni, and an episode of *Route 66.*

One of the two acting jobs that proved to be the most important in his life was in *They Came to Cordura* (1959). While on location in Mexico making the Gary Cooper-Rita Hayworth starrer, York severely injured his back.

Since then he has been hospitalized many times and has undergone a series of operations. He has also been addicted to drugs and alcohol. The pain that began then has never left him. The damage done to his spine has brought on a degenerative condition.

The other pivotal part was on *Bewitched,* a sitcom about an average male American married to a woman with supernatural powers. In the 1964–65 season, its first on the air, it was the second most popular show in the nation and the biggest hit ABC-TV had had up to that time.

York left *Bewitched* at the time of its highest ratings. It continued on the air for another three years with his replacement, Dick Sargent, giving a considerably different interpretation of "Darren Stephens."

York said he made the break and virtually ended his career for three pressing reasons: "My physical condition was rapidly deteriorating, my children and I were becoming virtual strangers, and the atmosphere on the set of *Bewitched* was extremely unpleasant. I left in an ambulance writhing in pain, but I never missed that show, nor have I ever regretted the decision to leave."

York has been married to the former actress Joan Alt since 1951. The couple met when they acted together on *Judy and Jane,*

Dick York lives in Rockford, Michigan.

Marty Jackson

a radio show in Chicago. Dick was fifteen and his future wife was twelve.

He has made only three appearances on television since *Bewitched.* The last one was on a made-for-TV movie, *High School, U.S.A.* (1983).

The Yorks raised their five children in Covina, California.

In 1985 the couple moved to Rockford, Michigan, to look after Mrs. York's ailing mother. Dick has not been out of the house since they arrived.

Asked in 1987 what he would like the public to know about Dick York, he replied: "I have the assurance of some very fine doctors that my life expectancy is zilch. But so is everyone else's the way countries and people are going at each other. I'd like to see all conflict abandoned. That is how I achieved peace."

Dick York has spent the last years of his life with tubes in his nostrils attached to a 24-foot cord linking him to an oxygen tank. Asked when he gave up cigarette smoking, he replied: "About twenty minutes ago."

The only time Loretta Young (center) *and her sisters appeared together on the screen was in* The Story of Alexander Graham Bell *(1939). Sally Blane*[8] *is upper left. Georgiana is upper right and Polly Ann is lower left.*

The Young Sisters

Shortly after the Young family moved from Colorado to Los Angeles in 1915, the father deserted his wife and their three children.

The first born, Jack, was adopted by two sisters who changed his surname to theirs, Lindley. He is now an attorney and the father of five. Jack has had very little contact with his blood relatives since then.

The Young children worked in motion pictures as extras during school vacations. Their mother ran a boardinghouse to support them.

Elizabeth Jane, the second oldest daughter, was the first to be cast in featured roles during the twenties. Her professional name was Sally Blane.[8]

Their mother Gladys eventually remarried and had a fourth daughter, Georgiana. Although her father's name was Belzer, she was billed as Georgiana Young throughout her brief career.

She spent three years under contract to David O. Selznick and was screen-tested for his production of *Gone with the Wind*. Selznick thought she might be right for the role of "Scarlet O'Hara's" young sister "Suellen," but even at the age of fourteen she was taller than Vivian Leigh. The part went to Evelyn Keyes.

Georgiana did very well as a model and continued in that profession until she retired.

She would have played a part in an "Andy Hardy" picture, had Mickey Rooney not been drafted. By the time he returned from service, Georgiana was married and unavailable.

In a recent interview published in the magazine *Beverly Hills (213)* Georgiana told reporter Margo Ravel: "I was scared to death in front of movie cameras, not like my sisters, who went on to have successful careers."

She met her husband, Ricardo Montalban, through her sister Sally and her husband, the late Norman Foster. Montalban had been directed in a Mexican film by Foster, who is credited as his discoverer.

Montalban insists that he had seen Georgiana in *The Story of Alexander Graham Bell* (1939) as a boy and vowed to have her as his mate.

Loretta Young[8] rose far beyond the leading-lady status her older sister, Sally Blane, achieved. After winning an Academy Award as Best Actress of 1947 in *The Farmer's Daughter,* she had a long and successful career on TV with her own series.

As late as 1986 Loretta Young received over-the-title billing when she starred in *Christmas Eve,* a rare TV appearance that was treated as something of an event.

Polly Ann Young was born in Denver, Colorado. Her birthday was October 25, 1908.

Jack Hamilton, coauthor of *They Had Faces Then,* called Polly Ann "the prettiest" of the four sisters. Her career, however, was very sporadic.

She was the girl John Gilbert jilts in *Masks of the Devil* (1928), a film noted for being the only Hollywood screen appearance of Eva von Berne, Irving Thalberg's "discovery."

Sally had supporting roles in the Constance Bennett starrer *Rich People* (1930) and in the Tim McCoy western *One Way Trail* (1931). Sally and the late Charles Starrett[8] were top-billed in *Stolen Sweets* (1934). She was John Wayne's leading lady in *The Man from Utah* (1934) and Buck Jones's in *The Crimson Trail* (1935). In *The Border Patrolman* (1936), a George O'Brien vehicle, she was the love interest.

In 1939 Polly Ann Young appeared in the screen version of the comic strip *Tailspin Tommy,* a low-budget feature entitled *Mystery Plane,* and in *Port of Hate,* which *Variety* dismissed as an "indie cheapie . . . pulp stuff." Her last lead was opposite Warren Hull in *The Last Alarm* (1940). Then she played minor parts in the Hal Roach comedies *Turnabout* (1940) and *Road Show* (1941). Horror fans know her for *The Invisible Ghost* (1941), a Bela Lugosi starrer.

Polly Ann Young-Herman is a widow and the mother of two. Her daughter acted briefly in the mid-sixties under the name Betty Jane Royale.

Sally Blane, widow of actor-director Norman Foster, leaving a Roman Catholic church where her sister, Loretta Young, narrated a Christmas pageant.

Marty Jackson

Polly Ann Young in the doorway of her home, which faces the Los Angeles Country Club.

Marty Jackson

Georgiana (left), since 1944 the wife of Ricardo Montalban, is the mother of four. When Loretta Young's second husband, producer Tom Lewis, died in 1988 they had been divorced for over nineteen years. The sisters were photographed in the autumn of 1988 leaving a party at the Bistro restaurant in Beverly Hills.

Marty Jackson

199

When Zorita and one of her two boa constrictors played Newark's Empire theatre, "Elmer" (above) fell out of their hotel room window onto the hood of a car. The stripper paid the $80 in damages, explaining to the press that "Elmer" was jealous of "Oscar," her other snake.

Zorita

The bad girl of burlesque was born Katherin Boyd in Youngstown, Ohio. Her birthday is August 30, 1915.

She was adopted when an infant from a Cleveland orphanage by a police officer and his wife, both staunch Methodists. Her adoptive parents took her to church every Sunday. After Mr. Boyd died in 1919, her mother took her frequently to hear Aimee Semple Mc-Pherson preach.

Her childhood was spent shuttling between Cleveland and Los Angeles, where her mother owned real estate. But wherever she attended school, any familiarity with boys was strictly forbidden. Her mother punished her for the slightest infraction of this rule by limiting her allowance.

Leaving school at fifteen, she worked for a year as a manicurist. Customers who got too fresh with her were doused with soapy water—at first. After observing that some of the other girls wore fur coats and took cabs to work, she realized that they were the same ones who took calls for room service.

"I was only sixteen then," she once told an interviewer. "But I finally got the message."

By 1935 she was appearing in the "Garden of Eden," one of the attractions of the California-Pacific Exposition in San Diego. The walled exhibit was supposed to be a nudist colony. Soon she was unencumbered by the attire all the girls were required to wear—sandals and a G-string. By the time fair officials were alerted, she had collected more than $300 in tips thrown over the wall by an appreciative audience.

In 1987 Zorita wrote of her beginnings as a stripper: "I got into burlesque after I had worked in niteries in Chicago with Nils Thor Granlund, the Ziegfeld of the nightclubs. I had been in nineteen beauty contests. That's where 'Granny,' as we all called him, got all the very young fifteen- to eighteen-year-old girls for his road shows. Then I went into Poppa Bushay's Villa Venice, also in Chicago. We just paraded around in big hats and pearls and high heels. But Poppa had a fag producer that taught us to dance a little. I was taught a snake dance with a live 8-foot boa, as I was the only one that was not afraid of it, out of twenty-eight girls. At the end of the big ninety-minute show, I was posed 99½ percent nude in a big half-circle moon, which I fell out of on the fourth night."

Working with a large snake set Zorita apart from the other strippers of the day. The act was highly publicized. Walter Winchell, then the most influential newsman in the nation, was an ardent fan. Her other trademark was the streaks of platinum running through her hair. Her "Dance of the Wandering Hands" was almost as well known on the runway as the one she did with a boa constrictor.

Zorita and her mother never came to an understanding about her profession or her life-style. Mrs. Boyd had wanted her daughter to become a physical education instructor. "That would have been awful," says Zorita, "because I hate kids."

Nor did she ever accept her mother's spiritual beliefs: "I'm religious in my own way. For instance, I help people when I can. But I don't go to church and they don't get a quarter out of me."

The only time Zorita's mother saw her act was at the New Follies Burlesque in downtown Los Angeles. Zorita told her she was wearing a flesh-colored bathing suit beneath the veil of black tulle, when actually she was stark naked.

On balance, however, Zorita feels her mother was "very good to me." She has inherited all of Mrs. Boyd's real estate in California.

Zorita was featured in the movie *Judy's Little No-No* (1969) and played a nightclub owner in *Lenny* (1974).

She worked as mistress of ceremonies at Café Society Downtown in Manhattan before opening the Key Hole Lounge, the first of two clubs in Miami Beach in 1954. It was then that she stopped stripping.

Zorita in 1987 with "Tamy," one of three prize-winning Persian cats she has at "Kittenhaven," her Florida estate.

Jackie Ritten

Says Zorita: "Most of my girls I taught myself, or improved their act. But I never taught any my Snake Dance—that was *my* gimmick."

In 1974 Zorita retired to live in Palm City, Florida, with her friend, Jackie, who had been her partner for sixteen years in Zorita's Sho-Bar. Their 4,000-square-foot home is on five fenced acres and has a fish pond and a swimming pool.

All of the snakes she used in her act eventually died. Boa constrictors, Zorita claims, are very sensitive to changes in temperature.

In the early years of her retirement Zorita bred and showed pedigreed Persian cats, but she concentrates now on the three she and her friend own. They also have two horses and two Doberman pinschers on their property.

Asked about her marriages, Zorita states: "I've been married to two lawyers and a nightclub owner—an Englishman, a Jew, and a Wop. My daughter, Tawny, is by the Wop."

201

Author Richard Lamparski (left) greeting Rose Hobart,[10] Regis Toomey, Bill Campbell,[9] Fayard Nicholas, and Billy Lee[10] at "The Night of Far More Than 100 Stars," the party Crown Publishers hosted at the Hollywood Roosevelt Hotel on December 4, 1986.

Alan Napier attended the Batman *cast reunion in early 1988 but left before this photograph was taken. Burt Ward, who played "Dick Grayson"/"Robin, the Boy Wonder," is on the left. Adam West, who portrayed "Bruce Wayne"/"Batman," is at the wheel of the Batcycle. Between them is Julie Newmar, one of those who appeared as the "Catwoman." Yvonne Craig, who played "Barbara Gordon"/"Batgirl," was also at the gathering, which featured the Batmobile parked outside the Pacific Stock Exchange in downtown Los Angeles throughout the evening.*

203

Biographical Notes on Personalities
Marked with an Asterisk (*) in the Text

ALLEN, REX The star of westerns lives in Sonoita, Arizona.

ANDERS, MERRY Best remembered for her roles in the TV series *How to Marry a Millionaire* and the Elvis Presley feature *Tickle Me* (1965). Married to an engineer and living in Encino, California. Has worked in the customer relations department of a large electronics firm for more than twenty years.

ANDES, KEITH Now a yacht broker, living in Marina Del Rey, California.

ANDREWS, DANA Living in Studio City, California, with his wife of fifty years.

BACHELOR, STEPHANIE Married and living in Las Vegas.

BARRYMORE, JOHN DREW Also known as John Barrymore, Jr. Unmarried and living in the Hollywood Hills. He is the father of Drew Barrymore.

BARTHOLOMEW, FREDDIE The major child star of the thirties retired some years ago as the senior vice president of one of the world's largest advertising agencies. He and his wife live in Beach Haven, New Jersey. Because his health does not permit him to fly, he keeps in close touch by telephone with his close friend of many years, Jimmy Lydon.[8]

BARTOK, EVA Former screen actress was last known to be a member of an eastern religious cult.

BENNETT, BARBARA Sister of stars Joan and Constance and mother of Morton Downey, Jr. Was married to the Irish tenor, Morton Downey, when she died at the age of fifty-one on August 8, 1958.

BENTLEY, IRENE Interest in the leading lady of the early thirties was aroused when *Ginger, Loretta and Irene Who?* was published in 1976. At the time the author, George Eells, was unable to discover what had become of her. Later it was revealed that she had died in Palm Beach, Florida, on November 24, 1965. She was sixty-one years old, was divorced, and had supported herself as a sales person.

BISHOP, JULIE Played in pictures originally as Diane Dubal, then as Jacqueline Wells. Retired as Julie Bishop when she married a physician. Now lives in Mendocino, California, but the couple make frequent trips to Los Angeles, flying their own plane.

BRANDON, HENRY Shares a house in West Hollywood with the actor Mark Herron, Judy Garland's fourth husband.

BRAZZI, ROSSANO Arrested in Italy in the mid-eighties for arms smuggling.

BRITO, PHIL The singer-actor is retired from a job in city government in South Orange, New Jersey. In 1987 he celebrated the fiftieth anniversary of his marriage to a nonprofessional.

BROMFIELD, JOHN Best known for his role of "Sheriff of Cochise" on television. Married and living in Costa Mesa, California.

BROOKS, HAZEL The widow of set designer Cedric Gibbon is now married to a socially prominent Beverly Hills physician. The couple live with their menagerie of animals in Bel Air, California.

BROOKS, PHYLLIS The widow of Congressman Torbert MacDonald lives in Cape Neddick, Maine.

CHAMPION, MARGE The widow of director Boris Segal lives in Stockbridge, Massachusetts.

CHATTERTON, RUTH Known today chiefly for her appearance in *Dodsworth* (1936), her last Hollywood film. She had gone into movies at the dawn of sound after winning Broadway stardom in *Daddy Long Legs* (1914). Her early screen vehicles, most of which were known as "women's pictures," were so successful she was billed for a time as "The First Lady of the Talkies." Married to and divorced from Ralph Forbes and George Brent, she was widowed by the actor Barry Thompson a year before she died in 1961 at the age of sixty-seven. She was an aviatrix and the author of four novels.

CHRISTY, JUNE Known as "The Misty Miss Christy" during her years as vocalist with Stan Kenton. Married to musician Bob Cooper and living in Sherman Oaks, California. She declines being interviewed because "I *hate* being interviewed!"

COGHLAN, FRANK ("Jr. Coghlan") Still acts occasionally. Married and living in Los Alamitos, California.

COOK, BILLY Boy actor best known for playing the title role in *Tom Sawyer, Detective* (1938). When he died in 1981 he was married to his fourth wife and teaching mathematics in Kennebunkport, Maine.

COOK, TOMMY Working as a professional tennis coach and, until recently, owned and operated a very upscale shop selling tennis togs and equipment in Los Angeles.

DAMITA, LILI Living in Palm Beach, Florida.

DARE, IRENE The ice skater never achieved her studio's goal of "RKO's answer to Sonja Henie." Her whereabouts are unknown.

DE FEE, LOIS Because of her height (over 6 feet) she was billed in burlesque as the "Eiffel Eyeful." Living in Miami, Florida, the retired stripper declines to be interviewed or photographed unless she is paid a substantial sum. Owns seventeen dogs.

DERR, RICHARD Best known to theatregoers for his appearances on Broadway in *Dial M for Murder* (1952) and *Plain and Fancy* (1955). Movie fans know him for his part in *When Worlds Collide* (1951). He is single, a real estate broker, and lives in West Hollywood.

DREW, ELLEN "Discovered" selling candy and ice cream in C.C. Brown's Confectionery on Hollywood Boulevard by then-agent William Demarest, she became Paramount starlet Terry Ray. As Ellen Drew she had the leads in *Christmas in July* (1940), *My Favorite Spy* (1942), and *Johnny O'Clock* (1947). Thrice divorced and retired from acting, her main residence is in Palm Desert. She also has a condominium near the ocean in Orange County, California.

DURBIN, DEANNA Has maintained a privacy on a par with Greta Garbo since her retirement from the screen forty years ago. Married to a French film executive and living in Seine et oise, France. She is and has been since the first volume of *Whatever Became of . . . ?* the most asked-about star of the past.

EGGERTH, MARTA The widow of Jan Kiepura lives in Rye, New York. The pair were often referred to as "Europe's MacDonald and Eddy." Kiepura, who died in 1981, was a Polish tenor, she, a Hungarian soprano.

ESMOND, JILL A well-known actress in her own right before she became the first Mrs. Laurence Olivier. Retired from acting, she shares a house in the Wimbledon area of London with a friend of many years. She never remarried.

EVANS, JOAN Married to a retired automobile dealer and living in a condominium in Solana Beach, California. She is a member of the UCLA choir.

FEARS, PEGGY The actress, nightclub singer, and producer resides in a sanitarium in Glendale, California.

FENTON, LESLIE Married to and divorced from Ann Dvorak, he acted in films and occasionally directed. Died in 1978.

HALL, RUTH The Wampus Baby Star of 1932 lives in the Park La Brea community in Los Angeles. She is a Christian Scientist and the widow of cinematographer Lee Garmes.

HATFIELD, HURD Single. Lives in Rathcormack, County Cork, Republic of Ireland.

HIATT, RUTH Screen player of the late twenties and the granddaughter of the Spanish playwright Vincente Blasco Ibanez. Lives in Hollywood.

HOMEIER, SKIP Known to his friends as "George," he lives in Palm Desert, California. A request for an interview was declined with the remark "I keep very busy."

HOMER & JETHRO A top comedy act in nightclubs and on recordings. Homer, whose real name was Henry Haynes, died at age thirty-nine in 1971. Jethro Burns lives in Evanston, Illinois, and appears frequently as a mandolin player.

HUSSEY, RUTH Living in Carlsbad, California.

JOHNSTON, JOHNNY The band leader–singer lives in Miami Beach, Florida.

KENNEDY, BILL After a brief movie career he spent many years as a host of televised movies on a Detroit channel. Single and retired, he now lives in Palm Beach, Florida.

KEYES, EVELYN Considers herself a writer and has retired from acting. Single and living in Beverly Hills.

KNOX, ELYSE The daughter of the Secretary of the Navy under President Roosevelt is married to football star—war hero—actor—sportscaster Tom Harmon. The couple live in the Brentwood area of Los Angeles and are the parents of Mark Harmon and Kris Harmon, the divorced wife of Rick Nelson.

LANG, JUNE Shares her North Hollywood home with her daughter.

LEE, DOROTHY Best known as the one-time Mrs. Jimmie Fidler and as the blonde foil of Wheeler and Woolsey. The widow of a prominent Chicago attorney, her main residence is in Galena, Illinois, but she maintains a winter home in San Diego.

LEE, PINKY Living with his wife of more than fifty years in Mission Viejo, California.

LIND, DELLA Best remembered for her appearance in the Laurel & Hardy film *Swiss Miss* (1938). The widow of Franz Steininger, composer of "Marching Along Together," she lives in Santa Monica.

LYNCH, CHRISTOPHER Studied with the great Irish tenor, Count John McCormack, and was expected to succeed him. Lynch concertized and appeared frequently on radio's *The Voice of Firestone* in the late forties and fifties. He declines to give any details of his present circumstances, but lives near Kidderminister, Worcestershire, England.

MANNERS, DAVID The leading man of early talkies lives in a retirement community in Santa Barbara, California.

MARIS, MONA The sultry Argentinian lives in Buenos Aires. She does not wish any publicity.

MARSHALL, BRENDA Known to her friends as "Ardis," the divorced wife of William Holden lives in Palm Springs. She does not grant interviews.

McCORMACK, PATTY Divorced. Lives with her son and daughter in North Hollywood.

MEEKER, RALPH Crippled physically and mentally by strokes in the early eighties, he spent the last years of his life in nursing homes. Divorced, he died at age sixty-seven in August 1988.

MONTENEGRO, CONCHITA "The poor man's Lupe Velez," as she was known by fans of fiery Latin ladies, lives in Madrid, Spain. She does not respond to fans or journalists.

MONTGOMERY, GEORGE Unmarried and living in West Hollywood. He sculpts and designs custom furniture.

MOORE, JUANITA Best known for her role in the remake of *Imitation of Life* (1959), which earned her an Oscar nomination as that year's Best Supporting Actress. Married to a bus driver and living in the Park La Brea apartment complex in Los Angeles. She is partnered in a Hollywood acting school.

MORRISON, HERB The radio announcer who made his reputation for his famed on-the-spot reportage of the von Hindenburg zeppelin disaster of 1937. Lives in retirement in Morgantown, West Virginia.

NADER, GEORGE After leaving Hollywood he made a series of features in Germany. While filming the last he was all but blinded in one eye. Since then he developed glaucoma and cannot act in films because of the glare of klieg lights. He and his companion of more than thirty years, who was a long-time employee of Rock Hudson, live on Maui, Hawaii.

O'BRIEN, MARGARET A resident of Thousand Oaks, California, a collector of pre-Columbian art, and the twice-divorced mother of a daughter born in 1976. Canadian journalist Jim McPherson described her in 1988 as "a rather plump middle-aged lady—gentle and immaculately mannered—likeable and poignantly vulnerable."

O'DAY, MOLLY The sister of the better-known Sally O'Neil lives in Avilla, California. Sally died in 1969.

O'HARA, MAUREEN Widowed and living on Christiansted, St. Croix, in the Virgin Islands, where she owns and operates a marina.

PARKER, JEAN A virtual recluse in her Glendale apartment with her small dog. The former actress does not even pick up her mail from the box. It, like everything else she requires, is brought to her several times a week by her son by the late Robert Lowery. She is not, however, an invalid.

PORTER, JEAN Living with her husband, director Edward Dmytryk, in Encino, California.

PUNSLEY, BERNARD One of the original "Dead End Kids." He refuses to be interviewed and, when approached by fans, denies who he is. True to his "nice boy" character, "Milty," he practices internal medicine in Torrance, California. "A doctor!" Leo Gorcey once exclaimed. "His dear Jewish mother must be so proud!"

QUIGLEY, JUANITA also known as "Baby Jane," which is how she was billed in *Imitation of Life* (1934), in which she played Claudette Colbert's daughter. She retired from the screen after *National Velvet* (1944) and for a while was a member of a Roman Catholic convent. Juanita is married to a former Jesuit seminarian by whom she has two children. She visits her sister Rita Quigley, who also acted in movies, in Los Angeles each summer. Juanita lives in Daylin, Pennsylvania, where she teaches school.

RAE, DOROTHY The singer is single and living in Saratoga, California.

RANDALL, JACK The singing cowboy was first married to western heroine Louise Stanley. His second wife was Barbara Bennett, sister of Joan and Constance. Contrary to published reports at the time of his death in 1945, he died from injuries sustained when his horse ran away with him during the filming of the serial *The Royal Mounted Rides Again*. He was replaced by Bill Kennedy.

REED, BARBARA Died in 1963 at the age of forty-six.

RICHARDS, JEFF A missing player of the fifties.

RIN TIN TIN The canine star of silent pictures is buried beneath a black onyx tombstone bearing the gold-leafed inscription "The greatest cinema star," in Cimetière du Chiens in Paris, France.

RODRIGUEZ, ESTELITA The Mexican actress died on March 2, 1966, at the age of thirty-seven.

ROLFE, GUY The spidery British leading man and heavy settled on a farm in the mountains of Spain after making *Taras Bulba* (1962). After being widowed he returned to London in the mid-seventies and shares a flat in Bryanston Square with a female friend and a three-legged cat.

SHEFFIELD, JOHNNY Best known for his role of "Boy" in several "Tarzan" features and as "Bomba the Jungle Boy" in the series of the same name, he lives with his wife in Chula Vista, California. He and his sons are part-nered in a construction business.

SHRIMPTON, JEAN The top fashion model of the sixties owns and operates the Abbey Hotel in Cornwall, Penzance, England. She declines to be interviewed.

SPENSER, JEREMY Last reported to be teaching school outside of London, England.

STANLEY, LOUISE The leading lady of westerns was a direct descendant of Mary Todd Lincoln. She died on December 31, 1982.

STOCKWELL, HARRY The father of Dean and Guy Stockwell, best remembered as the voice of "Prince Charming" in *Snow White and the Seven Dwarfs,* died on July 19, 1984, at the age of eighty.

STORM, GALE After the death of her first husband several years ago she has remarried. She lives in South Laguna, California.

STRATTON, GIL The sportscaster for the CBS television affiliate in Los Angeles.

SUZUKI, PAT As of 1985 she was living in Manhattan, was married, and had a daughter. She declined to be interviewed about her career or her recovery from drug addiction with the comment, "I'm grateful people remember me, but I want no publicity."

TAYLOR, KENT Best known for his portrayal of "Boston Blackie" on television. He died at the age of eighty in April 1987.

TERRY, DON Best known for his starring role in the serial *Don Winslow of the Navy* (1942). Married to the daughter of the founder of Starkist Tuna, he lived under his original name, Don Loker, after World War II. Died at the age of eighty-six on October 6, 1988, in Oceanside, California.

TERRY, RUTH Married and living in Rancho Mirage, California.

THOMPSON, KAY Lives in the same eastside Manhattan apartment building as the ninety-three-year-old silent screen star Aileen Pringle.

TOBIN, GENEVIEVE The soigné actress of stage and film is the widow of producer William Keighley. She lives in a nursing home in Pasadena, California.

TOUMANOVA, TAMARA The ballerina and sometime film actress is the widow of screenwriter Casey Robinson. She lives in Beverly Hills and is writing her memoirs.

TOWNSEND, COLLEEN Married to a minister and living in Washington, D.C.

TRENKLER, FREDDIE Known for more than forty years of comedic skating as "The Clown Prince of the Ice." He is married, retired, and living in Canoga Park, California.

TROUP, BOBBY Married to Julie London and living in Encino.

TWELVETREES, HELEN Died of an overdose of barbituates at the age of fifty in 1958. Her grandson, publisher of Twelvetrees Press, believes she did not intend to take her life.

VAUGHN, ALBERTA Best known as the star of *The Telephone Girl,* a series of silent two-reelers, and for her appearance, along with her sister Adamae, in the early talkie *Show of Shows* (1929). Adamae Vaughn died in 1943. Alberta ended her career as leading lady in early sound westerns. Single, she lives in one of several houses that stand on her property in Studio City, California. She chooses not to be interviewed.

VELOZ AND YOLANDA The ballroom dancing due of the thirties and forties were divorced when Frank died in 1981. Yolanda has never remarried. She lives in the San Fernando Valley and is active in real estate.

WALLACE, JEAN Married while a teenager to Franchot Tone, who eventually left her for Barbara Payton. A second marriage to Cornel Wilde[10] ended in a bitter divorce. Never remarried, she lives in Beverly Hills with her pets: two snakes, a Chihuahua, a parrot, two rabbits, a tarantula, and a duck.

WASHINGTON, FREDI Made an exceptionally strong impression as the daughter of Louise Beavers in the original screen version of *Imitation of Life* (1935). A widow and resident of Stamford, Connecticut, she chooses not to discuss her career.

WEAVER, MARJORIE Never lived up to the promise many saw in her in *Second Honeymoon* (1937). For more than twenty years she and her late husband owned and operated a liquor and gift store in Brentwood, California. Retired, she lives in Marina Del Rey.

WEAVER, DOODLES The TV comic was the brother of NBC president Pat "Sylvester" Weaver and the uncle of Sigourney Weaver. In 1983 at the age of seventy-one Weaver shot himself.

WHELAN, ARLEEN Screen actress and former wife of actor Alex D'Arcy.[10] When D'Arcy was advised that she was living in Laguna Niguel, California, he telephoned her. She had not heard his voice in more than forty two years. She immediately hung up.

WILLS, BEVERLY The comedic actress and daughter of Joan Davis was killed in a fire on October 24, 1963.

WRIXON, MARIS Leading lady of the forties, married to a former Warner Brothers executive. Of their four children, one daughter is a film editor. Maris still occasionally dubs foreign-language films under her husband's direction. They have been married for more than forty-nine years and live in the Hollywood Knolls area of Los Angeles.